PUBLISHER'S NOTE

In *An Eschatology of Victory,* in response to a growing demand, we have reprinted J. Marcellus Kik's expositions of Matthew XXIV and Revelation XX.

We have included a series of lectures by the same author on "Historic Reformed Eschatology," given at the Reformed Ministerial Institute at Westminster Theological Seminary in 1961.

TABLE OF CONTENTS

Section Three

REVELATION TWENTY

INTRODUCTION

One of the intellectual curiosities of the twentieth century is the unwillingness of scholars and Christian leaders to admit the existence of a major school of Biblical interpretation. Although postmillennialism has a long history as a major, and perhaps the central, interpretation of Biblical eschatology, it is summarily read out of court by many on non-Biblical grounds. According to Unger, "This theory, largely disproved by the progress of history, is practically a dead issue."[1] This note resounds in the critical literature, the appeal, not to Scripture but to history to read postmillennialism out of court.

Note, for example, the comments of Adams, ostensibly a Reformed scholar, when he touches briefly on the subject:

> The advent of two World Wars not only transformed yesterday's optimistic modernism into today's pessimistic Neo-orthodoxy, but virtually rang the death knell upon conservative postmillennialism as well. . . . Currently, postmillennialism is considered all but a dead issue. It is spurned as highly unrealistic because it predicts a golden age around the corner in a day in which the world nervously anticipates momentary destruction by nuclear warfare.[2]

Such comments are in principle modernistic, in that they assess Scripture, not in terms of itself, but in terms of the times, the modern age. In terms of this emphasis, Adams gives some attention to criticizing premillennialism, which seems relevant, he recognizes, because of its pessimism concerning history, and gives no attention to postmillennialism because history, not exegesis, has vir-

[1] Merrill F. Unger, *Unger's Bible Dictionary* (Chicago: Moody Press, 1957), p. 731.
[2] Jay E. Adams, *The Time Is at Hand* (Philadelphia: Presbyterian and Reformed Publishing Co., 1970), p. 2.

tually made it "a dead issue" for him. This constitutes Biblical interpretation according to the state of world affairs!

Not only are such newspaper exegetes neglectful of the primacy of Scripture as its own interpreter, but they also seriously misrepresent the facts. Witness the comment of Lindsey:

> There used to be a group called "postmillennialists." They believed that the Christians would root out the evil in the world, abolish godless rulers, and convert the world through ever increasing evangelism until they brought about the Kingdom of God on earth through their own efforts. Then after 1000 years of the institutional church reigning on earth with peace, equality, and righteousness, Christ would return and time would end. These people rejected much of the Scripture as being literal and believed in the inherent goodness of man. World War I greatly disheartened this group and World War II virtually wiped out this viewpoint. No self-respecting scholar who looks at the world conditions and the accelerating decline of Christian influence today is a "postmillennialist."[3]

Here again we have an implicit modernism: the "self-respecting scholar . . . looks at world conditions" rather than Scripture in order to decide on his eschatology!

The errors in Lindsey's brief statement are many, but one will suffice in this context. Which of the postmillennial scholars held to "the inherent goodness of man"? Did Calvin, Alexander, Charles Hodge, Warfield, or others? In our day, does this belief in the fallen man's goodness characterize Kik, Boettner, or this writer? Such a statement as Lindsey makes has no foundation in fact and maligns a great and growing school of thought.

Postmillennial thought will flourish because it is Biblical and is therefore *the eschatology of victory*, or of salvation in its full sense. It takes seriously all of Scripture and the resurrection. Christ's victory is in time and eternity, in the world of matter as well as in the realm of the spirit. "The accelerating decline of Christian influence today" of which Lindsey speaks is a product of Christian irrelevance. It was not World War I which led to an eclipse of postmillennialism; rather, the growing modernism and atheism led to a rejection by the natural man of that faith which asserted the

[3] Hal Lindsey with C. C. Carlson, *The Late Great Planet Earth* (Grand Rapids: Zondervan, 1970), p. 176.

"Crown Rights of King Jesus" over the world. False eschatologies, by surrendering history to the devil, hastened the retreat of Christian influence and power. Any true revival of Biblical faith will also be a revival of postmillennialism.

The sources of the modern dilemma are in part Manichaean. Basic to Manichaeanism is the belief that the world is divided into two realms, the realm of spirit, light, goodness, and the good god, and the realm of matter, darkness, evil, and the bad god. In terms of this faith, man's mission is not a missionary conquest of all things but a withdrawal from a hopelessly evil and satanic world into the world of spirit and light. Asceticism has been a major expression of neo-Manichaean thinking, and, in the early and medieval church, exercised a major influence. In modern Protestantism, neo-Manichaeanism manifests itself in eschatologies which surrender the world to the devil.

During the course of the past few years, this writer has been told repeatedly by persons dissenting with his postmillennialism that the world is ruled by Satan, and therefore postmillennialism is impossible. In the minds of church members, this conclusion that Satan is the ruler of time, matter, and history brings logical and radical conclusions. It means the surrender of the world to the enemy, the denial of the possibility of social reform, and a hostility to any note of victory in preaching. ("Victorious living" becomes a neo-Manichaean flight into the realm of spirit.) A prominent premillennialist preacher has declared, "You don't polish brass on a sinking ship," thereby denying the validity of any involvement in history. Others have insisted that Satan rules the world and history. The Christian hope has been turned into flight and despair.

Postmillennialism will again prevail, however, because it is the truth of God and His enscriptured word. As an eschatology of victory, it will inspire men with the power of God, and, as with great saints of old, and the Puritans of yesteryears, lead again and more enduringly to the triumph of Christ in every area, bringing every sphere of thought and action into captivity to Christ.

The writings of J. M. Kik give us that eschatology of victory which Scripture sets forth.

ROUSAS JOHN RUSHDOONY
March 4, 1971

SECTION ONE

HISTORIC REFORMED ESCHATOLOGY

TABLE OF CONTENTS

Section One

HISTORIC REFORMED ESCHATOLOGY

Chapter I

HISTORY OF THE REFORMED POSITION[1]

It is our purpose in a series of four lectures to give a historical, theological, and exegetical study of Historic Reformed Eschatology in so far as it deals with the progress of the church previous to the second coming of the Lord. It is at once obvious that we have taken in a large field of study and that the time limit alone necessitates the narrowing of that field. We have therefore limited our study to the concept of the millennium and here, too, there is a narrowing of the field as will be obvious later.

When we speak of the millennium immediately three schools of thought come to mind: the pre-, a-, and postmillenarian. As you know, the *premil* looks for the establishment of the millennial kingdom after the second coming of the Lord. As to the *amil* view we quote Prof. D. H. Kromminga: "The name literally means 'no millennium'; while as a matter of fact its advocates believe that the millennium is a spiritual or heavenly millennium rather than an earthly one of a literal reign of Christ on earth before the final judgment." Concerning the "thousand years" of Revelation 20 Prof. Kromminga states: "The Amillennialist interprets this as indicating the spiritual reign with Christ of the disembodied spirits in heaven during the thousand years."[1] Prof. Berkhof states: "The Amillennial view is, as the name indicates, purely negative. It holds that there is no sufficient Scriptural ground for the expectation of a millennium, and is firmly convinced that the Bible favors the idea that the present dispensation of the kingdom of God will be followed *immediately* by the kingdom of God in its consummate and eternal form."[2] We take it then that some *amils* relate

3

the millennial reign of the saints to the Messianic kingdom in the intermediate state; some relate it to the consummate kingdom; some to both. A few enlightened *amils* will grant that some of the millennial blessings may be enjoyed upon earth in the gospel dispensation but do not look for a golden age upon earth.

The *postmil* looks for a fulfillment of the Old Testament prophecies of a glorious age of the church upon earth through the preaching of the gospel under the power of the Holy Spirit. He looks forward to all nations becoming Christian and living in peace one with another. He relates all prophecies to history and time. After the triumph of Christianity throughout the earth he looks for the second coming of the Lord. There are, of course, differences of opinion concerning details among the *posts* as among other schools of thought.

It can be stated without fear of contradiction that the *postmil* position was the historic position of Princeton Theological Seminary. The Hodges were *postmils*. Charles Hodge writes: "The Scriptural doctrine therefore, is consistent with the admitted fact that separate nations, and the human race as a whole, have made great advances in all branches of knowledge and in all the arts of life. Nor is it inconsistent with the belief that the world under the influence of Christianity is constantly improving, and will ultimately attain, under the reign of Christ, millennial perfection and glory."[4]

A. A. Hodge writes: "The Scriptures, both of the Old and New Testament, clearly reveal that the gospel is to exercise an influence over all branches of the human family, immeasurably more extensive and more thoroughly transforming than any it has ever realized in time past. This end is to be gradually attained through the spiritual presence of Christ in the ordinary dispensation of Providence, and ministrations of his church."[5]

Warfield writes: "Surely, we shall not wish to measure the saving work of God by what has already been accomplished in these unripe days in which our lot is cast. The sands of time have not yet run out. And before us stretch, not merely the reaches of the ages, but the infinitely resourceful reaches of the promise of God. Are not the saints to inherit the earth? Is not the recreated earth

4

theirs? Are not the kingdoms of the world to become the kingdom of God? Is not the knowledge of the glory of God to cover the earth as the waters cover the sea? Shall not the day dawn when no man need say to his neighbour, 'Know the Lord,' for all shall know Him from the least to the greatest. O raise your eyes, raise your eyes, I beseech you, to the far horizon: let them rest nowhere short of the extreme limit of the divine purpose of grace. And tell me what you see there. Is it not the supreme, the glorious, issue of that love of God which loved, not one here and there only in the world, but the world in its organic completeness; and gave His Son, not to judge the world, but that the world through Him should be saved."[6]

This is also the position of Archibald Alexander and Joseph Addison Alexander. The latter's position comes out frequently in his work on Isaiah. He relates prophecies like Isaiah 2:2-4 to the church: "The Prophet sees the church, at some distant period, exalted and conspicuous, and the nations resorting to it for instruction in the true religion, as a consequence of which he sees war cease and universal peace prevail."[7] Perhaps the great stumbling block to the acceptance of the *postmil* position is the misunderstanding of the term "new heavens and a new earth." Many look upon this as a material concept rather than a term descriptive of the gospel economy. On Isaiah 65:17 Alexander writes: "Better than all these is the explanation of the verse as a promise of prediction of entire change in the existing state of things, the precise nature of the change and of the means by which it shall be brought about forming no part of the revelation here. That the words are not inapplicable to a revolution of a moral and spiritual nature, we may learn from Paul's analogous description of the change wrought in conversion (2 Cor. 5:17; Gal. 6:15), and from Peter's application of this very passage, 'Nevertheless, we, according to his promise, look for new heavens and a new earth wherein dwelleth righteousness' (2 Peter 3:13). That the words have such meaning even here, is rendered probable by the last clause, the oblivion of the former state of things being much more naturally connected with moral and spiritual changes than with one of a material nature."[8] This indicates that J. A. Alexander looks upon the term "new heavens and a new earth"

5

as a spiritual concept both in Isaiah and Peter. Would that more would understand it in that way!

Thus the Hodges, Warfield, and the Alexanders held to the general *postmil* position. It was not till the advent of Geerhardus Vos that the *amil* position was introduced. I am personally sorry that the remarkable talents of Vos were diverted from the historic Princeton position.

As in the Northern Church so the theologians of the Southern Presbyterian Church held to the *postmil* position. Dr. J. H. Thornwell, in writing against the premillenarian view of Dr. Breckinridge, has this thrilling passage: "If the Church could be aroused to a deeper sense of the glory that awaits her, she would enter with a warmer spirit into the struggles that are before her. Hope would inspire ardour. She would even now arise from the dust, and like the eagle plume her pinions for loftier flights than she has yet taken. What she wants, and what every individual Christian wants, is faith—faith in her sublime vocation, in her Divine resources, in the presence and efficacy of the Spirit that dwells in her—faith in the truth, faith in Jesus, and faith in God. With such a faith there would be no need to speculate about the future. That would speedily reveal itself. It is our unfaithfulness, our negligence and unbelief, our low and carnal aims, that retard the chariot of the Redeemer. The Bridegroom cannot come until the Bride has made herself ready. Let the Church be in earnest after greater holiness in her own members, and in faith and love undertake the conquest of the world, and she will soon settle the question whether her resources are competent to change the face of the earth."[9]

Dr. R. L. Dabney in his *Syllabus of Systematic Theology* has this to say: "Before this second Advent, the following events must have occurred. The development and secular overthrow of Antichrist (2 Thess. 2:3-9; Dan. 7:24-26; Rev. 17, 18), which is the Papacy. The proclamation of the Gospel to all nations, and the general triumph of Christianity over all false religions, in all nations (Ps. 72:8-11; Isa. 2:2-4; Dan. 2:44, 45; 7:14; Matt. 28:19, 20; Rom. 11:12, 15, 25; Mark 12:10; Matt. 24:14). The general and national return of the Jews to the Christian Church

(Rom. 11:25, 26). And then a partial relapse from this state of high prosperity, into unbelief and sin (Rev. 20:7, 8)."[10]

Another famous American divine who held this view is Jonathan Edwards. In his "Work of Redemption" he gives a fine exposition of the *postmil* position. I quote a small part: "The visible kingdom of Satan shall be overthrown, and the kingdom of Christ set up on the ruins of it, everywhere throughout the whole habitable globe. Now shall the promise made to Abraham be fulfilled, that 'in him and in his seed all the families of the earth shall be blessed;' and Christ now shall become the desire of all nations, agreeable to Haggai 2:7. Now the kingdom of Christ shall in the most strict and literal sense be extended to all nations, and the whole earth. There are many passages of Scripture that can be understood in no other sense. What can be more universal than that in Isa. 11:9, 'For the earth shall be full of the knowledge of the Lord, as the waters cover the sea.' As much as to say, as there is no part of the channel or cavity of the sea anywhere, but what is covered with water; so there shall be no part of the world of mankind but what shall be covered with the knowledge of God. So it foretold in Isa. 45:22, that all the ends of the earth shall look to Christ, and be saved. And to show that the words are to be understood in the most universal sense, it is said in the next verse, 'I have sworn by myself, the word is gone out of my mouth in righteousness, and shall not return, that unto me every knee shall bow, every tongue shall swear.' So the most universal expression is used. Dan. 7:27, 'And the kingdom and dominion, and the greatness of the kingdom under the whole heaven, shall be given to the people of the saints of the Most High God.' You see the expression includes *all* under the *whole heaven*."[11]

We leave now the American scene and go over to the British Isles. We should also have quoted from Dr. A. H. Strong, who holds forth this view in his *Systematic Theology*; Albert Barnes in his popular exposition of Isaiah 2:2-4; and Loraine Boettner in his book on predestination. We have narrowed our field to the English-speaking world with the exception of Witsius. However, Berkhof points out that during the 16th and 17th centuries it was the position of Reformed theologians in the Netherlands. He writes: "Among them were such well-known men as Coccejus, Alting, the two Vitringas, d'Outrein, Witsius, Hoornbeek, Koelman, and Brakel."[12] Kromminga writes that the influence of these men continued in the 18th century.

A few quotations from Witsius would be in order before turning to the English and Scotch writers. Witsius states that one of the benefits of the New Testament will be the restoration of the Israelites. From that section we quote these statements: "That when the fulness of the Gentiles is brought in, *all Israel shall be saved*, that is, as our Dutch commentators well observe, not a few, but a very great number, and in a manner the whole Jewish nation, in a full body. . . . As this is not yet accomplished, as to the whole body of the Israelites, and yet the scripture must be fulfilled, the apostle has justly inferred, that in the last times it will be perfectly fulfilled (Rom. 11:25-27). . . . To this restoration of Israel shall be joined the riches of the whole church, and, as it were, life from the dead, Rom. 11:12. The apostle intimates, that much greater and more extensive benefits shall redound to the Christian church from the fulness and restoration of the Jews, than did to the Gentiles, from their fall and diminution: greater, I say, *intensively*, or with respect to degrees, and larger with respect to *extent*. . . . For there is a certain fulness of the Gentiles, to be gathered together by the successive preaching of the gospel, which goes before the restoration of Israel, of which ver. 25, and another richness of the Gentiles, that comes after the recovery of Israel."[13]

We quote now from the "Reformed Presbyterian Testimony" (Belfast 1901) which gives the position of that church, J. G. Vos to the contrary. "Prophecy shows that a time is coming when the Kingdom of Christ shall triumph over all opposition and prevail in all the world. The Romish antichrist shall be utterly destroyed. The Jews shall be converted to Christianity. The fulness of the Gentiles shall be brought in and all mankind shall possess the knowledge of the Lord. The truth in its illuminating, regenerating, and sanctifying efficacy shall be felt everywhere, so that the multitudes of all nations shall serve the Lord. Knowledge, love, holiness, and peace shall reign through the abundant outpouring of the Holy Spirit. Arts, sciences, literature, and property shall

8

be consecrated to the advancement of the kingdom of Christ. The social institutions of men shall be regulated by gospel principles, and the nations as such shall consecrate their strength to the Lord. Oppression and tyranny shall come to an end. The nations, instead of being distracted by wars, shall be united in peace. The inhabitants of the world shall be exceedingly multiplied, and pure and undefiled religion shall exert supreme dominion over their hearts and lives so that happiness shall abound. This blessed period shall be of long duration. It will be succeeded by a time of general defection from truth and holiness, and of the prevalence of irreligion and crime. This will immediately precede the second coming of the Son of man from heaven."[14]

There was an excellent little volume published about 1850 entitled, *The Church in Earnest*, by John Angell James. He states in the concluding chapter of his work: "In the foregoing pages we have glanced at the state of the Christian church from its commencement to the present time; and we have seen the imperfections and corruptions which, in its best condition, have hitherto weakened its strength, impaired its beauty, limited its extent, and hindered its usefulness. An interesting inquiry now presents itself, 'Will it be always thus, till it is swallowed up of life, glory, and immortality? Is there no hope that it will arise from the earth, shake off the dust, put on its beautiful garments, and array itself as a bride adorned for her husband?' It were a melancholy thing, both for herself and the world, if there were no such expectation. It were a painful thing to look down the vale of time, and see the same divisions, errors, worldliness, and feebleness, ever within the church; the same Paganism, Mohammedanism, Judaism, and Popery, around it; and no visions of better things advancing to supplant these scenes of the moral world. If what we have seen, or read, is all that Christianity is to do for our race—if the world is never to be converted to Christ, nor the church brought into a nearer conformity to the New Testament—then would infidelity triumph, and exultingly affirm that the Son of God had *not* destroyed the works of the devil—that the gospel had been partially, and to a great extent, a failure, and therefore was a fable. We have no apprehension that such a ground of triumph will ever be given to the enemies of our faith. A brighter era is destined to arrive; a

9

golden age is to dawn upon us, when the predictions of prophets, and the descriptions of apostles, are all to be fulfilled, and the earth be full of the knowledge of the Lord."[15]

In his summation of the period of 1720 to 1840, Dr. K. R. Hagenbach has this to say in his *History of Doctrines*: "The prophetical parts of the Old and New Testament were also investigated anew in view of their didactic contents; what was veiled in vision and image was applied to the confirmation of a theosophic and apocalyptic eschatology. That the kingdom of God, which has its commencement and completion in Jesus Christ, the only-begotten Son of God, is ever approaching; that the idea of a glorified union of the human with the Divine, by means of a living faith in Christ, in relation to the whole as well as to individuals, will be more and more realized in the fulness of time; and that notwithstanding the manifold change of forms, the spirit of Christianity will always be the *incorruptible inheritance* of humanity—these are hopes reaching far beyond a sensuous millenarianism, and which we are justified in cherishing by the consideration of the course, which, amidst numerous conflicts and errors, the development of Christian theology has taken to the present hour."[16]

Dr. W. G. T. Shedd has this to say about the catholic or universal theory of the second advent: "The representations in Rev. 20 were once more interpreted by those in Matt. 25 which speak only of an advent at the day of judgment; and by the instructions given by St. Paul, in 2 Thess. 2 to correct the erroneous inference which the Thessalonian Church had drawn from his first Epistle to them, 'that the day of Christ is at hand.' The personal coming of Christ, it was now held, is not to take place until the final day of doom; until the gospel has been preached 'unto the uttermost part of the earth' (Acts 1:8); until the Jews have been converted to Christianity, after 'the fulness of the Gentiles be brought in' (Rom. 11); and until that great apostasy has occurred which is mentioned by St. Paul (1 Thess. 2:3)."[17] Thus, according to Shedd, the universal teaching of the church was that the second coming of Christ would not occur before the fulness of the Gentiles and the conversion of the Jews, the preaching of the gospel to all nations.

One of the best works of systematic theology that I know is that of Dr. John Dick. The first edition of his work was published in Scotland in 1834. He states this which was the prevalent view of the Scottish church: "As the new dispensation is universal in intention, no part of the human race being excepted in the apostolic commission, so we believe that it will be universal in fact. However improbable it may seem that the whole world should be Christianized, we know that God is able to perform what he has promised. The great revolution commenced immediately after our Saviour's ascension; and although for ages it was stationary, or rather retrograde, it has been advancing since the era of the Reformation, and is going on in our days with renovated vigour. A future generation will witness the rapidity of its progress; and long before the end of time, 'the knowledge of the Lord will cover the earth as the waters cover the sea.' Christianity will gain a complete triumph over all false religions; and the visible kingdom of Satan will be destroyed, or reduced within narrow limits, during the happy period when, in the figurative language of the Apocalypse, 'he shall be bound.' "[18]

Another well-known figure is Patrick Fairbairn, whose Typology is again coming to the fore. In his little book, *Prophecy*, he writes this: "And in regard to what still remains to be accomplished, though we cannot but see in the present state of the world, and even of the professing church, many great and discouraging obstacles in the way of success, yet when viewed in the light of what has already been achieved, they cannot with certainty be pronounced insurmountable to Christian effort and resources. The small mustard seed *has* sprung up into a lofty tree and whatever hindrances there may be tending to impede further progress, and prevent ultimate success, they are of the same kind with those over which the truth has in a considerable degree prevailed, and which no one has a right to say it cannot wholly overcome. . . . Christ shall reign till His enemies have become His footstool, and shall cause the knowledge of the Lord to cover the earth as the waters cover the sea. The word of prophecy can never reach its full accomplishment till this result is attained."[19]

The English divines of the seventh century also give expression to the belief that the whole world will be conquered and come under the domination of the gospel. Stephen Charnock, whose work on the attributes of God is one of the best in the English language, has this to say in his sermon on "The Church's Stability": "Here is comfort to expect the glory of the church: 'The Highest Himself shall establish her.' 'The mountain of the Lord's house shall be lifted up on the tops of the mountains,' Isa. 2:2. In the last days it shall be more glorious than any mountain dignified by God. . . . Abraham's conquests of the four kings, Gen. 14, seems to be a figure of the church's victories, when the captive *Lots* should be rescued, and Sodom itself should be something better for Sion. Then shall Christ meet her as King of Salem, King of Peace, with the blessing of the most high God. Then shall He, as He did at the feast in Cana, turn the church's water into wine. 'Idols shall be utterly abolished,' Isa. 2:18; dross and mixtures in doctrine and worship purged out: Rev. 22:1, 'The river of the water of life shall be as clear as crystal, proceeding from the throne of God, and of the Lamb;' 'The everlasting gospel preached,' Rev. 14:6; called *everlasting*, because it shall never more be clouded and obscured by the foolish inventions of men." Then Charnock quotes and comments on a number of passages which show the triumph of the gospel and states: "Now the church never yet found such a state suitable to those promises and predictions. Some great thing remains to be accomplished, which the world hath not yet seen, nor the church experienced; but that truth that will not lie, that truth which cannot lie, has assured it. 'The mystery of God shall be finished,' Rev. 10:7. The church hath hitherto been gasping in the fire and in the water. She has lived, but as wrapped in a winding-sheet. The saints under the altar have cried a long time for the vengeance of the temple to recompense their blood. There is a time when this Lazarus, that hath lain begging at the door of the rich and mighty, shall be mounted up to a better state. Sion shall enjoy a resurrection, and fling off all badges of a funeral, for 'the Highest Himself shall establish her.' "[20]

William Greenhill was one who took part in the assembly of divines at Westminster in 1643 and has written the classical work on Ezekiel. In writing of Ezekiel's vision of the temple, he states: "That which the vision doth chiefly hold out unto us is, the building of the christian temple, with the worship thereof, under Jewish expressions, which began to be accomplished in the apostles' days, Acts 15.16. . . . There is one thing more also intended, viz. the restoring of the christian church after its apostasy and suffering in spiritual Babylon under antichrist. Many are the breaches, rents, and ruins of the christian church to this day, and we may see the tabernacle of Christ is fallen. But it is expected that he 'whose appearance was like the appearance of brass, with a measuring line in his hand,' Ezek. 40:3, should come and raise it up, and build the ruins thereof, bringing in the fulness of Jew and gentile, that so the state of the church may answer those prophecies made of it, Isa. 60:17, 18; Ezek. 45:8. There shall be no violence, no oppression by princes, or others. Hitherto there hath been little else but oppression in all lands; and the new heaven, and new earth, wherein dwells righteousness, have not yet been created, but are to be expected as things intended in this vision."[21]

Among those who helped frame the Westminster Confession of Faith were two Puritan Independents, Dr. Thomas Goodwin and Rev. Philip Nye. They and about one hundred ministers of Independent churches differed on the stand taken regarding church polity on the part of the Westminster assembly. Under the authority of Cromwell they convened at the Savoy, in London, October 12, 1658. Along with John Owen, William Greenhill, and John Howe they drew up the Savoy Confession. It is practically like the Westminster Confession except on church polity. Of interest to the present subject is this statement: "As the Lord is in care and love towards his Church, hath in his infinite wise providence exercised it with great variety in all ages, for the good of them that love him, and his own glory; so, according to his promise, we expect that in the latter days, Anti-christ being destroyed, the Jews called, and the adversaries of the kingdom of his dear Son broken, the churches of Christ being enlarged and edified through a free and plentiful communication of light and grace, shall enjoy in this world a more quiet, peaceable, and glorious condition than they have enjoyed."[22]

That the Westminster divines would not differ from the Savoy Declaration in the above statement is revealed in the Westminster Standards. They are not without postmillennial indications. In Chapter V, section 7, we are informed that the providence of

God "after a most special manner, it taketh care of his Church, and disposeth all things to the good thereof." In Chapter VII, section 6, it relates that though the ordinances of the gospel are few "and administered with more simplicity and less outward glory, yet, in them it is held forth in more fullness, evidence, and spiritual efficacy, to all nations, both Jews and Gentiles." And in Chapter VIII, section 8, one of the things which Christ does for the elect is "overcoming all their enemies by his almighty power and wisdom, in such manner and ways as are most consonant to his wonderful and unsearchable dispensation." The answer to Q. 54 of The Larger Catechism states that Christ "doth gather and defend his Church, and subdue their enemies." The answer to Q. 191 states: "In the second petition (which is, Thy kingdom come) . . . we pray that the kingdom of sin and Satan may be destroyed, the gospel propagated throughout the world, the Jews called, the fullness of the Gentiles brought in; the Church furnished with all gospel officers and ordinances, purged from corruption, countenanced and maintained by the civil magistrate: etc." Thus these standards reveal that it was believed that Christ would dispose all things to the good of the church, that Christ would overcome the enemies of the church, that the church should pray that the kingdom of Satan be destroyed, the gospel propagated throughout the world, the Jews called, and the fullness of the Gentiles brought in. Surely the Westminster Standards would not encourage hope and prayer for things contrary to the Word of God.

NOTES

1. Lectures given at Women's College, Cambridge, England (1961).
2. D. H. Kromminga, *Millennium in the Church*, pp. 257, 258.
3. L. Berkhof, *Systematic Theology* (1941), p. 708.
4. Charles Hodge, *Systematic Theology*, Vol. II, p. 94.
5. A. A. Hodge, *Outlines of Theology*, p. 568.
6. B. B. Warfield, *The Saviour of the World*, p. 129.
7. J. A. Alexander, *Prophecies of Isaiah*, Vol. I, p. 96.
8. *Ibid.*, Vol. II, p. 452.
9. J. H. Thornwell, *Collected Writings (1871)*, Vol. II, p. 48.
10. R. L. Dabney, *Syllabus of Systematic Theology*, p. 837.

11. Jonathan Edwards, *Works* (1843), p. 488 ff.
12. L. Berkhof, *op cit.*, p. 716.
13. H. Witsius, *Economy of the Covenants* (1775), Vol. III, p. 352 ff.
14. *Reformed Presbyterian Testimony* (Belfast, 1901), p. 137.
15. J. A. Angell, *The Church in Earnest*, p. 283, 284.
16. K. R. Hagenbach, *History of Doctrines*, Vol. II, p. 518.
17. W. G. T. Shedd, *History of Christian Doctrine*, Vol. II, p. 398.
18. John Dick, *Lectures on Theology*, Vol. I, p. 156.
19. Patrick Fairbairn, *Prophecy*.
20. Stephen Charnock, *Works*, Vol. 5, p. 347 ff.
21. Wm. Greenhill, *The Prophet Ezekiel*, p. 775 ff.
22. Schaff, Savoy Confession, *Creeds of Christendom*, p. 723.

Chapter II

ALL NATIONS BLESSED

Does the Bible teach that the church of Christ will be established throughout the earth, that all nations will in time be predominately Christian, that the kingdom of Satan will be destroyed, and that there will be a universal prevalence of truth and peace throughout the earth? Does the Bible teach that this will be brought about by the preaching of the gospel along with the supernatural influence of the Holy Spirit? These questions will be answered in this lecture along the lines of Biblical theology.

Before doing so we must clear up a few misunderstandings and make a few definitions. For instance, Geerhardus Vos in his *New Testament Biblical Theology* writes of the postmillennial view with these expressions: "ideal perfection"; "convert every individual"; "universalism in the sense that all generations will be converted"; and "sinless individuals."[1] I know of no competent postmillennialist who teaches these things, nor is it the teaching of Scripture concerning the millennial blessings. It is Vos who puts that content into such expressions as "new heavens and new earth"; "the regeneration"; "the millennium"; etc. Relating these expressions to millennial blessings—to the gospel economy before the second coming—does not imply "ideal perfection"; "sinless individuals," etc. For instance, I feel that I am a regenerate person and a new creature. Yet I am very conscious of the fact that I am not sinless and that I am far from ideal perfection. Yet I maintain strongly that I am a new creature. Even so, the "new heavens and the new earth" can be applied to a corporate society upon earth without implying sinlessness or ideal perfection.

16

It is not my purpose to enter into a criticism of Vos's position, which is well known in our circles. But I do feel that he does not make a clear distinction between the Messianic kingdom and the consummate kingdom in his eschatology. Revelation is concerned almost entirely with the Messianic kingdom which begins in time and ends in time. For instance, the "thousand-year" period of Revelation 20 cannot refer to the consummate kingdom because it commences in time with the binding of Satan and ends in time with the short period of release of Satan. It deals with time before the last judgment. Also the Messianic kingdom, as such, ceases to exist, as is clearly indicated in I Corinthians 15:24-28, where it is stated: "Then cometh the end, when he shall have delivered up the kingdom of God, even the Father; . . . And when all things shall be subdued unto him, then shall the Son also himself be subject unto him that put all things under him, that God may be all in all." The eschatology of the Old Testament is chiefly concerned with the Messianic kingdom and its types speak of the Messianic kingdom. The predictive and didactic elements of New Testament prophecy deal with the Messianic kingdom. The consummate kingdom is not the great object either of Old Testament prophecy or New Testament prophecy. I may also add that I hold the position of the Westminster Confession that "The visible church . . . is the kingdom of the Lord Jesus Christ."[2]

So when we speak of the kingdom of God, the millennial kingdom, and even the kingdom (Christ's) of glory, we refer to the kingdom that God has given exclusively to the God-man for a definite period of time. The millennium, in other words, is the period of the gospel dispensation, the Messianic kingdom, the new heavens and new earth, the regeneration, etc. The millennium commenced either with the ascension of Christ or with the day of Pentecost and will remain until the second coming of Christ. There was a period of time when Jesus received the kingdom and there will be a period of time when He will surrender it to the Father. Now to go back to the answer the questions raised in the first paragraph.

"It Shall Bruise Thy Head"

The triumph of the church in history and upon the earth is first

17

clearly indicated in Genesis 3:15: "And I will put enmity between thee and the woman, and between thy seed and her seed: it shall bruise thy head, and thou shalt bruise his heel." That this is indicative of the triumph of the church upon earth is the interpretation of the prophets, the apostles, and our Lord.

Genesis 3:15 is part of the curse pronounced against the serpent and which commenced in verse 14. In the latter verse there is this expression: "and dust shalt thou eat all the days of thy life." This, of course, is aimed at Satan and his seed. Notice how the Scriptures use this expression to manifest the defeat of the enemies of the church. In Psalm 72 we read in verse 9 concerning the Messiah: "He shall have dominion also from sea to sea, and from the river unto the ends of the earth." And in the following verse we read the expression: "and his enemies shall lick the dust." In Micah 7:17 we read again of the defeat of the enemies of the church in these words: "They shall lick the dust like a serpent." In Isaiah 49 we read of the triumph of the future church and we read in verse 23: "And kings shall be thy nursing fathers, and their queens thy nursing mothers: they shall bow down to thee with their face toward the earth, and lick up the dust of thy feet." And in the glorious millennial blessings promised in Isaiah 65 we read in verse 25: "The wolf and the lamb shall feed together, and the lion shall eat straw like the bullock: and dust shall be the serpent's meat." This again signifies the defeat of the serpent in time and history. For surely verse 20 of the same chapter cannot be prophetical of heaven: "there shall be no more thence an infant of days, nor an old man that hath not filled his days: for the child shall die an hundred years old; but the sinner being an hundred years old shall be accursed." This speaks of a time on earth when there will be no premature death, as Alexander points out in his commentary. Isaiah 65:25 and Isaiah 65:20 are related to the same time.

But let us return to Genesis 3:15, which speaks of the crushing of the head of the serpent. All the cunning and poison of the serpent is in his head. The crushing of it means the defeat of the cunning and poison of the serpent. A fulfilment of this prophecy is indicated by our Lord in Luke 10, where the Lord said this after hearing the successful preaching mission of the

18

seventy: "I beheld Satan as lightning fall from heaven. Behold, I give unto you power to tread on serpents and scorpions, and over all the power of the enemy: and nothing shall by any means hurt you." Through the preaching of the gospel Satan was cast from his high heaven to the dust of the earth. Through the preaching of the gospel the disciples tread upon the serpent. Satan was to receive a crushing blow not through a cataclysmic act at the second coming but by the preaching of the gospel. Christ gave His disciples power to tread upon serpents. And, alas, we know it not!

Paul also refers to Genesis 3:15 to declare the victory of the church in time and upon earth. He says in Romans 16:20: "And the God of peace shall bruise Satan under *your feet* shortly." Not by a cataclysmic act but by the feet of Christians Satan was to be crushed in the Roman Empire. And again the decisive defeat of Satan is seen in Revelation 12:9, 11: "And the great dragon was cast out, that old serpent, called the Devil, and Satan, which deceiveth the whole world: he was cast out into the earth; and his angels were cast out with him. . . . And they overcame him by the blood of the Lamb, and by the word of their testimony." Here again it was by the preaching of the gospel as our Lord also revealed in Luke 10.

Thus the prophecy of Genesis 3:14, 15 relates to the earth and to time and history. The earth where he gained his initial victory over man shall also be the scene of his defeat. To this we add the following New Testament passages showing the triumph of Christ over Satan: Colossians 2:15, "And having spoiled principalities and powers, he made a shew of them openly, triumphing over them in it"; Hebrews 2:14, "that through death he might destroy him that had the power of death, that is, the devil"; I John 3:8, "For this purpose the Son of God was manifested, that he might destroy the works of the devil."

To say that the defeat of Satan will only come through a cataclysmic act at the second coming of Christ is ridiculous in the light of these passages. To think that the church must grow weaker and weaker and the kingdom of Satan stronger and stronger is to deny that Christ came to destroy the works of the devil; it is to dishonor Christ; it is to disbelieve His Word. We do not glorify God nor His prophetic word by being pessimists and defeatists. With sufficient faith in Christ we could crush Satan under our feet shortly. Or else these passages have no significance to the church of Christ.

All Families Blessed

Now let us turn to the covenant made with Abraham and his seed, particularly the promise: "and in thee shall all families of the earth be blessed."[3] Paul interprets this to mean that the seed of Abraham will inherit the world in Romans 4:13, "For the promise, that he should be the heir of the world, was not to Abraham or to his seed, through the law, but through the righteousness of faith." To this, surely, we can relate the promise of Christ in the Sermon on the Mount: "Blessed are the meek: for they shall inherit the earth." Also related to the Covenant promise is the commission of Christ: "Go therefore, and make disciples of all nations" (ASV). God is a covenant-keeping God. And Christ is He who commands His church to fulfill the covenant. We do not honor God by reducing the covenant concept of "all nations blessed" to a bare representation of all nations. We do not fulfill our obedience to the commission of Christ by merely witnessing to all nations. We, under the grace and power of Christ, are to make disciples of all nations. This means China as well as North America; this means Africa as well as Holland; this means Russia as well as Scotland.

In Revelation 21 and 22 we are given a picture of the church of Christ upon earth. An angel said to John: "Come hither, and I will shew thee the bride, the Lamb's wife." What did he show the apostle? He showed him that great city, the holy Jerusalem descending out of heaven from God. The bride of Christ is the holy city. This shows us immediately that we are dealing with figurative language, for Christ is not to marry a material city. And it is not heaven, for it comes down from heaven. It is not the consummate kingdom, for it is still upon earth to heal nations, and the gates are open to those who are outside. We mention the Holy City at this time to show its relationship to the covenant promises as indicated by several verses: Revelation 21:24, 26, "And the nations of them which are saved shall walk in the light of it: and the kings of the earth do bring their glory and honour into it. . . . And they shall bring the glory and honour of the nations into it." And to show that this still relates to time, history,

20

and the earth there is this passage: Revelation 22:2, "And the leaves of the tree were for the healing of the nations." This is just another way of stating the covenant promise that in thy seed shall all the nations of the earth be blessed. In heaven, of course, there will be no distinction of nations and they will not require healing. Thus in the last two chapters of the Bible the covenant concept of "all nations blessed" is related to earth and time.

In Genesis 13, where God repeated the covenant promise to Abraham after his separation from Lot, God states this: "Lift up now thine eyes, and look from the place where thou art northward, and southward, and eastward, and westward: for all the land which thou seest, to thee will I give it, and to thy seed for ever. And I will make thy seed as the dust of the earth: so that if a man can number the dust of the earth, then shall thy seed also be numbered." In looking toward four directions Abraham could look but for a few miles. In reality his vision took in the entire world, as Paul reveals in Romans 4:13. But notice how this expression, "north, south, east, and west," comes up throughout the Bible. In Genesis 28:14 it is repeated to Jacob: "And thy seed shall be as the dust of the earth, and thou shalt spread abroad to the west, and to the east, and to the north, and to the south: and in thee and in thy seed shall all the families of the earth be blessed." Moses relates in Deuteronomy 3:27 how the promise was repeated to him: "Get thee up into the top of Pisgah, and lift up thine eyes westward, and northward, and southward, and eastward, and behold it with thine eyes." In the Tabernacle the porters were to be at the gates: "In four quarters were the porters, toward the east, west, north, and south" (I Chron. 9:24). And the molten sea was supported by twelve oxen who looked towards the north, west, south, and the east, thus typifying that the cleansing signified by the molten sea was for the entire world.

The prophets also carry the thought of these directions as indicated in Psalm 107:3 and Isaiah 43:5. Our Lord indicated that His rejection by the Jews would not frustrate this promise of God as He relates in Luke 13:28, 29: "There shall be weeping and gnashing of teeth, when ye shall see Abraham, and Isaac, and Jacob, and all the prophets, in the kingdom of God, and your yourselves thrust out. And they shall come from the east, and from the west, and from the north, and from the south, and shall sit down in the kingdom of God." Here our Lord includes the Gentiles in the covenant promise. The Apostle John gathers in that aspect also in his vision of the Lamb's bride, the Holy City. In Revelation 21:13 we read: "On the east three gates; on the north three gates; on the south three gates; and on the west three gates." And these gates are open to the entire world as is stated in verse 25.

It was this Holy City, the Lamb's bride, the church of Christ, for which Abraham looked as a fulfillment of the covenant promise. Christ stated in John 8: "Your father Abraham rejoiced to see my day: and he saw it, and was glad." And it is stated in Hebrews 11:10, "For he looked for a city which hath foundations, whose builder and maker is God." Lest we think that this is heaven we are told in Hebrews 11:13, "These all died in faith, not having received the promises, but having seen them afar off." This is not meant of the happiness of the heavenly state, for that they received at death. But it is meant of the happiness of the gospel economy. They had but the types and shadows; we have the reality. They looked for the coming of Christ and His church. We obtained the promises; they did not at the time they dwelt upon earth.

The blessings offered in the covenant made with Abraham are ours. A vital part of that covenant is the promise that the church would be a blessing to all nations. Already we have seen that fulfilled in part. It should require but little faith on our part to believe in a greater fulfillment of the covenant promise. It should fill our hearts with hope and thankfulness that through Christ and His church all nations without exception will be blessed.

The Psalms

The covenant concept of "all nations blessed" comes to the fore in the poetry of the Psalter. The composers of the Book of Praise of the Old Testament looked for the triumph of the church upon earth. They rejoiced in this concept for it would redound to the glory of their God. There are no better missionary hymns than those contained in the Psalms. One of the contributing factors to the present day pessimism, gloominess, defeatism within the church is the omitting of the Psalms from the hymn books. They should have first place. The best musical talent of the church should be occupied in setting the Psalms to fitting music.

Right at the beginning of the Psalter we are introduced to the fact of the triumph of the Messiah. In Psalm 2:8 is the statement: "Ask of me, and I shall give thee the heathen for thine inheritance, and the uttermost parts of the earth for thy possession." That Christ did ask for the heathen as an inheritance and the uttermost parts of the earth for His possession is seen in the various expressions of the Great Commission. In Matthew it states: "Make disciples of all nations"; in Mark: "Go into all the world, and preach the gospel to every creature"; in Luke: "And that repentance and remission of sins should be preached in his name among all nations"; and in Acts: "Ye shall be witnesses unto me both in Jerusalem, and in all Judea, and in Samaria, and unto the uttermost part of the earth." The latter expression is borrowed from this second Psalm.

In Psalm 22, after a description of the crucifixion of the Messiah, the note of triumph is given in verses 27 and 28: "All the ends of the world shall remember and turn unto the Lord: and all the kindreds of the nations shall worship before thee. For the kingdom is the Lord's: and he is the governor among the nations." This not only shows that the world will turn to the Lord but that it will be the result of His crucifixion as is also clearly revealed in Isaiah.

After a wonderful description of the glory of the Messiah as King, we read in Psalm 45:17, "I will make thy name to be remembered in all generations: therefore shall the people praise thee for ever and ever." It is unfortunate that the word "people" is used in the singular form where the plural form, *peoples*, should have been used. It should so be used in the above verse. We see this also in Psalm 47, where the term *peoples* is the more accurate translation. Psalm 47 reveals that God is King of the whole earth and over all nations. It concludes: The princes of the peoples are gathered together to be the people of the God of Abraham; for the shields of the earth belong unto God: He is greatly exalted" (ASV). Here again the covenant promise to Abraham of "all nations" comes to the fore.

In Psalm 66:4 we read: "All the earth shall worship thee, and shall sing unto thee; they shall sing to thy name." In Psalm 67:4, "O let the nations be glad and sing for joy; for thou shalt judge the people righteously, and govern the nations upon earth." Let us not forget that the term "judge" is often used for ruling. And in Psalm 68:31 it is prophesied: "Princes shall come out of Egypt; Ethiopia shall soon stretch out her hands unto God. Sing unto God, ye kingdoms of the earth; O sing praises unto the Lord."

Psalm 72 is the classic of the universal triumph of Christ. Here are a few verses. "In his days shall the righteous flourish; and abundance of peace so long as the moon endureth. He shall have dominion also from sea to sea, and from the river unto the ends of the earth. . . . The kings of Tarshish and the isles shall bring presents: the kings of Sheba and Seba shall offer gifts. Yea, all kings shall fall down before him: all nations shall serve him. . . . All nations shall call him blessed."

Here are a few more samples of universal triumph: Psalm 82:8, "Arise, O God, judge the earth: for thou shalt inherit all nations." Psalm 86:9, "All nations whom thou hast made shall come and worship before thee, O Lord; and shall glorify thy name." In Psalms 96, 98, 100, 117, and 148 all nations are urged to sing praises to God for His righteous reign upon the earth.

One of the Psalms most frequently quoted in the New Testament is Psalm 110. The first verse reads: "The Lord said unto my Lord, Sit thou at my right hand, until I make thine enemies thy footstool." The Apostle Peter quotes this verse on the day of Pentecost. He declares that what happened at Pentecost was the fulfillment of Psalm 110:1. He did not interpret this as a cataclysmic act to be fulfilled at the day of judgment. He sees its fulfillment in the outpouring of the Holy Spirit upon the church.

Thus the Psalms give a glorious picture of the future under the reign of the Messiah. There is no room for pessimism or defeatism. They give a wonderful commentary on the covenant promise to Abraham that all nations will be blessed. They look for the fulfillment of this in time and upon the earth. As a matter of fact their wonderment was when at times their enemies seemed to triumph. Their faith was that the whole earth would be filled with the praises of God.

Isaiah's Millennialism

Even as the Psalms give us a picture of all nations blessed, so does the book of Isaiah. What a glorious prophecy is Isaiah 2:2-4: "And it shall come to pass in the last days, that the mountain of the Lord's house shall be stablished in the top of the mountains, and shall be exalted above the hills; and all nations shall flow unto it. And may people shall go and say, Come ye, and let us go up to the mountain of the Lord, to the house of the God of Jacob; and he will teach us of his ways, and we will walk in his paths: for out of Zion shall go forth the law, and the word of the Lord from Jerusalem. And he shall judge among the nations, and shall rebuke many people: and they shall beat their swords into plowshares, and their spears into pruninghooks: nation shall not lift sword against nation, neither shall they learn war any more." By no stretch of the imagination or by an act of gymnastics can this prophecy be related to life in heaven. There are no weapons in heaven to be turned into plowshares. And surely there will be no occasion for nations to say: "Come and let us go up to heaven to learn the ways of God." This is prophecy of what will happen upon earth in the gospel dispensation.

That the millennial blessings are to be brought in by the Messiah is indicated in Isaiah 9:6, 7, "For unto us a child is born, unto us a son is given: and the government shall be upon his shoulder: and his name shall be called Wonderful, Counsellor, The mighty God, The everlasting Father, The Prince of Peace. Of the increase of his government and peace there shall be no end, upon the throne of David, and upon his kingdom, to order it, and to establish it with judgment and with justice from henceforth even for ever. The zeal of the Lord of hosts will perform this." That this will be a process of time is seen in the expression, "Of the increase of his government and peace there shall be no end." That this is related to the *earth* is seen in the expression, "upon the throne of David."

A millennial picture is also given to us in Isaiah 11. Through the reign of the "Branch" the wolf shall dwell with the lamb. And in verse 9 it is stated: "They shall not hurt nor destroy in all my holy mountain: for the earth shall be full of the knowledge of the Lord, as the waters cover the sea." This is again a prophecy of the earth. It would be silly to prophesy that heaven, the dwelling place of God, will be filled with the knowledge of Him as the waters cover the sea. It relates to the earth under the reign of the Messiah. In every place upon earth and in every nation God will be known.

In Isaiah 40:4, 5 we read: "Every valley shall be exalted, and every mountain and hill shall be made low: and the crooked shall be made straight, and the rough places plain: and the glory of the Lord shall be revealed, and all flesh shall see it together: for the mouth of the Lord hath spoken it." Crooked places and rough places are only upon the earth, and in the earth they will be straightened. The thought of the church's triumph and the defeat of the enemies is revealed in chapters 41, 42, 43, 44, and 45. Then we read in Isaiah 49:6, "And he said, It is a light thing that thou shouldest be my servant to raise up the tribes of Jacob, and to restore the preserved of Israel: I will also give thee for a light to the Gentiles, that thou mayest be my salvation unto the end of the earth." And in the same chapter we read concerning the church in verse 23: "And kings shall be thy nursing fathers, and their queens thy nursing mothers: they shall bow down to thee with their face toward the earth, and lick up the dust of thy feet; and thou shalt know that I am the Lord: for they shall not be ashamed that wait for me."

In Isaiah 52:10 we read: "The Lord hath made bare his holy arm in the eyes of all the nations; and all the ends of the earth shall see the salvation of our God." And in verse 15 it is said of the Messiah: "So shall he sprinkle many nations; the kings shall shut their mouths at him: for that which had not been told them shall they see; and that which they had not heard shall they consider."

26

And the glorious conclusion of chapter 53 is: "Therefore will I divide him a portion with the great, and he shall divide the spoil with the strong." Who would dare to say that Christ's portion will be less than the devil's!

It is upon Christ's atoning sacrifice that the victory of the church is built. It is after chapter 53, which gives such a clear picture of the vicarious atonement, that we read these exultant words in chapter 54: "Sing, O barren, thou that didst not bear; break forth into singing, and cry aloud, thou that didst not travail with child: for more are the children of the desolate than the children of the married wife, saith the Lord. Enlarge the place of thy tent, and let them stretch forth the curtains of thine habitations: spare not, lengthen thy cords, and strengthen thy stakes; for thou shalt break forth on the right hand and on the left; and thy seed shall inherit the Gentiles, and make the desolate cities to be inhabited. . . . No weapon that is formed against thee shall prosper."

From Isaiah 54 and 66 we have various pictures of the millennium. In these chapters we are informed of the destruction of Israel after the flesh for their refusal to behold and accept the Messiah. But this will not hinder the progress of the gospel church. For instance, it is stated to the church in Isaiah 60:1, 3: "Arise, shine, for thy light is come, and the glory of the Lord is risen upon thee. . . . And the Gentiles shall come to thy light, and kings to the brightness of thy rising." And in Isaiah 62 is the vow of the Lord to accomplish it: "For Zion's sake will I not hold my peace, and for Jerusalem's sake I will not rest, until the righteousness thereof go forth as brightness, and the salvation thereof as a lamp that burneth, and the Gentiles shall see thy righteousness, and all kings thy glory." And we are urged to remind God of His vow in 62:6, 7: "Ye that make mention of the Lord, keep not silence, and give him no rest, till he establish, and till he make Jerusalem a praise in the earth."

We can challenge the Lord to fulfill the prophecies of Isaiah. We are glad to give God no rest till He makes the church a praise throughout the earth. Of course, a church which is ignorant of these promises or who evades the truth of them or who dares not believe them will never challenge God to bring about a universal peace through the spread of the gospel.

The New Testament

We cannot, of course, go fully into the New Testament teachings of the millennium but merely indicate a few. We have mentioned some already. Luke 10 indicates the fall of Satan through the preaching of the gospel. Romans 16:20 states that Satan will be crushed under the feet of the church. Revelation 12:9, 11 states the defeat of Satan through the preaching of the blood of Christ. There are passages like Colossians 2:15; Hebrews 2:14; I John 3:8 which bring out the triumph of Christ. There is Romans 4:13 to the effect that the church is the heir of the world, and Christ states that the meek will inherit the earth. His Great Commission implies the fulfillment of the Covenant promise through the preaching and teaching of the gospel. Paul is able to say in II Corinthians 2:14, "Now thanks be unto God, which always causeth us to triumph in Christ, and maketh manifest the savour of his knowledge by us in every place."

There are the parables such as the mustard seed and the leaven. The grain of mustard seed, which though the least of all seeds is the greatest of herbs. The leaven pervaded the whole. Both of these parables indicate the slow but progressive growth of the kingdom of God. Both point to the ultimate triumph of the gospel.

Romans 11 surely speaks of the conversion of Israel after the flesh. If the fall of the Jews brought richness to the Gentiles, how much will it add to the riches of the Gentiles when the Jews are restored. It will be like life from the dead. I have never been able to understand how people can interpret the "fullness of the Gentiles" to be the emptiness or poverty of the Gentiles. When the Gentile world is converted then will come about the conversion of the Jews as a nation.

The book of Revelation, of course, is the book which speaks of the ultimate triumph of Christ and His church. It is terrible ignorance of this book that causes some to think it speaks only of a triumph by a cataclysmic act at the second coming of our Lord.

The poor church, according to some, is only to struggle without hope till that day. Rightly interpreted, Revelation reveals a triumph of the church in time and history. It sums up for us the promise of 3:15; it gives reason to the triumphant poetry of the Psalter; it indicates the fulfilment of the covenant promise that all nations will be blessed.

NOTES

1. Geerhardus Vos, *Outline of Notes on New Testament Biblical Theology*, pp. 89. 90.
2. Westminster Confession of Faith, chap. XXV,2.
3. Genesis 12:3; 17:5, 6; 22:18; 28:14, etc.

29

Chapter III

MATTHEW TWENTY-FOUR

In treating this prophetic chapter of Matthew 24 in one lecture it is quite impossible to touch the majority of verses. I can only refer you to my book on Matthew 24,* which deals with each verse in detail. It is my purpose in this lecture to take one or two of the most difficult verses and deal with them.

It is my contention that Matthew 24:34 gives the key to the understanding of the entire chapter. If we accept the ordinary sense of that verse the chapter becomes understandable. Verse 34 reads, "Verily I say unto you, This generation shall not pass, till all these things be fulfilled." If we were to take the words "this generation" in the ordinary sense we would think of them as indicating a contemporary race, people living at the same time, the generation then living. That is the only sense we will find in all other passages in Matthew where the word *generation* occurs (Matt. 1:17; 11:16; 12:38-45; 16:4; 23:26). To get around the obvious meaning of verse 34, some would substitute another idea for the word *generation*. They substitute the idea of "race," "nation," or "Israel." But there is no scriptural warrant for so doing because the word *generation* nowhere in the Scriptures has the idea of a nation in its successive generations.

Dr. J. A. Alexander in his remarks on the parallel passage, Mark 13:30, and basing his remarks on his study of the word as found throughout the New Testament, states: "Common to all these cases is the radical idea of *contemporaneous existence*, which

* Section II of this book.

30

it would be monstrous therefore to exclude in that before us, as we must do, if we understand it of the whole race in its successive generations."[1] Dr. Geerhardus Vos states: "To be sure, the solution should not be sought by understanding 'this generation' of the Jewish race or of the human race. It must mean, according to ordinary usage, the then living generation."[2] Spurgeon writes: "It was just about the ordinary limit of a generation when the Roman armies compassed Jerusalem, whose measure of iniquity was then full, and overflowed in misery, agony, distress, and bloodshed such as the world never saw before or since."[3] Dr. J. A. Broadus in his commentary on Matthew writes: "The word cannot have any other meaning here than the obvious one. The attempts to establish for it the sense of *race* or *nation* have failed."[4]

Since, then, the obvious sense of the word *generation* must be taken, then the obvious sense of the sentence in which it appears must also be taken, which is, that all the things which Christ mentioned previously occurred before the passing away of the generation living at the time when Jesus spoke. And this would mean that it has found fulfillment in the destruction of Jerusalem in the year A.D. 70. But some think that the language is too strong to be descriptive of that event and therefore will not take the obvious meaning of verse 34. They, as it were, say: "Nay, Lord, thou doest not mean this present generation. Thou hast some greater event in mind." Such will not subject themselves to the words of Christ. They say that all things were not fulfilled before the passing of that generation. They take issue with the words of Christ.

That some of the expressions Christ used previous to verse 34 may be used to describe events at the second coming is possible. But similar expressions do not necessitate similar events. Christ used the expressions to describe what will happen to the generation then living, and we have absolutely no right because of the similarity of expression to assume that Jesus did not mean what He clearly said.

Many commentators see that the destruction of Jerusalem and of the Jewish economy adequately fulfills the words of Matthew 24:4-28, but the great majority cannot grant it of verses 29-31. These words, they say, can only find fulfillment at the second coming of the Lord and have nothing whatsoever to do with the destruction of the Jewish dispensation and the city of Jerusalem. In other words, these things, verses 29-31, did not occur before the passing of the then living generation. The honest conclusion then is: Our Lord was mistaken when He said, "This generation shall not pass, till all these things be fulfilled." He should have said: "This generation shall not pass, till some of these things be fulfilled." But that is not what He said.

However, if one interprets Scripture by Scripture one will have no difficulty in believing that the language used in verses 29-31 finds adequate fulfillment in the generation indicated by Christ. Let us study in some detail verse 29.

> *Immediately after the tribulation of those days shall the sun be darkened, and the moon shall not give her light, and the stars shall fall from heaven, and the powers of the heavens shall be shaken.*

The word *immediately* binds this verse to the events which are described in verses 4-28. You cannot excise this verse from the events mentioned previously for it states: "*Immediately* after the tribulation of those days shall the sun be darkened." Of course, you could say that *immediately* does not mean immediately, even as this generation does not mean this generation. That is rather a dishonest way of getting out of a seeming difficulty and does away with all meaning of language and the science of exegesis. If verses 4-28 are descriptive of the destruction of Jerusalem, then verse 29 must find its fulfillment immediately after that event. And so it does.

In the light of prophetic language and pronouncements, this verse is descriptive of the passing away of Judaism. It describes the eclipse of the Old Testament dispensation. It describes the passing away of Jewish privileges and glories. This can be readily seen when this passage is interpreted in its well-defined Biblical sense. Let us turn to the Scriptures.

In verse 10 of Isaiah 13 we find the same language as in the verse before us. Herein is a reference to the judgment of God against the nation of Babylon. It reads: "For the stars of heaven and the constellations thereof shall not give their light; the sun shall be darkened in his going forth, and the moon shall not cause her light to shine." Babylon in all its shining beauty and its marvelous glory was to be totally eclipsed. Hence the use of such highly figurative language. If the Holy Spirit speaking through the prophet Isaiah uses such figurative language to describe the downfall of a heathen nation like Babylon, *how much more* would not such language be used to describe the downfall of the chosen nation of Israel?

The same vivid language meets us in Isaiah 34:4, 5. Here it is used in regard to the terrible and sudden judgment of God against Idumea. It reads: "And all the host of heaven shall be dissolved and the heavens shall be rolled together as a scroll: and all their host shall fall down, as the leaf falleth off from the vine, and as a falling fig from the fig tree. For my sword shall be bathed in heaven: behold, it shall come down upon Idumea, and upon the people of my curse, to judgment." Surely, no one will maintain that when the judgment of God came upon Idumea the host of heaven were dissolved and the heavens were rolled together as a scroll and that all the stars fell down as leaves falling from a vine! Surely, no one will maintain that a literal sword came down from heaven upon Idumea. If the Holy Spirit speaking through the prophet Isaiah uses such figurative language to describe the downfall of such an insignificant nation as Idumea, *how much more* would not such language be used to describe the downfall of the Jewish nation!

The same type of language confronts us in Ezekiel 32:7, 8. It comes in a lamentation against Egypt. It reads: "And when I shall put thee out, I will cover the heaven, and make the stars thereof dark; I will cover the sun with a cloud, and the moon shall not give her light. All the bright lights of heaven will I make dark over thee, and set darkness upon thy land, saith the Lord God." If the Holy Spirit speaking through the prophet Ezekiel uses such figurative language to describe the downfall of Egypt, *how much more* would not such language be used to describe the downfall of the Jewish nation!

We have an infallible interpreter of this figurative language in the person of the Apostle Peter. Peter states that the events of the day of Pentecost fulfilled the prophecy of Joel 2:28-32, which he quotes in these words: "And it shall come to pass in the last days, saith God, and I will pour out my Spirit upon all flesh: and your sons and your daughters shall prophesy, and your young men shall see visions, and your old men shall dream dreams: and on my servants and on my hand-maidens I will pour out in those days of my Spirit; and they shall prophesy: and I will shew wonders in heaven above, and signs in the earth beneath; blood, and fire, and vapour of smoke: the sun shall be turned into darkness, and the moon into blood, before that great and notable day of the Lord come: and it shall come to pass, that whosoever shall call on the name of the Lord shall be saved."

In Joel two things were prophesied: the outpouring of the Holy Spirit and judgment upon Israel. Peter declares that the prophecy is fulfilled in regard to the Spirit. Quoting both elements of the prophecy, Peter indicates that he also expected the fulfillment of the judgment prophesied by Joel. Since the one was fulfilled Peter also expected the other. As he stated in Acts 2:16, "But this is that which was spoken by the prophet Joel." He expected a judgment upon Israel along with the outpouring of the Holy Spirit. The judgment through the grace of God was delayed but came in the year A.D. 70 with the complete destruction of Jerusalem and the Jewish economy.

In spite of the analogy of many Old Testament passages there are those who will not grant that the figurative language can be applied to the destruction of Jerusalem alone. It must take in that judgment, to be sure, but it has its greatest fulfillment at the second coming. Rev. Arthur W. Kuschke in his review of my book, *Matthew 24*, finds his escape in the meaning of the word "fulfilled." He points out meanings given in Thayer's *Lexicon* for *ginomai* as "to begin to be," "to come to pass, happen," "to arise, appear in history," and "to be done, finished." Then he states, "It is apparently in the last sense that Kik takes the word 'fulfilled' in verse 34; but with what justification does he exclude 'begin to be' or 'arise'? This question leads, of course, to the problem of the whole structure of Matthew 24 and whether there can be reference both to the destruction of Jerusalem and to the Second Coming in the very same verses."[5] According to this, at the destruction of Jerusalem the sun "began to be" darkened; the moon "began to be" reluctant of giving light; and the stars began their

34

falling. If you interpret verse 29 literally you cannot apply it to the generation living at the time of Christ. And so, again, you must quarrel with the obvious meaning of the words of Christ in verse 34.

Another critic has stated that one must be governed by the analogy of New Testament language rather than that of the Old. If it therefore can be shown that the New Testament does use similar figurative language to describe an event other than the second coming, then our case should be settled without a question of doubt. Fortunately, there is such a passage. It is Revelation 6:12-17, "And I beheld when he had opened the sixth seal, and, lo, there was a great earthquake; and the sun became black as sackcloth of hair, and the moon became as blood; and the stars of heaven fell unto the earth, even as a fig tree casteth her untimely figs, when she is shaken of a mighty wind. And the heaven departed as a scroll when it is rolled together; and every mountain and island were moved out of their places. And the kings of the earth, and the great men, and the rich men, and the chief captains, and the mighty men, and every bondman, and every free man, hid themselves in the dens and in the rocks of the mountains; and said to the mountains and rocks, Fall on us, and hide us from the face of him that sitteth on the throne, and from the wrath of the Lamb: for the great day of his wrath is come; and who shall be able to stand?"

This judgment came at the opening of the sixth seal. It was not the end of the world nor of history, for the seventh seal was not yet opened. In Revelation 8:1 the seventh seal was opened and there was silence in heaven about the space of half an hour. Then John saw the seven angels which had the seven trumpets. The trumpets are occupied with time and not with a cataclysmic act. It speaks of a third part of trees burnt up; a third part of the sea becoming blood; one great star falling; a third part of the sun, moon, and stars smitten; men being tormented for 5 months; a third of men being slain. Then after the blowing of the trumpets we have the outpouring of the seven vials also occupied with a period of time. Now if the sixth seal finished the sun, moon, and the stars in one final cataclysmic act, history would have been finished and there would be no time for the trumpets and vials.

Surely the language of Revelation 6:12-17 is figurative of some great judgment previous to the second coming of Christ. In Revelation we are dealing with figurative language, as we so often remind the premillenarian. But it is a figurative language which has already been interpreted by the prophets. And as in the context Revelation 6:12-17 cannot mean the cataclysmic act at the second coming of Christ, neither are we compelled to interpret Matthew 24:29 as the final cataclysmic act.

I would like to quote a statement from Dr. Milton S. Terry in his *Biblical Hermeneutics*, which is well to the point. He writes: "We might fill volumes with extracts showing how exegetes and writers on New Testament doctrine assume as a principle not to be questioned that such highly wrought language as Matt. 24:29-31; 1 Thess. 4:16; and 2 Peter 3:10, 12, taken almost verbatim from Old Testament prophecies of judgment on nations and kingdoms which long ago perished, must be literally understood. Too little study of Old Testament ideas of judgment and apocalyptic language and style, would seem to be the main reason for this one sided exegesis. It will require more than assertion to convince thoughtful men that the figurative language of Isaiah and Daniel, admitted on all hands to be such in those ancient prophets, is to be literally interpreted when used by Jesus and Paul."[6]

Coming in the Clouds

In verse 30 there is an expression used which it is claimed can only signify the second coming of the Lord. The expression is: "And they shall see the Son of man coming in the clouds of heaven with power and great glory." Does this only signify the personal, visible, second coming of the Lord? I think that it can be shown that such expressions are also used of times of judgments before the final judgment.

The expression which Jesus uses in Matthew 24:30 is taken from Daniel 7:13 and was well known to the Jews as significant of the Messiah and His reign. It reads: "I saw in the night visions, and, behold, one like the Son of man came with the clouds of heaven, and came to the Ancient of days, and they brought him near before him. And there was given him dominion, and glory, and a kingdom, that all people, nations, and languages, should serve him: his dominion is an everlasting dominion, which shall not pass away, and his kingdom that which shall not be destroyed."

Surely, no one would say that this vision of the Son of man coming in the clouds and presented to the Ancient of days is indicative of the second coming. The vision is given in the midst of a judgment against the fourth beast, which Dr. Edward J. Young and many others state is a symbol of the Roman Empire. The symbol, *coming in the clouds*, is indicative of the deity, power, glory, and reign of the Messiah. I quote Dr. E. J. Young: "The judgment which Daniel beheld does not end in the destruction of the world-powers. It is continued in the foundation of the kingdom of God by the Son of Man. . . . It is the coming in accompaniment with clouds that is indicative of Deity. . . . Driver, therefore, is correct in interpreting 'in superhuman majesty and state.' Among the Jews the Messiah came to be known as *canani*, 'Cloudy One,' or *bar nivli*, 'Son of a Cloud.' "[7]

The significance of *clouds* is well summed up by Dr. E. B. Pusey: "As God manifested Himself in the cloud in the Exodus, the wilderness, the tabernacle, or the temple, as the clouds hide from us what is beyond them, so they are spoken of as the visible hiding-place of the Invisible Presence of God. To ascribe then to any created being a place there, was to associate him with the prerogative of God. Holy Scripture says of God, *He maketh the clouds His chariot; clouds and darkness are round about Him; His pavilion round about Him were dark waters and thick clouds of the sky; the clouds are the dust of His Feet, behold the Lord rideth upon a swift cloud, and shall come into Egypt.*[8]

Daniel 7:13, 14 is the coronation scene of Christ, which took place after His ascension. When Jesus ascended to the Father, the eyes of His disciples followed Him, till "a cloud received him out of their sight" (Acts 1:9). He made that cloud His chariot and entered into the presence of the Ancient of days and gave evidence of the sacrifice He had made at Calvary. This coronation is also vividly brought before us in Revelation 4 and 5. There Daniel 7:13, 14 is expanded. The *Lamb* is presented to Him who is seated upon the throne and is considered worthy to open the seals of history and control the events of history.[9]

Daniel 7:13, 14 is therefore basic to the understanding of the Messianic concept: the Son of man coming in the clouds of heaven. It gives meaning to Matthew 16:28, "Verily I say unto you, there be some standing here, which shall not taste of death, till they see the Son of man coming in his kingdom." There were people standing before Him who would not die until they saw the Son of man coming in His kingdom. This could not possibly refer to the second, personal, visible coming. It must be interpreted in the light of Daniel 7:13, 14.

The high priest understood the meaning of the statement of Christ, recorded in Matthew 26:64, "Jesus saith unto him, Thou hast said: nevertheless I say unto you, Hereafter shall ye see the Son of man sitting on the right hand of power, and coming in the clouds of heaven." Caiaphas understood this as claiming deity and condemned Him for blasphemy. The phrase, "sitting on the right hand of power," would also preclude the second coming of Christ.

The only other place where the exact phrase is used, "coming in the clouds," is Revelation 1:7, "Behold, he cometh with clouds; and every eye shall see him, and they also which pierced him: and all kindreds of the earth shall wail because of him." Generally this is taken to mean the second coming of the Lord, although some commentators take this in relationship to Daniel 7:13, 14 in connection with the judgment against the fourth beast, the Roman Empire. I think they are right. Surely the book of Revelation concerns itself with the destruction of pagan Rome. We are told in Daniel 7:11 that the beast (Roman Empire) would be destroyed. Its fulfillment is revealed to us in Revelation 13 and 14. It is to call to our attention that Daniel's prophecy would be fulfilled that the words of Daniel 7:13 are given in Revelation 1:7.

We quote a few authors who support this view. Hengstenberg writes: "The clause, 'Behold he comes with the clouds,' points to Daniel, the rest to Zechariah, the clouds with which, or accompanied by which, the Lord comes, are not 'the symbol of glory, of elevation above all nature,' but they are the shadow of judgment. This even in the O.T. is the regular signification of the clouds, when employed in such a connection. Isa. 19:1; Ps. 97:2; Ps. 18:10; Nahum 1:3. The Lord does not come once merely with clouds at the end of the world, but through all periods of the world's history. . . . The opinion, which would confine the expression to an externally visible appearance of the Lord, is already excluded by the fundamental passages of the O.T. But of special importance for the right understanding of it is Matt. 26:64, where Jesus says to the high priest, 'But I say unto you, from henceforth ye shall see the Son of man sitting on the right hand of power, and coming in the clouds of heaven.' There the Lord comes upon the clouds to the judgment of Jerusalem, as a manifest proof that we are not to think merely of His coming at the last day, and that the words do not point to a visible appearing. There also the Lord does not come merely to the proper catastrophe on the clouds; He comes *from henceforth*; so that His whole secret and concealed agency towards the destruction of Jerusalem is comprehended under His coming. But if there the coming on the clouds refers to the judgement on Jerusalem, and here *primarily* to the judgment on persecuting Rome, then we obtain the result, that thereby the judicial activity of the Lord in its whole compass, according to its different objects and manifestations, is indicated."[10]

Vitringa writes: "Nor is it necessary that the words of John (Rev. 1:7) should be restricted to the last advent of Christ. For, Christ is said in Scripture style to come in the clouds of heaven, as often as He displays His glory, and shows Himself as present to the church. And there are various gradations of that advent of Christ, in which He is seen by His hardened enemies themselves with the greatest anguish and lamentation."[11]

Excluding parallel passages there are four which speak of the Son of man coming with clouds: Daniel 7:13; Matthew 24:30; 26:64; and Revelation 1:7. The basic passage, Daniel 7:13, cannot refer to the second advent, as there Christ is presented to the Father, the Ancient of days. Matthew 26:64 cannot refer to the second advent in its primary significance, for the high priest, Caiaphas, would not be upon earth. Revelation 1:7 need not be related to the second advent but to the promised destruction of the Roman Empire. Matthew 24:30 is held in bounds by our Lord in the words of Matthew 24:34, "Verily I say unto you, This generation shall not pass, till all these things be fulfilled." In the meaning of Daniel 7:13 Christ did come with the clouds and in the meaning of Daniel 7:14 His kingdom was established, and we all know by history that the kingdom of Christ did destroy the Roman Empire.

NOTES

1. J. A. Alexander, *Mark*, pp. 362, 363.
2. G. Vos, *International Standard Bible Dictionary*, Vol. II, p. 218.
3. C. H. Spurgeon, *The Gospel of the Kingdom*, p. 218.
4. J. A. Broadus, *Matthew*, p. 491.
5. A. W. Kuschke, *The Westminster Theological Journal*, May, 1949, pp. 166, 167.
6. M. S. Terry, *Biblical Hermeneutics*, p. 468.
7. E. J. Young, *The Prophecy of Daniel*, p. 154.
8. E. B. Pusey, *Daniel the Prophet*, p. 131.
9. Comp. Daniel 7:9, 10, 13, 14 with Revelation 4:2, 3; 5:9-13.
10. E. W. Hengstenberg, *Revelation of St. John*, Vol. I, pp. 101-103.
11. Vitringa, quoted by Hengstenberg, *op. cit.*, p. 103.

Chapter IV

REVELATION TWENTY

In dealing with Revelation Twenty we are limiting our study chiefly to verses 4 and 5, which, if not the heart of the chapter, are certainly the heart of the controversy regarding this chapter. The *thousand years* mentioned in verse three make up the gospel dispensation from the first coming of Christ till that brief period of apostasy expressed in the words: "and after that he must be loosed a little season." The binding of Satan is, as is stated in verse 3, in regard to deceiving the nations. During that period Satan will not be able to control the nations as he did before the first coming of Christ. Notice that verses 4-6 explain what is happening while Satan is bound in respect to the nations. They form a parenthesis between verses 3 and 7. Verse 7 resumes the thought of verse 3. Let us read the two verses together: "And cast him into the bottomless pit, and shut him up, and set a seal upon him, that he should deceive the nations no more, till the thousand years should be fulfilled: and after that he must be loosed a little season. . . . And when the thousand years are expired, Satan shall be loosed out of his prison." You see how verse 7 resumes the thought of verse 3. The intervening verses give a picture of what the saints are doing during the thousand-year period when Satan is bound.

I feel that the Apostle John through the Holy Spirit has given a key which will unlock the meaning of the chapter. It is the expression in verse 5: "*This is the first resurrection.*" It is verse 4 that is most difficult to understand. It seems like a picture of a different type of life than that which is experienced at this present time upon earth. It pictures saints seated upon thrones, living and

41

reigning with Christ a thousand years. The premillennialist says: "This must be *upon earth* and *after the second coming of Christ.* They must be *resurrected saints, reigning with the Lord upon earth.*" "No," says the amillennialist, "it must be the intermediate state in heaven because it speaks of souls." But the Apostle John, the author of Revelation, states definitely: "This is the first resurrection."

The Apostle John wanted no misunderstanding. He did not want anyone to think that verse 4 had reference to the general resurrection and the period following. He halts us from such a thought by abruptly stating: "This is the first resurrection." If we can determine by Scripture what the first resurrection is, we will go a long way in the understanding of the entire chapter.

Resurrection is "a rising again from the dead." That which was dead is brought to life again. This is very important to keep in mind. Whatever the term *first* may signify, the word *resurrection* means a rising again from the dead. The fact that it is a resurrection knocks out the thought that it is descriptive of the life of the soul in the intermediate state. It has been maintained that when the soul leaves the body at death it enters into the millennial state and lives and reigns with Christ for a thousand years and that this is the first resurrection. But when the Christian soul leaves the body to dwell in heaven, it is not a *resurrection.* The soul in the Christian is alive; it is not in a dead state. Its removal from the body could be better termed an ascension or a translation. To state that the translation of the soul into heaven is a resurrection is to contradict directly the teaching of Christ that "whosoever liveth and believeth in me shall never die." The very fact that this twentieth chapter deals with a resurrection knocks out the whole amillennial interpretation that the chapter is speaking of the intermediate state of the soul.

But what is the *first resurrection* if it is not the translation of the soul to heaven? The way to discover that is to discover what is the first death. What needs to be resurrected first. The first death is described to us in Genesis 2:17, "Thou shalt surely die." The primary meaning of that is the death of the soul. Upon the act of disobedience the soul was separated from God. Included in the death of the soul was the death of the body, which came later. This death of the soul is also brought out in passages like Ephesians 2:1; I Timothy 5:6; Matthew 8:22. Since the first death is primarily the death of the human soul, it is the soul that must be resurrected *first*. Consequently we must expect to find in the New Testament references to the resurrection of the soul. This we find in abundance.

An important passage is Ephesians 2:5, 6, which reads: "Even when we were dead in sins, hath quickened us together with Christ, (by grace ye are saved;) and hath raised us up together in heavenly places in Christ Jesus." The soul is "quickened" or "made alive." This is brought out clearly in the expression: "And hath raised us up together, and made us sit together in heavenly places in Christ Jesus." "To raise up" is to resurrect. Even while upon earth the resurrected saints sit with Christ in heavenly places. This points to the interpretation of Revelation 20:4. Other passages are Colossians 2:12, 13; I John 3:14. Ephesians 1:19, 20 brings out the fact that the same mighty power of God that was used to resurrect Christ was used in respect to the soul of the believer. The second resurrection is that of the body which occurs at the second coming of Christ.

The classic passage which deals with the two resurrections is John 5:24-29. It is well to allow John to interpret John. John 25:24, 25 speaks of the resurrection of the soul: "Verily, verily, I say unto you, He that heareth my word, and believeth on him that sent me, hath everlasting life, and shall not come into condemnation; but is passed from death unto life. Verily, verily, I say unto you, The hour is coming, and now is, when the dead shall hear the voice of the Son of God: and they that hear shall live." The second resurrection, that of the body, is given in John 5:28, 29, "Marvel not at this: for the hour is coming, in the which all that are in the graves shall hear his voice, and shall come forth; they that have done good, unto the resurrection of life; and they that have done evil, unto the resurrection of damnation." Please take for granted that this is the correct exegesis as there is no time to develop it. However, I would like to quote from Shedd's *Dogmatic Theology*: "The regeneration of the soul, according to Paul, results in the resurrection of the body (Rom. 8:11). It should be noticed, that while Christ, in John 5:25-29, mentions directly both resurrections, John, in Rev. 20:5, 6, directly mentions only one, namely the 'first resurrection.' He leaves the 'second resurrection,' namely that of the body, to be inferred. That the 'first resurrection,' in Rev. 20:6 is spiritual, is proved still further by the fact that those who have part in it are 'blessed and holy,' and not 'under the power of the second death,' and are 'priests of God.' The literal resurrection is not necessarily connected with such characteristics, but the tropical is."[1]

Surely John of Revelation would not contradict John of the Gospel and Epistle. There was no confusion in the mind of John as to what the first resurrection actually was as he records the teaching of Christ concerning it in his Gospel. Those who were acquainted with his Gospel would know immediately to what he referred when he wrote: "This is the first resurrection." It is the resurrection experience of the soul.

I shall exegete Revelation 20:4 clause by clause. First of all, 4a: "*and I saw thrones, and they sat upon them.*" What, when, and where are the questions about the thrones. And also who sat upon them. *What* thrones? Surely they are not material, literal thrones. Surely we do not expect to see a million or more earthly kingdoms with a saint seated upon a throne ruling a number of subjects. Christ says: "But so shall it not be among you: but whosoever will be great among you, shall be your minister: and whosoever of you will be the chiefest, shall be servant of all." In the light of this teaching it is rather strange how a material, earthly, and carnal conception of the thrones continues to hold sway over some minds. *Throne* is a figure of speech indicating the reign of the saint. That the saints reign is indicated in a number of verses. II Timothy 2:12 states: "If we suffer, we shall also reign with him." Revelation 5:10 reads: "And has made us unto our God kings and priests; and we shall reign on earth." Romans 5:17 states: "much more they which receive abundance of grace and of the gift of righteousness shall reign in life by one, Jesus Christ." The type of "lordship" in this life is revealed in I Corinthians 3:21, 22, "For all things are yours: whether Paul or Apollos, or Cephas, or the world, or life, or death, or things present, or things to come; all are yours." The thrones stand for the saints' spiritual dominion within themselves and over the world. Through the grace of Christ they reign in life over the flesh, the world, and the devil. In all things they are more than conquerors through Christ.

Where are the thrones located? In verses 8 and 9 of Revelation 20 we are informed that at the end of the thousand years Satan will deceive the nations again. These nations are upon earth. The deceived nations compass the camp of the saints and the beloved city. Satan and his hosts do not set siege to the saints in heaven. The thrones, the camp, and the beloved city all have reference to the church upon earth.

When were these thrones in existence? In verses 4-6 we have a period synchronous with the binding of Satan. Therefore the reigning takes place before the second coming of the Lord. Then another important thing must be noted in regard to the time of the thrones. According to the King James Version the verbs *sat, was given, lived, reigned*, are in one tense, while the verbs *had worshiped, had received* are in another tense. It would seem from this that the period of not worshiping the beast and not receiving his mark was before the sitting, living, and reigning. Actually all the verbs are in the same tense, the aorist. This is corrected in the American Revised Version, which reads: "and such as worshiped not the beast, neither his image, and received not the mark upon their forehead and upon their hand; and they lived, and reigned with Christ a thousand years." The time of sitting on the thrones and reigning with Christ is the same as that of not worshiping the beast. It was while the saints were actually seated upon the thrones that they were refusing to worship the beast and to receive his mark.

Who are they that are seated upon the thrones? Every saint of the new dispensation is seated upon a throne. The thrones were not limited to those who were martyred when the beast prevailed, nor were they limited to those who refused to worship him. Otherwise the thrones are limited to only a small portion of the saints of Christ. All are not martyred, nor do all live during the period of the beast.

Now let us turn to Revelation 20:4b, "*And judgment was given unto them: . . . and they lived and reigned with Christ a thousand years.*" I have left out the clause dealing with the martyrs, for later in this lecture. I feel that the clause is a parenthesis. I am going to be far too brief in explaining the sense of "judgment was

45

given unto them." It is a fulfillment of Daniel 7:22, which Dr.
Young feels signifies the final judgment.² There is no possibility
in the passage before us of being the final judgment. Whatever
this judgment is, it is continuous throughout the millennium. It is
during the entire period of the thousand years. And saints do not
occupy the throne in the final judgment. They, too, are judged.
The sense of judging is that of ruling, as we see in the book of
Judges and passages like I Corinthians 6:2; John 12:31; Psalms
72:2; Matthew 19:28. Luther states concerning John 12:31, "And
the Gospel shall not only be judge over flesh and blood, and, not
only over some of Satan's angels or devils, but over the prince
himself, who has the whole world mightily in his hands." During the
millennium the saints rule over the flesh, the world, and the devil.

During the thousand years the saints live with Christ. They live
in contrast with the rest of the world, who are dead even though
they think they live. As all Christians live with Christ we need
say no more. But they also reign with Christ in this life. Notice
carefully that it does not state that Christ is reigning with the saints
on earth or in heaven but that the saints are reigning with Him.
But how can the saint reign with Christ while the saint lives upon
this sinful earth? In the very same manner as Enoch walked with
God. The fact that Enoch walked with God did not mean that
Enoch was in heaven. Nor did it mean that God was in bodily
form upon the earth. Enoch walked with God in a spiritual
sense. The saint upon earth reigns with Christ in the same manner
as Enoch upon earth walked with God. Revelation 5:10 states:
"and we shall reign on the earth." It cannot be the so-called
renewed earth here, because it occurs before final judgment of
the great white throne of verse 11. And may we again call your
attention to the fact that Gog and Magog make siege to the church
upon earth and not in heaven. I would say in light of the context
that it is exegetically impossible to relate the thrones and the
reign of the saints to heaven. And by the way, II Timothy 2:11, 12
gives the same truth as verse 4b in these words: "It is a faithful saying: for if we be dead with him, we shall also live with him:
if we suffer, we shall also reign with him." Though dead, we live;
though suffering, we reign.

We come now to Revelation 20:4c, and we use the American

Standard Version: *"And I saw the souls of them that had been beheaded for the testimony of Jesus, and for the word of God, and such as worshipped not the beast, neither his image, and received not the mark upon their forehead and upon their hand."* I have shown that the terms *thrones, judgment, living,* and *reigning* relate to the life of the saint upon earth. Now what may seem to contradict all this is the experience of the Christian martyrs and others who live in periods of persecution. As the book of Revelation deals with the persecution of the saints under the two beasts of Revelation, they are the martyrs that are picked out for illustration. The first beast is the pagan Roman Empire. The second beast, who "had horns like a lamb" is papal Rome. The first beast was revived in the Holy Roman Empire. I do not demand that you accept this, but may I call your attention to the fact that according to verse 10 the beast and the false prophet were already in the lake of fire before Satan was cast in. So their period of time upon earth was limited. Some mentioned in 4c were not martyred but are described as not worshiping the beast nor receiving his mark.

Now it is said of both martyrs and others that they were seated upon thrones and that they lived and reigned with Christ. How can that be? How can they be said to be enthroned when the beasts had the upper hand? How can they be said to live in the midst of the terrible persecution of the beasts? How can they be said to reign in the midst of apparent defeat? How can they be pictured as triumphant when it is apparent that the two beasts were triumphant over the Christians? The question is, did the beasts triumph? Their aim was to crush Christianity and cause Christians to apostatize from the faith. In this the beasts failed and the Christians were triumphant. The martyrs never showed their kingship more strongly than when confronted with the axe, the lion's den, and the torch. They had control over their souls, over sin, over temptation, over the beasts, and over the devil. They could not be dethroned! They were living! They were reigning! They were in all these things more than conquerors.

Psuchai

But, it is said by the amillennialist, the Apostle John did not see living persons; he saw *souls*. These *souls*, he explains are disembodied spirits. A recent writer of this school states: "The word here translated 'souls' (Psuchai) is found a hundred times or more in the New Testament for the soul, as distinct from the body." This statement is open to serious challenge. The New Testament, as we shall see, very, very seldom uses the Greek term *psuche* to describe the disembodied spirit.

The premillennialist, on the other hand, thinks that he is perfectly justified in translating the Greek terms *psuche* by the word "person." This would include both the body and soul. This is a possible interpretation if the context warrants it. In the following passages the term *psuche* is used of the entire person: Acts 2:41, 43; 3:23; 7:14; 27:37; Romans 13:1; I Peter 3:20; Revelation 16:3. The interpretation would then read: "I saw the persons (bodies and souls) of them who had been beheaded." But John tells that he is describing the first resurrection, which is that of souls only. The context, therefore, forbids this translation of *psuche*.

There is another sense in which *psuche* is used frequently in the New Testament, and that is in the sense of *life*. There are over thirty-five clear cases where *psuche* is translated in this sense. Among them is Matthew 2:20, "For they are dead which sought the young child's life." Luke 12:22, "Take no thought for your *life*, what ye shall eat." Acts 20:10, "Trouble not yourselves; for his *life* is in him." The Apostle John, who wrote the book of Revelation, uses *psuche* almost exclusively in that sense: John 10: 11, 15, 17; 12:25; 13:37, 38; 15:13; I John 3:16; Revelation 8:9; 12:11. It is therefore entirely permissible to translate the *psuchai* of Revelation 20:4 by the word "lives." The clause would then read: "and I beheld the lives of them that were beheaded for the witness of Jesus." It might seem, on the face of it, that the martyrs had not reigned in life. But the apostle sees them also as enthroned in life. In their lives upon earth they also were more than conquerors.

Verse 4 of Revelation Twenty may be paraphrased in this fashion: "I beheld the saints seated upon thrones, ruling over the flesh, the world, and the devil; yea, I beheld the victorious lives of those who had been beheaded and also those who suffered

48

because they refused to worship the beast! As a matter of fact, all saints live and reign with Christ a thousand years."

Now another question which remains is: How can it be said concerning the saints upon earth that they live and reign with Christ a *thousand years*? Three score years and ten is the average life of the saint upon earth. This, however, is no more different statement than to say that the Romans ruled over the world for many centuries. This does not mean that each individual Roman lived for that period. It refers to the Roman Empire. Even so the Apostle John is speaking of the church in relation to the binding of Satan. He is speaking, as it were, of the body of Christ. As the Roman Empire is one so is the body of Christ. The body of Christ is always represented upon earth. The church never ceases but reigns throughout the thousand-year period.

It is our contention that Revelation 20:4 speaks of the gospel dispensation. It reveals the victorious reign of the saints upon earth regardless of martyrdom and suffering. In all these things they are more than conquerors. The use of the word *psuche* in the New Testament shows how difficult it is to apply it to the intermediate state of the believer's soul. And to relate this verse to a kingdom to be established after the second coming of Christ brings such a host of problems and contradictions as to bring hopeless confusion.

NOTES

1. Shedd, *Dogmatic Theology*, Vol. II, p. 645.
2. Young, *Daniel*, p. 159.

SECTION TWO

MATTHEW TWENTY-FOUR

AN EXPOSITION

Preface

The first edition of this work was published in 1948 and it is indeed gratifying that the demand for it has necessitated a second edition. The particular interpretation represented in this book found slow acceptance but in recent years approval has multiplied, especially with the decline of the dispensational position. While very little new has been added to the second edition, it has been carefully corrected throughout.

The need for a correct interpretation of the Olivet Discourse has been heightened by the growing prominence of the modern school of "realized eschatology." Most of this school follow David Strauss' opinion that "Jesus at first speaks of the destruction of Jerusalem and farther on, and until the close, of his return at the end of all things, and that he places the two events in immediate connection" (*Life of Jesus,* Vol. III, p. 95). From this incorrect exposition Strauss came to the conclusion, with which many today concur, that since Christ's visible return has not taken place "the announcement of Jesus appears so far to have been erroneous" (*ibid.* p. 85).

Several generations ago Albert Schweitzer in his *The*

Quest of the Historical Jesus (1911) maintained that Jesus believed himself to be Israel's Messiah of the end-time but embraced death because the consummation did not arrive when he expected it. Schweitzer believed that Jesus shared the apocalypticism of his day. How utterly ridiculous this contention is can be seen in the parable of the Ten Pounds which Jesus used to counteract such expectations, "And as they heard these things, he added and spake a parable, because he was nigh to Jerusalem, and because they thought that the kingdom of God should immediately appear" (Luke 19:11).

Others have followed the lead of Strauss and Schweitzer and claim that either Jesus was mistaken or that his prophetic discourses are interpolations. C. C. McCown writes, "Either Jesus is mistaken or these discourses are not from him. The Christian Church cannot without disloyalty escape this dilemma" (*The Search of the Real Jesus*, pp. 243-244). In his book, *The Historic Mission of Jesus*, C. J. Cadoux suggests, "It seems on the whole preferable to explain such discrepancies as the chapter contains partly by the natural tendency of Mark (as of the other evangelists) to put in close proximity to one another sayings originally spoken on different occasions, and partly to the tendency of the early Church to modify radically certain remembered sayings of Jesus and even to ascribe to him (without any dishonest intent) some sayings which in point of fact he never actually uttered."

Even scholars who lean to the conservative position have yielded to the opinion that Jesus was wrong in his prophecies. G. R. Beasley-Murray in his book, *Jesus and the Future*, writes that he "hesitated long before capitulating before the facts." But capitulate he did: "Yet facts they appear to be and the Christian must come to terms with them; to resist what appears to be truth is to deny the Lord in whose interest it is done." He would seek to explain Christ's mistaken confidence of the nearness of the final kingdom on the ground "that his conviction of the nearness of the victory was due to the clarity of that vision." Dr. Beasley-Murray disregards the teaching of the parables of the Mustard Seed and the Leaven that a process of time is involved in the establishment of the kingdom. Christ does not confuse the consummate kingdom with his messianic kingdom as so many scholars seem to do.

Another scholar, Oscar Cullmann, takes issue with the school of "thorough-going eschatology" in his statement, "In the Church of Christ, eschatology is, in fact, an absolutely chronological concept, and it cannot be conceived as the expression of 'our permanent availability for existential decision' (Bultmann). Eschatology must not be interpreted so metaphysically as to dispel its substance altogether" (*The Early Church*, p. 144). However, Cullmann also believes that Christ taught his imminent return and that this was the belief of the early Church, "it must be recognized that in the early Church, just as much as in Mark 9:1, Matthew 10:23 and Mark 13:30 no one reckoned on the period between the ascension and the return of the Master lasting for centuries" (*ibid.* p. 152). Cullmann argues for the return of Christ to earth. This has caused another scholar to charge: "It is a strange commentary upon Dr. Cullmann's work that many of his arguments and diagrams bear a close resemblance to those of the older fundamentalist distinction, also emphasized by Dr. C. H. Dodd, between the kingdom of Christ and the kingdom of God, and sees them as successive stages in the realization of the divine purpose of the ages" (J. E. Fison, *The Christian Hope*, p. 57).

Sufficient has been quoted to evidence an utter confusion among scholars as to the interpretation of the teachings of the New Testament. There seems to be a unanimity that Christ was mistaken as were the apostles; no thought is allowed that the exegesis of the scholars may be at fault.

Without question modern scholars follow the "literalist" interpretation, popularized by the premillennial school and formerly condemned by the same scholars. The misunderstanding of the Thessalonians has become traditional. The admonition of Paul is wasted on many students of eschatology, "that ye be not soon shaken in mind, or be troubled, neither by spirit, nor by word, nor by letter as from us, as that the day of Christ is at hand" (II Thess. 2:2). Neither Paul nor Christ taught the "imminent" parousia as popularly conceived. And certainly there is no basis for it in the Olivet Discourse of our Lord. What has been ignored in the interpretation of this prophetic discourse is the existence of an "apocalyptic dialect"—a traditional language employed by the prophets and used by Christ and the apostles.

The author planned at first to include a criticism of the school of "thorough-going eschatology" in this second edition but came to the opinion that a positive exposition of the Matthew account of the Olivet Discourse would be the best answer.

J.M.K.

Table of Contents

Section Two
MATTHEW TWENTY-FOUR

Chapter I

The Time Text

Verily I say unto you, This generation shall not pass, till all these things be fulfilled (Matthew 24:34).

A storehouse to prophetic students, a perplexity to lay readers, and to others a labyrinth of errant eschatological notions—such are the reactions to Matthew Twenty-four. Many will agree that this Chapter, with its vivid prophetical language, is difficult to understand. Commentators have only added to the confusion of interpretation by indicating their "double meanings," "prophetic perspectives," and "partial and complete fulfillments." These intended solutions to the exegesis of difficult verses have in no way contributed to a right understanding of Jesus' prophetic discourse. Yet, to those who will allow Scripture to interpret Scripture, there is a key that unlocks simply for us the meaning of this difficult passage. The key to Matthew Twenty-four is verse 34.

We might term this key verse the "time text" of the Chapter. If the literal and well-defined meaning of this verse be accepted, then we shall quite readily perceive that the verse divides the entire Chapter into two main sections. Section One speaks of events which were to befall the contemporary generation of Jesus. Section Two relates to events that are to occur at the second coming of the Lord. Verse 34 thus is the division point of the two sections.

There are some who would maintain that the vivid language of Section One (Matthew 24:1–35) militates against such a division. *False Christs—wars, famines, pestilences, earthquakes—the Gospel preached to all nations—the abomination of desolation—great tribulation—false prophets—sun and moon darkened—stars falling from heaven—Son of Man coming in the clouds:* all these things seem to indicate the time of the end. The Church has been acclimatized so to regard these phrases as indicative of the second coming of Christ. Indeed, that some of the events of the first section did find fulfillment, or at least partial fulfillment, during the generation of Christ no one will seriously argue. But that all the events were fulfilled at this particular time is debatable. Many insist that the majority of events mentioned by our Lord will only find fulfillment in the period immediately preceding the second coming. Nevertheless, a literal, well-defined meaning of verse 34 can be accepted, and that all the events of Section One have been fulfilled in the generation specified by our Lord.

Our Lord made the definite pronouncement that "This generation shall not pass, till all these things be fulfilled." Viewing what is obvious from this sentence, one would judge that every thing mentioned in the previous verses were to be fulfilled before the contemporary generation would pass away. That is certainly the evident meaning, and one that may be taken as literal. The generation living at the time of

Christ would not pass away until all the things he had mentioned hereto were manifested.

The Meaning of "Generation"

To obviate what seems to be the clear statement of verse 34, some interpreters would substitute another meaning for the word "generation." The idea of "race," "nation," or "Israel," replaces that of contemporary generation. For instance, Dr. L. S. Chafer in his book, *The Kingdom in History and Prophecy,* states: "Israel, as a nation, not one generation, is to be divinely preserved until all be fulfilled: 'Verily I say unto you, This generation (genea, race, or stock, Israel) shall not pass, till all these things be fulfilled. Heaven and earth shall pass away, but my words shall not pass away' " (p. 137). Dr. Chafer indicates that Christ intended to teach that Israel as a nation would not pass away till all these things be fulfilled. But he has no warrant for that claim because the word "generation" nowhere in Scripture suggests the idea of a nation in its successive generations. One must conclude that an extraneous meaning is imported into *generation* simply because its inherent meaning does not fit a certain bent of interpretation.

The best way to determine the meaning of a word in the New Testament is to see how it is used in its various passages. By noting that word in other parts in the gospel of Matthew, one thereby gathers the sense in which the author has used it. Wherever the word in question is used in Matthew, it means a contemporary race, people living at the same time, the generation then living.

Matthew 1:17 states, "So all the generations from Abraham to David are fourteen generations; and from David until the carrying away into Babylon are fourteen generations; and from the carrying away into Babylon unto Christ are fourteen generations." Here the sense of the word is that of the average life-time of man which may be anywhere from thirty to a hundred years. One cannot possibly substitute the notion "nation" in this passage.

Matthew 11:16 states, "But whereunto shall I liken this generation? It is like unto children sitting in the markets, and calling unto their fellows." Jesus is speaking of those living in his day who criticized John for his fasting and Jesus for his eating and drinking. It was not Israel in successive generations who made this criticism but that *present* generation. The idea of a nation in its successive generations cannot be substituted for the meaning obvious here.

In the passage, Matthew 12:38–45, *generation* is used four times. The scribes and Pharisees were demanding a sign, and Jesus stated that the only sign for this evil and adulterous generation would be the sign of the prophet Jonah, which was indicative of his death and resurrection within the present generation. It was only the generation then living that witnessed the death and resurrection of Christ. So again it is not possible to substitute the idea of the nation in its successive generations. Jesus also stated in the same passage that the men of Nineveh and the queen of the south would rise up in judgment over this generation and condemn it. Neither would condemn every generation of the Jewish race, only would they condemn the present generation because it did not repent at the preaching of one greater than Solomon. Again Jesus is speaking of the *present* generation.

Matthew 16:4 is similar to the early verses of the above passage. Jesus warns the scribes and the Pharisees that to the present generation there would be no sign given except the sign of the prophet Jonah. Jesus again could only be speaking of the generation then living.

Matthew 23:36 is conclusive in the words, "Verily I say unto you, All these things shall come upon this generation."

As the verse stands in its context, no other generation could be meant but the one living at the time of Christ. This verse is practically identical to Matthew 24:34.

Thus the understanding common to all the passages in Matthew where the word generation appears is that of a contemporary race, people living at the same time of Christ, the generation then living. It is further emphasized by the demonstrative pronoun "this." It is *this* generation, not a generation or generations in the future.

Dr. J. A. Alexander, discussing a parallel passage, Mark 13:30, and basing his conclusions on the study of this word as he found it throughout the New Testament, remarks: "Common to all these cases is the radical idea of *contemporaneous existence,* which it would be monstrous therefore to exclude in that before us, as we must do, if we understand it of the whole race in its successive generations." To change the meaning of "this generation" to that of the Jewish nation in its successive generations would indeed be unwarranted and unscriptural. Only the stress of having to fit this word to some "prophetic scheme" has brought about such interpretation, along with a misunderstanding of the true meaning of previous verses in the Chapter. As Dr. David Brown wrote, "Nothing but some fancied necessity arising out of their view of prophecy, could have led so many sensible men to put this gloss upon our Lord's words" (p. 464, *Second Advent*). Surely the gospel of Matthew indicates the precise meaning of the word *generation.*

Corroborating Texts

In the twenty-third chapter of Matthew, Jesus denounces the scribes and Pharisees for their hypocrisies and sins. In verse 32 he exhorts them, "Fill ye up then the measure of your fathers." Jesus is saying that the cup of the iniquity of the Jewish nation is just about filled to the brim. The present generation would completely fill that cup and cause the judgment of God to fall upon it. The cup was filled to the brim by the greatest work of iniquity—the crucifixion of the Son of God and the persecution of his apostles and prophets (23:34). Jesus concludes his judgment (23:35, 36): "That upon you may come all the righteous blood shed upon the earth, from the blood of righteous Abel unto the blood of Zacharias, son of Barachias, whom ye slew between the temple and the altar. Verily I say unto you, all these things shall come upon this generation." As the contemporary generation filled the cup of iniquity by rejecting and crucifying the Lord of glory, so God would fall upon it the heaviest stroke of his judgment. That Christ meant the generation then living is obvious. Since the meaning of Matthew 23:36 is so clear, the similar expression in Matthew 24:34 must certainly be as well.

That some great catastrophe was to happen to the present generation is the burden also of Matthew 16:28: "Verily I say unto you, There be some standing here, which shall not taste of death, till they see the Son of man coming in his kingdom." Surely no one can twist the expression, "some standing here" to mean a generation removed by several thousand years. Jesus was coming in judgment upon the existing generation and this verse points to the meaning of Matthew 24:34. Some maintain that the strong and vivid language used to describe the sufferings of those upon whom the judgment would fall is too strong for the generation of that day, and must refer therefore to events previous to the second coming. However, in Luke 23:28–30 Jesus states, "Daughters of Jerusalem, weep not for me, but weep for yourselves, and for your children. For, behold, the days are coming, in the which they shall say, Blessed are the barren, and the wombs that never bare, and the paps which never gave suck. Then shall they begin to say to the mountains, Fall on us; and to the hills, Cover us." Here Jesus employs the same type of language as in the first portion of Matthew Twenty-four where he is describing the sufferings and anguish that were to come upon the present generation. Surely no one can mistake the daughters of Jerusalem and their children for a generation several thousand years hence.

Continuous Fulfillment

A rather desperate attempt to escape the obvious meaning of the time-text is the explanation by some that the verb for "be fulfilled" should be translated "shall begin to be fulfilled." Thayer's *Greek-English Lexicon* gives "to begin to be" as a possible meaning for *ginomai* although it indicates the meaning of this verb in Matthew 24:34 as "to come to pass, happen." Suppose, for a moment, that "to begin to be" is the correct meaning of the verb in verse 34: then it involves the whole structure of what precedes as well as allowing reference both to the destruction of Jerusalem and the second coming. According to this meaning, at the destruction of Jerusalem the sun "began to be" darkened; the moon "began to be" reluctant in giving light; the stars began their falling; the Son of man began coming in the clouds of heaven, and so forth. The mere statement of how this meaning would affect the structure of the preceding verses in sufficient to show that Thayer is correct in indicating that *ginomai* means "to come to pass, happen" in verse 34.

Destruction of Jerusalem

What great event, then, was to occur to the existing generation that Christ should use such strong and vivid language in describing it? The event was the destruction of Jerusalem in the year 70 A.D. and the excision of the Jewish nation from the Kingdom. All the verses of Matthew Twenty-four up to verse 34 depict this disaster. All the verses up to 34 describe the destruction of the Holy City and the events leading up to this destruction. "All these things," as Jesus indicates, were to come upon the generation then living. John the Baptist had warned the nation that the ax was at the roots (Matt. 3:10); Jesus shows exactly how and when the ax would fall. Furthermore, Jesus gives emphasis to this prophecy by stating in verse 35, "Heaven and earth shall pass away, but my words shall not pass away." He wanted no one to be in doubt that all the things which he prophesied would be fulfilled in the contemporary generation.

Chapter II

The Transition Text

But of that day and hour knoweth no one, not even the angels of heaven, neither the son, but the Father only (Matthew 24:36, ARV).

The first thirty-four verses of Matthew 24, along with verse 35 in which Jesus confirms the certainty of his prophesies, deal with the destruction of Jerusalem and its temple. After Jesus had asserted that the buildings of the temple would be completely demolished, the puzzled and astonished disciples asked, "When shall these things be?" Jesus had answered their question in the first part of his discourse. He had given a detailed picture of the events which were to occur within the present generation. Now with verse 36 Christ commences a new subject, namely, his second coming and the events preceeding it. This verse may be termed the "transition text" of the chapter.

Jesus had been definite about the circumstances and time of the destruction of Jerusalem; but in his Messianic capacity he disclaimed knowledge about the time of his second coming. That moment when the Messianic age would be completed and the world destroyed was known only to God the Father. As a consequence Jesus did not disclose the time of his coming in judgment upon the entire world like he did with the coming of judgment upon the contemporary generation.

The Day and Hour

A common expression in the Scriptures for the final and universal Judgment is that which Jesus utters in the transition text: *that day and hour*. That phrase, with reference to the final Judgment, must have been a familiar one to the disciples who would perceive it as the answer to their question concerning the time of the end of the age (24:3). Other parts of Scripture employ the same expression:

"Many will say to me in that day, Lord, Lord, have we not prophesied in thy name? and in thy name have cast out devils? and in thy name done many wonderful works?" (Matt. 7:22). "But I say unto you, It shall be more tolerable for Tyre and Sidon at *the day of judgment,* than for you" (Matt. 11:22).

"Marvel not at this: for *the hour* is coming, in the which all that are in the graves shall hear his voice, and shall come forth; they that have done good, unto the resurrection of life; and they that have done evil, unto the resurrection of damnation" (John 5:28,29).

Besides finding reference to these expressions in the Gospels we find frequent reference to "the day" and "that day" in the Epistles, i.e., I Thess. 5:2; II Thess. 1:10; II Tim. 1:12,

18; 4:8; and Jude 6. These passages reveal that "the day" and "that day" have reference to the time when Christ comes with his holy angels to reward his saints and pass final and complete judgment upon his enemies. It was not necessary for Christ to explain that he was now turning to the subject of the final Judgment, because the disciples were acquainted with the significance of the phrase, "that day and hour."

It becomes apparent that in Matthew 24:36 Christ passes from the subject of the destruction of Jerusalem, or his judgment against the Jewish nation, to his second coming at the end of the age when he would judge the world. He had given the time of the former, but of the latter ". . . that day and hour knoweth no one, not even the angels of heaven, neither the Son, but the Father only." As Spurgeon states in his commentary: "There is a manifest change in our Lord's words here, which clearly indicates that they refer to his last great coming to judgment" (*The Gospel of the Kingdom*, p. 218).

Vivid Contrast

Further evidence that verse 36 is a transition verse can be seen from the contrast in content between the two sections of Matthew Twenty-four and Twenty-five. In the First Section (24:4–35), Jesus is very definite in his description of the events and the time of his judgment against the Jews. In the Second Section (24:36–25:46), however, Jesus cannot give the time of his second coming nor an indication of the events that are to precede it.

We may notice in the First Section how definite Christ is about his coming in judgment. He tells of things which are to precede this coming, i.e., false christs, wars and rumors of wars, famines, pestilences, earthquakes, persecutions, betrayals, false prophets, and apostasy. One explicit sign of the end is to be the preaching of the Gospel as a witness to all nations. Another sign will be the abomination of desolation

69

spoken of in Daniel. Then there would be a terrible tribulation. This was to be followed by the sun and moon being darkened and the stars falling from the heavens. Christ concludes his precise description with these words: "Now learn a parable of the fig tree; when his branch is yet tender, and putteth forth leaves, ye know that summer is nigh: so likewise ye, when ye shall see all these things, know that it is near, even at the doors." The disciples by the signs and events which Jesus enumerated could judge the exact time of his judgment. They would be able to tell when it was at the door. All these signs are clear.

But now notice the vivid contrast in the Second Section which deals with his second coming. Everything about it is indefinite. Christ states that no man, nor angels, nor even the Son of man knows the day and hour of his second coming. This thought is emphasized throughout the Second Section: v. 42, "Watch therefore: for ye know not what hour your Lord doth come"; v. 44, "Therefore be ye also ready: for in such an hour as ye think not the Son of man cometh"; v. 50, "The Lord of that servant shall come in a day when he looketh not for him, and in an hour that he is not aware of"; and v. 13 of chapter 25, "Watch therefore, for ye know neither the day nor the hour wherein the Son of man cometh."

In the Second Section Jesus compares the days previous to his coming to the days of Noah. There was to be eating and drinking, marrying and giving in marriage. What a contrast this is to the famines, pestilences, and wars of the First Section! As the flood came without "signs," even so would be the coming of the Son of man. There would be normal occupation—two in the field and two grinding at the mill. But in the suddenness of his second coming men will have no time to flee to the mountains.

Another thing to note is that Christ compares his coming to a thief in the night. The whole point is that the thief would give no warning. On comparing the parable of the thief with the parable of the fig tree one discovers that they are a direct contrast. The fig tree gives warning of the approach of summer; the thief gives no warning.

The emphasis in the Second Section is also that of delay. The evil servant was able to say, "My Lord delayeth his coming." In the parable of the Ten Virgins the bridegroom tarried. And in the parable of the Talents we read, "After a long time the Lord of those servants cometh." The stress on delay is apparent in all these parables.

Thus the contrast between the two Sections is so vivid that one cannot help but notice it. The two cannot refer to the same event; the only logical explanation is that the First Section refers to Christ's coming in judgment against the Jews, and the Second Section speaks of his second coming.

Local Events

It is apparent that the First Section is limited to the locality of Palestine and to Jerusalem and its Temple in particular. That whole discourse was incited by Jesus' pronouncement that the Temple at Jerusalem was to be completely destroyed. The disciples had asked when this destruction was to take place. Christ did not ignore the question; he dealt with it. The abomination of desolation mentioned in verse 15 was definitely limited to the Temple. And it was the Temple that Christ indicated would be destroyed. Then in this First Section we learn that those who were in Judea were to flee to the mountains. The reference to the Sabbath Day proves also that the coming of Christ was to be limited to Palestine. Only in that country would travel on the Sabbath increase hardship, for the Jews would not help those who traveled on that day. All these references make it clear that the events of the First Section were local and limited to Palestine.

Commentators have recognized, of course, that some of the

events must find their realization in the destruction of Jerusalem and its Temple. Some premillennialists overcome this difficulty by building another Jerusalem and Temple in the future. They have no scriptural warrant for doing this. Christ was talking about the Temple then existing. "There shall not be left here one stone upon another, that shall not be thrown down." That is the Temple he had reference to in his prophecy. However, premillennialists are consistent in building another Jerusalem and Temple in the future, because in this way they can take the events of the First Section and relate them to the second coming.

Some amillennialists are not so consistent. In arbitrary fashion they relate some of the events to the destruction of Jerusalem and some to the second coming. They even rend asunder a sentence in order to make it fit with their conception. For instance, Professor Berkhof in his *Systematic Theology* (p. 697) refers to Matthew 24:5–14, 21, 22, 29–31 as describing the important events which have to occur before Christ's physical return at the last day. He omits reference to verse 20, as though verse 21 were not the concluding part of the sentence begun in verse 20! If verse 21 refers to what is to take place just previous to the Second Coming then verse 20 must also. And so must verses 15–19. How much more consistent in this instance is the premillennialist than the amillennialist!

Other commentators seek their way out of the difficulty by using the concept "prophetic perspective." In the Old Testament, they say, the prophets sometimes blend the first and second coming of Christ together. This is called the prophetic perspective. So, they claim, in this First Section, we have an example of the prophetic perspective. Jesus, the greatest prophet of them all, blends together the destruction of Jerusalem with the final destruction of the world. But this view cannot hold water in the presence of verse 34, "time text."

The Prophet definitely limits the perspective to the present generation. Who are we to extend his limitation?

The Second Section does not deal with a local judgment upon one nation. Matthew 25:31–46 gives us a picture of universal judgment. All the nations are gathered before the judgment seat of Christ. The scene of judgment is not upon earth, as in the First Section, but in Heaven. Hence in the Second Section there is no warning to flee to the mountains. The picture of the First Section is judgment upon earth in Palestine; the picture of the Second Section is judgment in Heaven upon all nations.

Therefore, when the "time text," verse 34, and the "transition text," verse 36, are considered together, it is not difficult to see that there are two definite Sections relating to two distinct matters. This is borne out by the contrast of subject matter which the two sections disclose. Section One (Matt. 24:4–35) refers to the destruction of Jerusalem and the excision of the Jewish nation from the Kingdom; and Section Two (Matt. 24:36–25:46) refers to the second coming of Christ.

73

Chapter III

The Context

Many passages in Scripture can only be understood when we study closely their context, immediate and remote. This is true not only of a single text we may be considering, but also an entire chapter. A whole section may depend, for proper exposition, upon our understanding the scope and plan of the writer's argument. Even the main thread of the entire Scriptures must be kept in mind if we are to interpret any part of them properly. The consideration of context is certainly important to the interpretation of Matthew Twenty-four. This Chapter does not stand by itself but is the culmination of a series of prophecies and warnings against the representatives of the Jewish nation. One of the main dramas of Matthew's Gospel, as well as the other Gospels, is the conflict between Christ and those who were the leaders of the Jewish nation.

One of the chief reasons why many commentators reject the idea that the First Section refers only to the destruction of Jerusalem is that they think the language of that Section too striking and bold for a description of such a local event. Such vivid language, they believe, can refer only to the events just previous to the second coming of the Lord. They forget that the destruction of Jerusalem, which resulted in the excision of the Jewish nation from the Kingdom, was one of the most important events that has ever occurred on earth, and that it had tremendous consequences. The destruction of Jerusalem signalized that the old dispensation was over and was never to return. And since the prophets in the Old Testament used such vivid language to announce the destruction of Gentile nations, should not our Lord have used the same type of language to announce the destruction of what was once his chosen nation and center of true worship?

In viewing Church history, one can see how under the providence of God the destruction of Jerusalem and its Temple was a definite blessing to the world. Paul indicates this in Romans 11 where he declares that the fall of the Jews would work to the salvation and riches of the Gentiles. One of the sharpest battles fought in the early Church was that against the judaizing tendencies of Jewish Christians. They continually tried to bring the Gospel under the carnal elements of the old dispensation. But God had made clear to them that he was through with the old material Jerusalem and the earthly Temple. The Kingdom as spiritually conceived and taught by Christ and the apostles would have met even greater opposition had the old City and Temple not been totally destroyed.

Even in the present time there are some within the Church who simply cannot believe that the old dispensation has been terminated. They still look for a temporal Jewish kingdom whose capital, Jerusalem, will hold sway over all the earth. This was the carnal conception of his kingdom which Christ fought and the apostles opposed, and against which his

Church must still fight. It is true that we look forward to the conversion of the Jewish nation, and that the whole world will be blessed by this conversion. But that is something entirely different from the idea of a temporal Jewish kingdom holding sway over all the nations of the world.

That the destruction of Jerusalem and its Temple would be one of the consequences of Christ's coming to earth is clear throughout the Gospels.

The Witness of John the Baptist

John the Baptist received the revelation that one of the consequences of the coming of the Messiah would be a visitation of God's wrath upon the Jewish nation. When the scribes and Pharisees came to his baptism he said to them, "O generation of vipers, who hath warned you to flee from the wrath to come?" (Matthew 3:7). He then warned them to repent if they be spared from the wrath to come, and not to rely upon the fact that they were the children of Abraham. In Matthew 3:10 he declares, "And now also the ax is laid unto the root of the trees." So near was the time of their excision that the ax was at the very roots. Only repentance would cause the ax to be withdrawn.

The Scriptures and history reveal that the Jews did not repent. Matthew Twenty-four simply states how and when the ax would fall. It is remarkable that in Matthew 23:33 Jesus uses almost word for word John's greeting to the scribes and Pharisees: "Ye serpents, ye generation of vipers, how can ye escape the damnation of hell." Thus the Lord links his warning of Jerusalem's destruction with that of John the Baptist.

The Jews Cast Out

Early in his ministry Christ gave similar warning and prophecy to the Jews. At the faith of a Roman centurion, he declared, "And I say unto you, That many shall come from the east and west, and shall sit down with Abraham, and Isaac, and Jacob, in the kingdom of heaven. But the children of the kingdom shall be cast out into outer darkness: there shall be weeping and gnashing of teeth (Matt. 8:11, 12)." Herein Jesus was declaring that the Jewish nation as a nation was to be cut off from the Kingdom because the people did not manifest true faith as did the Roman centurion. The privileges of the Kingdom were not for those who boasted of being children of Abraham according to the flesh, as many Jews believed, but on being children of Abraham by faith. Thus, believing Gentiles were to inherit the covenant blessings promised to Abraham, Isaac, and Jacob.

C. I. Scofield's reference to Matthew 11 describes a pivotal point in the ministry of Jesus in relation to an offer he makes of the Kingdom to the Jews. He comments: "The rejected King now turns from the rejecting nation and offers, not the kingdom, but rest and service to such in the nation as are conscious of need. It is a pivotal point in the ministry of Jesus." Scofield's references in the Bible place the emphasis on the rejected Christ; Scripture itself, however, places the emphasis on the rejected Jewish nation. Matthew 8:11,12 clearly indicates that the Kingdom was to be given to believing Gentiles while the Jews were to be cast into outer darkness. Even at an earlier period than that indicated in Matthew 8, Christ had said that the center of worship was not to be at Jerusalem of Palestine. In John 4 Jesus declares to the woman of Samaria, "Woman, believe me, the hour cometh, when ye shall neither in this mountain, nor yet at Jerusalem, worship the Father." The earthly Jerusalem was not to be the center of true worship in the New Dispensation. This revelation was made early in the ministry of Christ and not at some pivotal point referred to by Scofield's Bible reference.

Parables of Matthew Twenty-one

The antagonism between Christ and representatives of the Jewish nation becomes more and more apparent as Matthew continues the narrative of his Gospel. The parables of Matthew Twenty-one are aimed against the Jews and teach that the Jewish people would not possess the Kingdom. Jesus declares in one parable, "Verily, I say unto you, That the publicans and the harlots go into the kingdom of God before you" (v. 31). Publicans and harlots, who had been excommunicated from the theocracy of Israel, would enter into the kingdom of God before scribes and Pharisees.

The Parable of the Wicked Husbandmen had direct application to the chief priests and Pharisees, which they sensed. Jesus concluded that parable with the statement, "Therefore say I unto you, The kingdom of God shall be taken from you, and given to a nation bringing forth the fruits thereof" (v. 43). There is no indication of a "postponed kingdom" here but rather a kingdom taken away from the Jews and given to a nation bearing the fruits thereof. "The children of the kingdom" were to be cast out for their unbelief and the Gentiles would take their place.

The Final Debate

Matthew Twenty-two relates the final debate between Christ and various representatives of the Jewish nation. First, the Pharisees in company with the Herodians sought to entangle Jesus by asking whether it was lawful for a Jew to give tribute unto Caesar. Jesus silenced them with the reply, "Render therefore unto Caesar the things which are Caesar's; and unto God the things that are God's." Then the Sadducees sought to embarrass him by asking a question concerning the marital state of a woman who had been wife to seven brothers. Jesus silenced them also by stating that in the resurrection persons neither marry, nor are given in marriage. Later, a Pharisee sought to trap him with a question on the law, or which of the commandments was greatest. Christ answered, and then countered him with a question which the Pharisee did not dare to answer. From that day Jewish leaders asked him no more questions of that nature. Jesus had vanquished his enemies which in turn increased their antagonism.

The Judicial Sentence

The antagonism between Christ and the Jewish religious leaders came to a climax so far as Christ was concerned in Matthew Twenty-three. In this terrible chapter Christ like a lawyer sums up the crimes which the leaders of the nation have committed, and then like a judge he gives this sentence: "Behold, your house is left unto you desolate" (v. 38).

In a series of woes Christ denounces the scribes and Pharisees as hypocrites, blind guides, fools, whited sepulchres, serpents, and generation of vipers. He accuses them of shutting up the kingdom of heaven against men. He accuses them of extortion, false teaching, of lack of judgment, mercy and faith. Throughout this terrible denunciation and accusation one can catch the intense righteous indignation of Jesus —an indignation which abandons the objects of it as past all hope of reform and repentance.

In verse 32 of this denunciatory chapter, Christ declares, "Fill ye up then the measure of your fathers." The picture is that of a cup nearly filled and now being filled to overflowing by the present generation of Jews. National sin, accumulated over many centuries, had been trying the patience of God. Again and again the Jews had sinned against their God and forsaken him for idols. God had manifested to them his forbearance and longsuffering and had pleaded with the Jews to repent and return unto him. Now, with the rejection of his Son and the crucifixion approaching, the patience of God had come to an end. The cup of sin through this greatest of all crimes would overflow and bring upon the nation the terrible stroke of divine judgment.

In verse 34 Jesus shows how they would continue their wrath against those whom Christ would send to them after his ascension. They would kill, crucify, scourge, and persecute his apostles and prophets, as indeed they did. Consequently upon their generation would come the payment for all the righteous blood which had been shed by the hands of the wicked throughout preceding generations. So Jesus declares in Matthew 23:36, "Verily I say unto you, All these things shall come upon this generation." Jesus is emphasizing again that it was "this generation" that would fill the cup to overflowing and experience the terrible wrath of God.

The judicial sentence declared in verse 38 was, "Behold, your house is left unto you desolate." This was truly the sentence of death. God, as it were, forsook the Temple which had once been his dwelling place, and by his departure the Temple was left a sepulchre. It would henceforth be a blot upon the earth and fit only to be destroyed. Christ no longer calls it "*my* house" as he did in Matthew 21:13, but "*your* house left unto *you* desolate." The Temple thus was forsaken by the living God. No longer would he dwell in the Holy of Holies of the earthly Temple. The House of God was now the House of Desolation. And being the House of Desolation its destruction was inevitable.

Destruction of the Temple

After Jesus pronounces his judicial sentence, he departs from the Temple never to return. His disciples, so stunned by that pronouncement, come to him to show him the buildings of the Temple. It seems as though they try to say, "How could such a beautiful building become desolate? Surely, Master, you did not mean that this Temple will become desolate!" But Jesus answers, "See ye not all these things? Verily I say unto you, There shall not be left here one stone upon another, that shall not be thrown down." This prophecy was literally fulfilled in the year 70 A.D., and was accompanied with a tribulation such as the world had never witnessed. It was this prophecy that caused the disciples to ask when the time of the destruction of the Temple would be. Jesus informs them, and the record of this information is contained in Matthew 24:4-35. That marks the climax of the antagonism between Christ and the Jews. For their unbelief and apostasy, God was going to visit them in wrath. Surely in the light of this terrible catastrophe to the Jewish nation, once beloved of God, we can hardly say that the language of Matthew 24:4-35 is too strong and too vivid. In the context it is something we would expect.

A Hint of Future Repentance

In the concluding verse of Matthew Twenty-three, Christ states that the Jewish nation would be desolate until such a time as the Jews would say, "Blessed is he that cometh in the name of the Lord." The Jews, who are not now the "chosen" race, will some day be included amongst the chosen. The Apostle Paul also indicated this in Romans 11. When the Jews accept the messenger of the Gospel, Christ will dwell with them again. Jesus declares, "For I say unto you, Ye shall not see me henceforth, till ye shall say, Blessed is he that cometh in the name of the Lord." Until that time the Jewish nation will be desolate as history has so clearly revealed. God will not dwell with them until they accept the message of the Messiah.

Chapter IV

The Question of the Disciples

Tell us, when shall these things be? and what shall be the sign of thy coming, and of the end of the world? (Matthew 24:3).

In the Twenty-third chapter of Matthew, Christ summed up the crimes of the representatives of the Jewish nation and further declared that the present generation would fill the cup of iniquity to overflowing. This they did by the crucifixion of Christ and the persecution of his followers. Christ indicated that God would thus visit upon them "all the righteous blood shed upon the earth, from the blood of righteous Abel unto the blood of Zacharias" (Matt. 23:35). Following these words Christ pronounced the judicial sentence, "Behold, your house is left unto you desolate."

Christ prefigured the desolation of the Jewish House of God by his departure from it: "And Jesus went out, and departed from the Temple" (Matt. 24:1). This meant he would never return until he returned in judgment. When Christ pronounced that the Temple would be desolate, the disciples were horrified. "Master, behold," they exclaimed, "what manner of stone and what manner of buildings!" (Mark 13:1). How could the living God desert the beautiful Temple wherein God had promised to dwell? The Jews expected that the Temple of Jerusalem would be the center of worship for the entire world in the days of the Messiah. They believed that in his days the Temple would be the glory and beauty of the earth, and God would manifest himself there. It was unimaginable that God would forsake the Temple at Jerusalem during the Messianic age!

In order to convince his disciples that the desolation of the Temple meant utter destruction, Jesus added, "See ye not all these things? Verily, I say unto you, There shall not be left here one stone upon another, that shall not be thrown down" (Matt. 24:2).

Jesus meant to impress it upon their minds that he was speaking about the Temple which they were admiring. Was it in vain that Jesus had tried to instruct them to look for a spiritual fulfillment of many prophecies? The disciples apparently could not eliminate from their thoughts the notion that the material Temple would be the center of worship for the entire world. For them the destruction of the Temple would be the end of the world. Yet Jesus clearly informed them, "There shall not be left here one stone upon another, that shall not be thrown down." This prophecy, as we mentioned before, was literally fulfilled in 70 A.D. Titus, the Roman general who led the siege of Jerusalem, ordered the walls of the city and those of the Temple to be demolished. So thoroughly was this accomplished that Josephus, the historian, commented: "there was left nothing to make those who had come thither believe it had ever been inhabited."

Significance of the Question

The disciples do not doubt, of course, that Christ's words would be literally fulfilled for we read that upon the Mount of Olives they ask him privately, "Tell us, when shall these things be? And what shall be the sign of thy coming, and of the end of the world?" This question is important in our understanding of the prophecy that follows. We must never forget that the Olivet discourse was given in answer to that specific question. This is not to say that the disciples had a distinct understanding of what their question involved. They had frequently revealed their confusion about the true nature of the Messiah and his Kingdom, and Christ had upbraided them for their defective understanding. Even after his resurrection he called several of them, "fools and slow of heart to understand all that the prophets have spoken." Nevertheless, despite the confusion evidenced in this disciples' question, we must discover what they had in mind when they interrogated Jesus concerning the destruction of the Temple.

To ascertain this, we may consult parallel passages. For instance, the question of the disciples is recorded a little differently in Mark and Luke than it is in Matthew. Here is a comparison of the three:

"Tell us, when shall these things be? and what shall be the sign of thy coming, and of the end of the world?" (Matt. 24:3).

"Tell us, when shall these things be? and what shall be the sign when these things are all about to be accomplished" (Mark 13:4).

"Master, when therefore shall these things be? and what shall be the sign when these things are about to come to pass?" (Luke 21:7).

84

The above parallel passages suggest that there are two things which the disciples desire to know. First, they want to know *when* these things would come about, and second, they desire to know the *sign* as to when these things were about to be accomplished. The *time* and the *sign* of the time figure prominently in the question of the disciples. That their question relates to the destruction of the Temple is obvious from the context. They had just been pointing to the Temple and Jesus had declared concerning it, "See ye not all these things? Verily I say unto you, There shall not be left here one stone upon another, that shall not be thrown down." Immediately then the disciples ask, "When shall these things be?" What could be more obvious than that the disciples are asking about the time when not one stone would remain upon another of the Temple?

If the writer has labored the point in showing that Christ's pronouncement concerned the Temple then standing in Jerusalem, and that the disciples' question relates to the same Temple, it is to be apologized. I have done this because I am aware that some premillennialists refer the Olivet discourse to some future Temple. They claim that Christ does not answer the question of the disciples in regard to the existing Temple. Yet that is precisely what Christ is talking about, and that is the main concern of the disciples. Christ had made a prophecy of the destruction of the Temple standing before him and his disciples, and they are asking him when this destruction would take place. Had a future Temple been the subject of consideration, Christ would have so informed the disciples. Hardly would he have misled them in thinking he was speaking about a contemporary building when he had a future one in mind. We can thus rest assured that Christ gives the disciples a direct answer.

The Sign

The disciples want to know not only the *when* of the destruction, but the *sign* that would precede it. Notice that where Matthew declares, "what shall be the sign *of thy coming?*" Mark writes, "what shall be the sign *when these things are all about to be accomplished?*" and Luke states, "what shall be the sign *when these things are about to come to pass?*"

After asking when *these things* shall be, the disciples ask, "what shall be the sign when *these things* are about to come to pass?" "These things" refer to the same matter both times. And as Christ also uses the expression "these things" in answer to them, we would have to admit to a sad state of confusion if Christ and his disciples had not been talking about the same subject.

The form of the disciples' question in Matthew is different from that in Mark and Luke. Instead of the sign as to when these things would come to pass, the question reads, "what shall be the sign of thy coming?" The expression "sign of thy coming" equates the expression "sign when these things are about to come to pass." Matthew reveals that in the mind of the disciples the destruction of the Temple indicated the coming of the Lord. The word he uses for "coming" is "parousia," indicating the second coming of Christ. The question as stated in the Gospel of Matthew reveals that to the disciples the destruction of the Temple was to occur at the second coming of the Lord.

The disciples shared the common belief that the Temple would remain throughout the new age introduced by the Messiah. The Jews thought that the Temple would last until the end of time and this idea was based on their interpretation of Old Testament prophecy. God had declared to Solomon, "I have hallowed this house which thou hast built, to put my name there forever." Psalm 78:68,69 declares, "He chose the tribe of Judah, the Mount of Zion which he loved. And he built his sanctuary like high palaces, like the earth which he had established for ever." Jewish interpretation of these biblical prophecies took for granted an everlasting Temple that would become especially glorious when the Messiah came upon the earth. Their error consisted of the failure to realize that the earthly Temple was but a type of the spiritual Temple: Christ Jesus and his Church.

Even as the disciples did not understand that the Kingdom would be spiritual, neither did they understand that the Temple would be spiritual. There was no excuse for their ignorance since Christ had indicated the spirituality of the Temple during the Gospel dispensation. In Matthew 12:6 he declared, "But I say unto you, That in this place is one greater than the Temple." He asserted in John 2:19,21, "Destroy this temple, and in three days I will raise it up. . . . But he spake of the temple of his body." And to the Samaritan woman he said, "Woman, believe me, the hour cometh, when ye shall neither in this mountain, nor yet at Jerusalem, worship the Father." In spite of these clear teachings the disciples at this time could not grasp the reality of a spiritual Temple: their thoughts were still on the material Temple at Jerusalem. So when Christ told them that the material House of God would be desolate they could not help pointing at the Temple and saying, "Master, see what manner of stones and what buildings are here!" Surely this Temple would remain until the end of time!

Throughout the ministry of Christ the disciples had been taught about the coming Day of Judgment (Matt. 10:15; 11:22; 12:36,41,42; 13:39,49). Therefore, when they heard Christ pronounce a judgment against Jerusalem and its Temple, it seemed natural for them to associate it with that great Day of Judgment about which they had heard so much. And as they had also been taught that the Day of Judgment was to occur at the second coming of the Lord, they associated the destruction with his second coming. That is why the question reads in Matthew, "And what shall be the sign of thy coming?" They thought that the Saviour would not destroy Jerusalem and its Temple until he came to put an end to the present state of the world at the Day of Judgment.

The End of the Age

Matthew adds another clause which is not expressed in the parallel passages of Mark and Luke: "And of the end of the world." The word "world" is not an exact translation of the Greek "aionos." The Greek word means "age." The disciples asked when the end of the age would be and what would be the sign of it. According to Matthew the disciples associated the "parousia" of Christ with the end of the age. Their question is "what shall be the sign of thy coming and of the end of the age?"

The fact that the disciples asked Christ concerning the end of the age presents a problem of interpretation. What was in the minds of the disciples when they asked concerning the end of the age? There is no doubt the disciples believed that the destruction of the Temple and the end of the age were one and the same thing. The fact that both Mark and Luke omit the expression, "the end of the age," would indicate this. If the expression represented a totally different idea, undoubtedly Mark and Luke would have included it. The destruction of the Temple, however, was associated in their minds with the end of the age and the mention of the one would bring to mind the other.

According to the Jews there were to be two ages: "This age" and "the age to come"—the pre-Messianic age and the Messianic age. We believe that in Matthew the question has reference to the end of the Messianic age. In the parable of the Tares (Matt. 13:39,40) the disciples were taught that the

Judgment would come at the end of the age. This could only be the Messianic age. The same teaching comes to the forefront in the parable of the Drag Net (Matt. 13:47–50). This parable pictures the Judgment. "So shall it be at the end of the world: the angels shall come forth, and sever the wicked from among the just, and shall cast them into the furnace of fire: there shall be wailing and gnashing of teeth." These parables indicate the writer's concept when he used the expression "the end of the age." So when we read this expression in the disciples' question, we may be sure that they are asking for the sign of the end of the Messianic age.

Whatever confusion there may have been in the minds of the disciples, Jesus in his answer separates the destruction of Jerusalem and its Temple from the end of the Messianic age. He rightly divides their question into two parts. First, he speaks of the *when* and the *sign* of the destruction of Jerusalem, and secondly he speaks of the *when* and the *sign* of the end of the Messianic age which would be contemporaneous with his second coming. The destruction of Jerusalem forms the content of Section One (24:4–35) and the end of the age forms the content of Section Two (24:36–25:46).

Chapter V

Misleading Signs of the End

And Jesus answered and said unto them, Take heed that no man deceive you. For many shall come in my name, saying, I am Christ; and shall deceive many. And ye shall hear of wars and rumors of wars: see that ye be not troubled: for all these things must come to pass, but the end is not yet. For nation shall rise against nation, and kingdom against kingdom: and there shall be famines, and pestilences, and earthquakes, in divers places. All these are the beginning of sorrows. Then shall they deliver you up to be afflicted, and shall kill you: and ye shall be hated of all nations for my name's sake. And then shall many be offended, and shall betray one another, and shall hate one another. And many false prophets shall rise, and shall deceive many. And because iniquity shall abound, the love of many shall wax cold. But he that shall endure unto the end, the same shall be saved (Matthew 24:4-13).

The disciples had asked Jesus for a sign that would signalize the destruction of Jerusalem and its Temple. Before giving them this peculiar sign, Christ proceeds to mention other signs that might mislead them in believing that the end of Jerusalem was at hand. That the disciples needed this caution is seen by the fact that even today these misleading signs are quoted as symbolizing the end of the world. How frequently are we not informed that the end of the world is at hand because we are having wars and rumors of wars? Christ stated explicitly that these are not signs indicating either the immediate end of Jerusalem or the end of the world. These signs that might have misled the disciples to believing that the end was at hand are given to us in Matthew 24:4–13. The passage reveals what is to occur in the period previous to the destruction of Jerusalem, 70 A.D.

False Christs

What the Jews expected was a Messiah who would set up a political kingdom and deliver them out of their grievous bondage to the Romans. The power of any political leader, of course, would be enhanced by a claim of Messiahship. For that reason Christ gives warning of false messiahs: "Take heed that no man deceive you. For many shall come in my name, saying, I am Christ, and shall deceive many."

History records but few of the names of those who claimed to be the Messiah in the period from the ascension of Jesus Christ to the destruction of Jerusalem. Undoubtedly many were too insignificant to be recorded by historians. But we do have allusions to those who tried to deceive the people by their claims. For instance, as early as in Acts 8:9,10, we read concerning a Simon Magus: "But there was a certain man, called Simon, which before time in the same city used sorcery, and bewitched the people of Samaria, giving out that himself was some great one: to whom they all gave heed, from the

91

least to the greatest, saying, This man is the great power of God." Several of the early Christian writers refer to Simon Magus. Justin relates that, in the time of Claudius Caesar, Simon was worshiped as a god at Rome on account of his magical powers. Jerome quotes Simon Magus as saying, "I am the Word of God, I am the Comforter, I am Almighty, I am all there is of God" (Mansel, *The Gnostic Heresies,* p. 82). And Irenaeus tells us how Simon claimed to be the Son of God and the creator of angels.

Origen informs us of a Dositheus who claimed that he was the Christ foretold by Moses. The historian Josephus describes the time of Felix as mentioned in Acts: "Now as for the affairs of the Jews, they grew worse and worse continually, for the country was again filled with robbers and impostors, who deluded the multitude. Yet did Felix catch and put to death many of those impostors every day, together with the robbers." This gives some idea of the number of persons who sought to deceive the multitudes with their false claims. To protect his followers from such impostors, Jesus foretold them and warned against being deceived by their claims.

Wars, Famines, Pestilences, and Earthquakes

The beginning of sorrows for the Jewish nation would consist of wars, famines, pestilences, and earthquakes. All these things would occur sometime previous to the destruction of Jerusalem. At the time Jesus revealed this state of affairs, the Roman Empire was experiencing peace within its borders. However, it was not long after the Olivet Discourse that strife, insurrections, and wars were filling both Palestine and other parts of the Roman Empire. In Rome itself, four emperors came to a violent death in the short space of eighteen months. Were one to give account of all the disturbances that actually occurred within the Empire after Jesus' death, he would be constrained to write a separate book.

To the Jews it was a highly turbulent time. There was an uprising against them in Alexandria. In Seleucia 50,000 were slain. In Caesaria a battle between Syrians and Jews brought death to about 20,000 Jews. The fight between Syrians and Jews divided many villages and towns into armed camps. Constant rumors of wars kept the Jewish people in an unsettled state. Josephus mentions how Caligula, the Roman Emperor, made orders that his statue be placed in the Temple of Jerusalem. Because the Jews refused to allow this, they lived in constant fear that the Emperor might send an army into Palestine. Some Jews lived in such fear that they dared not even plow and seed the ground.

Acts 11:28 makes mention of a famine which occurred in the day of Claudius Caesar. It was a famine that spread not only in Judea but other parts of the world, and like all famines, it was followed by pestilences that caused the death of thousands. And as to earthquakes, many are mentioned by writers during a period just previous to 70 A.D. There were earthquakes in Crete, Smyrna, Miletus, Chios, Samos, Laodicea, Hierapolis, Colosse, Campania, Rome, and Judea. It is interesting to note that the city of Pompeii was much damaged by an earthquake occurring on February 5, 63, A.D.

From the above evidence one may conclude that the prophecy of Jesus was literally fulfilled as to wars, famines, pestilences, and earthquakes. Christ told his disciples that they were not to be troubled by these things because these calamities did not indicate the end. Throughout history there have been those who have taken these signs as indicating the approaching end of the world. Even today, national and international calamities are said to be decisive proofs that the world is coming to its end. The Lord, however, teaches that these signs did not even mean the end of Jerusalem. He says, "But the end is not yet." Hence the disciples were not to be troubled when they beheld these events.

In verse 8 Jesus says, "All these are the beginning of sorrows." The word rendered "sorrows" in reality means "birth-pains." It is rightly translated in the American Revised Version as "travail." The word "travail" is a word of hope. It speaks of better things to come—of a new birth. It speaks of the regeneration of the world. As these "birth-pains" were to be in the earth, so would the birth or regeneration occur upon the earth. Thus, the "birth-pains" which Christ revealed in the First Section were not indicative of the final experience of the world: better things were going to come.

The Persecution of the Church

Beginning with verse 9 Jesus passes from the general sphere of the world to the particular sphere of the Church. He tells his disciples of the persecution and troubles they themselves would have to endure before the destruction of Jerusalem. These are his words: "Then shall they deliver you up to be afflicted, and shall kill you: and ye shall be hated of all nations for my name's sake."

One need go no further than the book of Acts for evidence of the fulfillment of this prophecy. Almost immediately after the preaching of the Gospel, the Apostles were put in prison and beaten. Stephen was stoned. James was killed by Herod. And there was great persecution against the Church in Jerusalem (Acts 8:1). Wherever the early missionaries went they were hated, persecuted, jailed and killed. Not only does the book of Acts record the hatred of all nations against the followers of Christ, but so do the works of Roman historians.

We get another true prophetic picture of the days previous to the destruction of Jerusalem in verse 10: "And then shall many be offended, and shall betray one another, and shall hate one another." Paul indicates the fulfillment of this state of affairs in a number of passages: "This thou knowest, that all they which are in Asia be turned away from me; of whom

94

are Phygellus and Hermogenes" (II Tim. 1:15); "For Demas hath forsaken me, having loved this present world, and is departed into Thessalonica; Crescens to Galatia, Titus unto Dalmatia. . . . at my first answer no man stood with me, but all men forsook me: I pray God that it may not be laid to their charge" (II Tim. 4:10,16). During the persecution instituted by Nero, it was common for Christians to betray their fellow Christians. Tacitus, the Roman historian, records, "that several Christians at first were apprehended, and then, by their discovery, a multitude of others were convicted, and cruelly put to death, with derision and insult."

That the period previous to the destruction of Jerusalem would produce many false prophets, as Christ had said, is revealed in Acts and in the Epistles. Serious conflicts between the Judaizers and true disciples are recorded in the book of Acts. Paul says, "For I know this, that after my departing shall grievous wolves enter in among you, not sparing the flock" (Acts 20:29). Almost every Epistle of Paul deals directly or indirectly with the harmful teachings of false prophets. Typical of his statements is that of Romans 16:17,18: "Now I beseech you, brethren, mark them which cause divisions and offenses contrary to the doctrine which you have learned; and avoid them. For they that are such serve not our Lord Jesus Christ, but their own belly; and by good words and fair speeches deceive the hearts of the simple." Peter warns, "But there were false prophets also among the people, even as there shall be false teachers among you, who privily shall bring in damnable heresies, even denying the Lord that bought them, and bring upon themselves swift destruction" (II Pet. 2:1). The Apostle John gives a similar warning in his first Epistle: "Beloved, believe not every spirit, but try the spirits whether they are of God: because many false prophets are gone out into the world" (I John 4:1). These are only a few of many New Testament passages that indicate the fulfillment of Christ's prohecy with regard to the time previous to the destruction of Jerusalem.

During this period there would not only be danger from false prophets, but the influence of prevalent wickedness dampening Christian zeal and love. Christ had indicated that the love of many would wax cold because of the prevalence of iniquity. This does not speak of apostasy but rather of spiritual deterioration. The Epistles give abundant evidence of the decrease of spirituality on the part of the churches. This was the burden of many Epistles. Again and again Paul had to admonish the Christians for their lack of zeal and love and for their lack of discernment. Hebrews 10:25 indicates that many forsook the assembling of themselves together for public worship. In Galatians 3:1-4, Paul complains that the foolish Galatians were soon bewitched by false prophets. To Timothy Paul revealed how the love of the world had caused Demas to leave him.

One of the most remarkable things about the siege of Jerusalem was the miraculous escape of the Christians. It has been estimated that over a million Jews lost their lives in that terrible siege, but not one of them was a Christian. This our Lord indicated in verse 13: "But he that shall endure unto the end, the same shall be saved." That the "end" spoken of was not the termination of a Christian's life but rather the end of Jerusalem is evident from the context. Immediately after this verse Christ goes on to relate the exact time of the end. Christians who would live to the end would be saved from the terrible tribulation. Christ indicates also the time for the Christian to flee from the city so that he could be saved during its destruction. This is verified in a parallel passage (Luke 21:18): "But there shall not an hair of your head perish." In other words, during the desolation of Jerusalem, Christians would be unharmed, although in the period previous to this some would lose their lives through persecution.

There are those who insist that verse 13 has reference to the salvation of the soul and that the endurance has reference to faithfulness to Christ. No doubt it may have such significance. But since Jesus immediately goes on to explain in detail how they may escape the terrible end of Jerusalem, it is more reasonable to think that Jesus is here signifying the saving of such followers alive at that time. Its primary application is to this life rather than the life hereafter. It was a remarkable fulfillment of that prophecy that none of Christ's disciples are known to have perished in the siege and destruction of Jerusalem.

Thus in the passage of our study, Matthew 24:4–13, Christ informs his disciples of signs that must not be taken to mean the immediate end of Jerusalem. These were but the beginning of sorrows. All these things would come to pass before the actual destruction of the city. History reveals that these signs did find fulfillment in the period designated.

Chapter VI

The Approximate and Real Sign
of the End

And this gospel of the kingdom shall be preached in all the world for a witness unto all nations; and then shall the end come. When ye therefore shall see the abomination of desolation, spoken of by Daniel the prophet, stand in the holy place, (whoso readeth, let him understand:) Then let them which be in Judea flee into the mountains (Matthew 24:14-16).

After indicating signs that might mislead the disciples to think that the time of the destruction of Jerusalem was at hand, Jesus gives what would be the approximate sign and the definite sign of that future event. Numerous incorrect interpretations have resulted from the Lord's statement that the Gospel of the Kingdom would be preached in all the world for a witness unto all nations. Many commentators

98

cannot see how this was fulfilled before the year 70 A.D. Yet the New Testament itself reveals that this prophecy was fulfilled, and for those who regard the New Testament as authoritative, this should be convincing enough.

How often have prophetic teachers, premillennial and amillennial, insisted that the end of the world would come after the Gospel has been preached as a witness to all nations. In saying this they have wrenched the verse out of its context. We see in the passage that Christ indicates no change of subject; he is still answering the disciples' question as to the destruction of Jerusalem and its Temple. And the verses that follow (15–21) show that he is speaking of an event in the locality of Judea. In other words, he is not speaking of the end of the world.

Christ says that before the end of Jerusalem the Gospel of the Kingdom would be preached for a witness to all nations. By this he does not mean that they would become Christian nations, but that they would have the opportunity of accepting the Gospel. It was no doubt an opportunity given to the Jews who were dispersed among the nations to embrace the Gospel. The custom of the Apostles was to witness to the Jews first with the message of the crucified Messiah. Then, such a proclamation of the Gospel would let the habitable world know the justification for the destruction of Jerusalem.

That all nations of that day heard the Gospel is definitely told in the book of Acts and the Epistles. Particular emphasis is given in the second chapter of Acts concerning the Jews from all nations of the world present on the day of Pentecost when the Gospel was proclaimed. "And there were dwelling at Jerusalem Jews, devout men, out of *every nation under heaven*" (Acts 2:5). The eighth chapter of Acts records how the Gospel went to Ethiopia, and we can well believe that there were similar incidents not recorded.

Paul, in writing to the Romans, rejoiced that their faith was known throughout the whole world. "First, I thank my God through Jesus Christ for you all, that your faith is spoken of *throughout the whole world*" (Rom. 1:8). The same fact is proclaimed in Colossians 1:6: "Which is come unto you, as it is *in all the world;* and bringeth forth fruit, as it doth also in you." In verse 23 of the same chapter Paul states: "If ye continue in the faith grounded and settled, and be not moved away from the hope of the gospel, which ye have heard, and which was preached to *every creature which is under heaven.*"

The above verses indicate beyond a doubt that the Gospel was preached by the apostles and their fellow laborers throughout the habitable world before the destruction of Jerusalem. Those who deny this must quarrel with the statements of Scriptures. All nations of the world heard the Gospel proclaimed before the year 70 A.D.

As a matter of interest, though not demonstrable proof, here is a quotation from Qualben's *History of the Christian Church* with regard to the traditional labors of the Apostles: "Tradition assigns the following fields to the various apostles and evangelists: Andrew is said to have labored in Scythia; hence the Russians worship him as their apostle. Philip spent his last years in Hierapolis in Phrygia. Bartholomew is said to have brought the gospel according to Matthew into India. The tradition concerning Matthew is rather confused. He is said to have preached first to his own people, and afterward in foreign lands. James Alphaeus is said to have worked in Egypt. Thaddeus is said to have been the missionary to Persia. Simon Zelotes is said to have worked in Egypt and in Britain; while another report connects him with Persia and Babylonia. The evangelist John Mark is said to have founded the Church at Alexandria."

This reference illustrates the ground for the Apostle Paul's frequent declarations—"throughout the whole world"; "in all the world"; "to every creature which is under heaven." We may be assured that the inspired writer spoke from authority. The Gospel was proclaimed as a witness to all nations dwelling upon earth at that time.

It is worthwhile to take notice of the difference between the prophecy of Matthew 24:14 and the Great Commission of Matthew 28:19,20. In the first, Christ speaks of witnessing to all nations; in the second, of making disciples of all nations. With regard to the former, Christ has Jerusalem in view; in the latter, he refers to the conversion of the world. The Great Commission states, "Go ye therefore, and make disciples of all nations, baptizing them in the name of the Father and of the Son and of the Holy Spirit: teaching them to observe all things whatsoever I command you: and lo, I am with you always, even unto the end of the world" (ARV). We cannot say with complacency, as so many do, that the mission of the Church is merely to witness to all nations. According to the Great Commission the Church's work is to make disciples of all nations and for the accomplishment of this, Christ has assured the Church of his presence.

The Real Sign of the End

Such signs as false Christs, wars, famines, pestilences, earthquakes, persecutions, false prophets, and spiritual coldness were not to be taken by the disciples as indicative of the time of the judgment upon Jerusalem. The real sign that the time was at hand is given in verse 15 to which we add verse 16 in order to supply the context: "When ye therefore shall see the abomination of desolation, spoken of by Daniel the prophet, stand in the holy place, (whoso readeth, let him understand:) then let them which be in Judea flee into the mountains."

The warning sign for the disciples to flee to the mountain

was the abomination of desolation standing in the holy place. Fortunately, we are not left to our imagination as to what the "abomination of desolation" would be. Luke tells us in the parallel passage that it refers to the Roman army. "And when ye shall see Jerusalem compassed with armies, then know that the desolation thereof is nigh. Then let them which are in Judea flee to the mountains; and let them which are in the midst of it depart out; and let not them that are in the countries enter thereinto" (Luke 21:20,21). To those who, believing in the authority of the Bible, interpret Scripture with Scripture, the phrase "abomination of desolation" affords no great difficulty. Luke, speaking of the same matter as Matthew in similar context, declares that it is the Roman army.

Many cling tenaciously to a preconceived theory on this subject, and dismiss this parallel passage of the Luke as not dealing with the same thing as Matthew. In comparing the two passages, however, we find that Luke introduces his passage the same way as Matthew, namely, with the question of the disciples in regard to the destruction of the Temple; and he records the same preliminary signs of false Christs, wars, earthquakes, and so forth. As Matthew's account warns those in Judea to flee when they see the abomination of desolation, so does Luke's Gospel warn those in Judea to flee when they see the army of desolation. The conclusion of both Matthew and Luke are similar. Can we honestly deny that both Matthew and Luke were writing of the same thing?

Why then was the Roman army designated "the abomination of desolation?" The Roman army carried ensigns consisting of eagles and images of the emperor to which divine honors were often paid by the army. No greater abomination could meet the eye of the Jew than the ensigns to which idolatrous worship was rendered. Josephus gives us an incident in his Eighteenth Book of the *Antiquities of the Jews* illustrating how the Roman ensigns were an abomination to the Jews.

"But now Pilate, the procurator of Judea, removed the army from Cesarea to Jerusalem, to take their winter quarters there, in order to abolish Jewish laws. So he introduced Caesar's effigies, which were upon the ensigns, and brought them into the city; whereas our law forbids us the very making of images; on which account the former procurators were wont to make their entry into the city with such ensigns as had not those ornaments. Pilate was the first who brought those images to Jerusalem, and set them up there; which was done without the knowledge of the people, because it was done in the night time; but as soon as they knew it, they came in multitudes to Cesarea, and interceded with Pilate many days that he would remove the images; and when he would not grant their request, because it would tend to the injury of Caesar, while yet they persevered in their request, on the sixth day he ordered his soldiers to have their weapons privately, while he came and sat upon his judgment-seat, which seat was so prepared in the open place of the city, that it concealed the army that lay ready to oppress them; and when the Jews petitioned him again, he gave a signal to the soldiers to encompass them around, and threatened that their punishment should be not less than immediate death, unless they would leave off disturbing him, and go their ways home. But they threw themselves upon the ground, and laid their necks bare, and said they would take their death very willingly, rather than the wisdom of their laws should be transgressed; upon which Pilate was deeply affected with their firm resolution to keep the laws inviolable, and presently commanded the images to be carried back from Jerusalem to Cesarea."

The above incident bears out the fact that the ensigns of the Romans were an abomination to the Jews—such an abomination that they were willing to die rather than tolerate them in their sacred city. The word "abomination" in Daniel has a definite connection with idolatry. The same word is used in I Kings 11:5,7 in reference to the idols of the Ammonites and the Moabites. (See also II Kings 23:13; Jer. 4:1, 7:30; 13:27; Ezek. 5:11). In all these passages the word "abomination" has reference to idolatrous worship. It cannot be denied that the idolatrous ensigns of the Romans fit very well into the biblical significance of the term "abomination."

Josephus gives this description of the city of Jerusalem after it was taken: "And now the Romans, upon the burning of the holy house itself, and of all the buildings round about it, brought their ensigns to the Temple, and set them over against its eastern gate; and there did they offer sacrifices to them" (*Wars of the Jews*, Book 6, chap. 6). In this incidence was the complete fulfillment of the prophecy of Daniel. The mere approach of these ensigns was sufficient to cause the Christians to flee. They remembered the word of the Lord, "Whoso readeth, let him understand." The city of Jerusalem and its temple were destroyed and made utterly desolate. The abomination did indeed cause desolation and another prophecy was remarkably fulfilled.

The Prophecy of Daniel Nine

Because our Lord quotes from the prophecy of Daniel, it may be profitable to study that passage to determine whether the above interpretation agrees with it. The reading is from Daniel 9:24–27; and following the American Revised Version, let us consider it verse by verse.

Seventy weeks are decreed upon thy people and upon thy holy city, to finish the transgression, and to make an end of sins, and to make reconciliation for iniquity, and to bring in everlasting righteousness, and to seal up vision and prophecy, and to anoint the Most Holy (Dan. 9:24).

The seven weeks are, in prophetic language, weeks of years. The period in which the above was to find fulfillment consisted of 490 years. During this period four things were to be accomplished: (1) reconciliation for inquity, (2) righteousness established, (3) sealing up vision and prophecy, and (4) the anointing of the Most Holy. All these things were to be accomplished by the Messiah.

The whole design of Christ's coming upon earth and dying upon Calvary's Cross was "to finish transgression, and to make an end of sins, and to make reconciliation for iniquity." Daniel, in his prayer previous to this particular prophecy, was deeply concerned with the forgiveness of both his and the people's transgressions, sins, and iniquities. God assures him that within the prophetic seventy weeks one would come who would remove these things. The whole of the New Testament proclaims that Christ did exactly what Daniel prophesied. For example, Peter declares, "But those things, which God before had shewed by the mouth of all his prophets, that Christ should suffer, he hath so fulfilled. Repent ye therefore, and be converted, that your sins may be blotted out. . . . Unto you first God, having raised up his Son Jesus, sent him to bless you, in turning away every one of you from his iniquities" (Acts 3:18,19,26).

Everlasting righteousness has been brought into this world by the incarnation, life, death, and resurrection of Jesus Christ. In the Gospel, says Paul, "Is the righteousness of God revealed from faith to faith" (Rom. 1:17). He further declares "For Christ is the end of the law for righteousness to everyone that believeth" (Rom. 10:4). And the apostles declare to the Philippians "and be found in him, not having mine own righteousness, which is of the law, but that which is through the faith of Christ, the righteousness which is of God by faith" (Phil. 3:9). Not only is the objective righteousness brought into this world but also the subjective righteousness: "That the righteousness of the law might be fulfilled in us, who walk not after the flesh, but after the Spirit" (Rom. 8:4). The New Testament indeed declares that Christ has brought in everlasting righteousness according to this prophecy of Daniel.

Also Christ sealed up both vision and prophecy by fulfilling the same. That is why Simeon could say upon beholding Christ: "Lord, now lettest thou thy servant depart in peace, according to thy word: for mine eyes have seen thy salvation." All things that were written concerning the Messiah, in the law, the prophets, and the psalms were fulfilled in and by Christ.

This period, referred to in Daniel, saw also the fulfillment of the anointing of the Most Holy. This anointing took place at the baptism of Jesus. Therefore, the Apostle Peter could declare, "How God anointed Jesus of Nazareth with the Holy Ghost and with power" (Acts 10:38).

Know therefore and discern, that from the going forth of the commandment to restore and to build Jerusalem unto the anointed one, the prince, shall be seven weeks, and threescore and two weeks: it shall be built again, with street and moat, even in troublous times (Dan. 9:25).

The seventy weeks are divided into three divisions: 7-62-1. They form in years: 49-434-7. At the time Daniel made this prophecy the children of Israel were in captivity and Jerusalem and its Temple were in ruins. The first period of 49 years was to accomplish the rebuilding of the city. This actually took place when Zerubbabel was governor over Judah. A number of Israelites were released from captivity, and they rebuilt the city. The books of Nehemiah and Ezra relate the troublous times that were experienced in the rebuilding. However, in spite of all these handicaps, the city was rebuilt.

And after the threescore and two weeks shall the anointed one be cut off, and shall have nothing: and the people of the prince that shall come shall destroy the city and the sanctuary; and the end thereof shall be with a flood, and even unto the end shall be war; desolations are determined (Dan. 9:26).

Notice that the above verse states *after* the threescore and two weeks shall the anointed one be cut off. The Anointed One is, of course, Christ Jesus. The 483 years (7 plus 62 weeks) takes us up to the ministry of Christ. During the last week of years the Messiah was to be cut off. We know that after three and a half years of his ministry the Anointed One suffered a violent death. Isaiah used the same expression in his fifty third chapter: "He was cut off out of the land of the living."

The prophecy records that this cutting off of Christ was *after* the sixty ninth week. There are those who maintain that the last week of this prophecy has as yet not been fulfilled in history. This amounts to a denial of the plain import of the prophecy that the death of the Anointed One was to be after the sixty ninth week and during the seventieth week. H. A. Ironside writes: "between the sixty ninth and the seventieth weeks we have a Great Parenthesis which has now lasted over nineteen hundred years. The seventieth week has been postponed by God Himself who changes the time and the seasons because of the transgressions of the people." Notice that it is Dr. Ironside who declares that the week has been postponed. God does not state it, nor does his Written Word. Although God does change the times and the seasons he does not change his infallible Word. How thankful we are that the week was not postponed and that the Messiah was actually cut off, as the prophecy declares, so that the wonderful promises of Daniel 9:24 were fulfilled in a real

107

and genuine way. If the seventieth week were postponed we would still be in our sins!

The expression, "And shall have nothing," seems to refer to the city and its Temple. In Matthew 23 Christ disowned Jerusalem with the statement, "Behold, your house is left unto you desolate." No longer was he saying "my house." The Temple and the city were nothing to Christ after their rejection of him. And it was because of this cutting off of the Messiah that the destruction of the city and its sanctuary was determined. Christ points out particularly in the parable of the Wicked Husbandmen that the killing of the Son was related as cause and effect to the rejection and punishment of the Jews (Matt. 21:33–46).

Dr. Edward J. Young points to another interpretation of the above expression. He writes: "They seem to indicate that all which should properly belong to the Messiah, he does not have when he dies. This is a very forceful way of setting forth his utter rejection, both by God and man. 'We have no king but Caesar,' cried the Jews. 'My God, my God, why hast thou forsaken me?' were the words from the Cross. In that hour of blackness he had nothing but the guilt of sin of all those for whom he died" (*The Prophecy of Daniel*, p. 207). The prophecy indicates that the destruction was to be accomplished by the people of the Prince, namely, the Romans under the command of the general Titus. As a matter of fact, the Roman soldiers destroyed the city and its sanctuary directly against his wishes. And that destruction was certainly as a flood, for the city and its Temple were completely destroyed.

And he shall make a firm covenant with many for one week: and in the midst of the week he shall cause the sacrifice and the oblation to cease: and upon the wing of abominations shall come one that maketh desolate; and even unto the

108

*full end, and that determined, shall wrath be poured out
upon the desolate"* (Dan. 9:27).

That firm covenant is none other than that which Christ
made with many. "For this is my blood of the new convenant,
which is shed for many for the remission of sins (Matt. 26:28).
We know that Christ by his death caused the sacrifice and
oblation to cease by fulfilling the shadow and becoming the
substance. "Who needeth not daily, as those high priests, to
offer up sacrifice, first for his own sins, and then for the
people's: for this he did once, when he offered up himself"
(Heb. 7:27). When Christ died upon the Cross the veil of
the Temple was rent in twain. Gone was the old system with
its shadows. Even for the unbelieving Jews, Jesus caused
the sacrifice and oblation to cease by the destruction of the
Temple and the city and by the dispersion of the Jews. This
is true even unto this day. Thus the prophecy of Daniel
9:24–27 finds its fufillment in the atoning sacrifice of Christ
and the destruction of Jerusalem. Dr. E. P. Pusey has stated:
"All this meets in one in the Gospel. He, the so long looked-
for, came: He *was* owned as the Messiah; he *did* cause the
sacrifices of the law to cease; he *was* cut off; yet he *did* make
the covenant with the many; a foreign army *did* desolate
the city and Temple; the Temple for these 1800 years (ed.
now 1900) has lain desolate; the typical sacrifices have
ceased, not through disbelief in their efficacy on the part of
those to whom they were once given."

A Possible Objection

The only valid objection against this general interpretation is that the destruction of Jerusalem did not occur within
the seventieth week—within the period of seven years. The
seventy weeks extended to about 33 A.D. The destruction of
Jerusalem, of course, came in 70 A.D. A close examination

of the passage in Daniel does not disclose any definite statement that the people of the prince were to cause this destruction within the seven years. Within the seven years the destruction of the city *was determined* by its rejection of Christ and his apostles. Because of this rejection "the people of the prince that shall come shall destroy the city and the sanctuary."

Christ himself stated that for a short period after his death he would send his prophets: "Wherefore, behold, I send unto you prophets and wise men, and scribes: and some of them ye shall kill and crucify; and some of them shall ye scourge in your synagogues, and persecute them from city to city." This actually happened before the seven year period was up. After the stoning of Stephen, the Church was scattered abroad and the message went to the Samaritans and Gentiles. Jerusalem, by the crucifixion of Christ and the persecution of his followers, overflowed the cup of iniquity. Jerusalem was nothing but a stinking carcass. As Jesus stated: "For wheresoever the carcass is, there will the eagles be gathered together." Jerusalem became a "carcass" during the seventieth week. It was only a matter of time when the "eagles" would come with the outward destruction.

Daniel prophesied that the events he enumerated were to occur in the continuous period of 490 years. Would not God have revealed to him that the last seven years were not to be joined to the 483? Did not God know that the Jews would reject his Son? The Scriptures and history have revealed that the prophecy of Daniel has been wonderfully fulfilled. The Scriptures do not tell us that the seventieth week has been postponed. If it were postponed, I repeat, we would still be in our sins and without hope.

If one can believe Luke, that the abomination of desolation is the Roman army, then the passage of Matthew 24:4–15 retains its unity. Verses 4–14 are the preliminary signs of the

110

destruction of Jerusalem. It is hard to see how one can divorce verse 15 and what follows it from verses 4–14. Dr. J. A. Alexander has stated: "The full force of this exhortation cannot be perceived except by viewing it in contrast with the former part of the discourse." Christ does not in the course of a sentence start with the destruction of Jerusalem and end with the destruction of the world. The whole scene of verses 15–21 is placed in Judea. What right have we to extend it outside the limits revealed to us?

Chapter VII

Great Tribulation

Let him which is on the housetop not come down to take any thing out of his house: Neither let him which is in the field return back to take his clothes. And woe unto them that are with child, and to them that give suck in those days! But pray ye that your flight be not in the winter, neither on the sabbath day: For then shall be great tribulation, such as was not since the beginning of the world to this time, no, nor ever shall be. And except those days should be shortened, there should no flesh be saved: but for the elect's sake those days shall be shortened (Matthew 24:17–22).

The great signal for the destruction of Jerusalem was to be the abomination of desolation spoken of through Daniel the prophet. This, Luke informs us, would consist of the armies surrounding Jerusalem. The warning was that when the Christians beheld the Roman armies they were to flee from Judea to the mountains. So great would be the need for haste that they were not even to descend from the housetops nor enter their homes for their personal belongings.

This admonition would have no significance to dwellers in twentieth century homes or penthouses, for it describes a situation peculiar to Jerusalem. The housetops of Jerusalem were flat. It was easy to walk from one roof to another. People, therefore, could actually flee the city at once along the tops of the houses, and thus escape to the mountains for safety. This is exactly what the Christians did and they were spared from the terrible horror of the siege of Jerusalem.

Josephus throws an interesting sidelight on this matter of the necessity of haste. Those within the city were not only prevented from escape by the enemy but also by the Zealots within the city. He writes: "And now the war having gone through all the mountainous country, and all the plain country also, those that were at Jerusalem were deprived of the liberty of going out of the city; for as to such as had a mind to desert, they were watched by the Zealots; and as to such as were not yet on the side of the Romans, their army kept them in, by encompassing the city round about on all sides."

In the midst of his warning, Christ mourns over the distress that would overcome expecting mothers and those with infants. Horrifying are the things which Josephus relates concerning them. He writes: "But the famine was too hard for all other passions, and it is destructive to nothing so much as to modesty; for what was otherwise worthy of reverence was in this case despised; insomuch that children pulled the very morsels that their fathers were eating out of their mouths, and what still more to be pitied, so did the mothers do as to their infants; and when those that were most dear were perishing under their hands, they were not ashamed to take from them the very last drops that might preserve their lives."

Josephus recounts a story about a wealthy and cultured woman that will illustrate the truth that Christ's description of the terrible tribulation was not extravagant. This woman had stored up a great deal of food. But during the siege, she was robbed of all that she had. Cursing the villains in her despair, "she then attempted a most unnatural thing: and snatching up her son, who was a child sucking at her breast, she said, 'O thou miserable infant: for whom shall I preserve thee in this war, this famine, and this sedition? As to the war with the Romans, if they preserve our lives, we must be slaves. This famine also will destroy us, even before than slavery comes upon us. Yet are these seditious rogues more terrible than both the other. Come on; be thou my food, and be thou a fury to these seditious varlets, and a by-word to the world, which is all that is now wanting to complete the calamities of us Jews.' As soon as she had said this, she slew her son, and then roasted him, and ate the one-half of him, and kept the other half by her concealed. Upon this the seditious came in presently, and smelling the horrid scent of this food, they threatened her that they would cut her throat immediately if she did not show them what food she had gotten ready. She replied that she had saved a very fine portion of it for them, and withal uncovered what was left of her son. Hereupon they were seized with a horror and amazement of mind, and stood astonished at the sight, when she said to them, 'This is mine own son, and what hath been done was mine own doing! Come, eat of this food; for I have eaten of it myself. Do you not pretend to be either more tender than a woman, or more compassionate than a mother; but if you be so scrupulous, and do abominate this my sacrifice, as I have eaten the one-half, let the rest be reserved for me also.' After which those men went out trembling, being never so much affrighted at anything as they were at this, and with some difficulty they left the rest of that meat to the mother."

In the light of this and other things too horrifying to mention it is no wonder that Christ wept as he thought of this tragedy, and cried out to the wailing women of Jerusalem, "Daughters of Jerusalem, weep not for me, but weep for yourselves, and for your children. For, behold, the days are coming, in the which they shall say, Blessed are the barren, and the wombs that never bare, and the paps which never gave suck."

Another hardship which Jesus forsaw for the Christians was that their flight might be in the winter or upon the Sabbath. Christians were to pray that no natural impediments might obstruct their flight from the scene of horror. In the winter traveling would be difficult and the days short. The Jewish law for Sabbath traveling was also a hindrance. On that day, they could not travel more than a mile or two, and Jews along the way would deny them hospitality. This is again a revelation that Christ was speaking of a local event, one that was limited to Palestine, and not descriptive of a world-wide happening. Least of all it is a description of the second coming when the elect will be taken up with Christ. At that time there will be no necessity for believers to flee to the mountains.

Great Tribulation

Next we come to verse 21 which both premillennarians and amillennarians relate to the end of the world and the period just previous to the second coming of Christ. "For then shall be great tribulation, such as was not since the beginning of the world, to this time, no, nor ever shall be."

First of all, it should be obvious that this verse is directly connected with the previous verses. When the Christians beheld the abomination of desolation, they were to flee to the mountains without a moment's hesitation, and they were to pray that their flight might not be in the winter or on the Sabbath, "*for then* shall be great tribulation, such as was not since the beginning of the world to this time, no, nor ever shall be." They were to flee to the mountains *because* of the great tribulation coming upon Jerusalem.

Some amillennialists overlook this obvious connection, and are guilty of careless exegesis. Professor Berkhof in his *Systematic Theology* always excises verses 14 and 21 from verses 15–20, even though verse 21 is subjoined to verse 20. Verses 15–20 are embarrassing to those who would refer the preaching of the Gospel to all the world for a witness to all nations and the great tribulation to the time of the second coming of our Lord. Verses 15–20, which describe a local situation, do not fit in with such an interpretation.

The premillennialist is more consistent in his position because he relates this prophecy directly to the city of Jerusalem and its Temple. His exegesis, therefore, is more sound. But since Jerusalem and its Temple have already been destroyed, he must reconstruct them in some future period. For this he has no scriptural warrant. Apparently ignoring the fact that the prophecy has already been literally fulfilled, he must construct ideas of a "parenthesis" and "postponement," and resurrect "shadows" and the "carnal hopes" of the Jews. In actuality he wants a repetition of the tribulation that occurred in the year 70 A.D.

Men have thought that the words of verse 21, being as strong and vivid as they are, could only describe a worldwide catastrophe anticipatory of the second coming of our Lord. It is indeed a tremendous assertion, this verse concerning the tribulation. The nature of it would be "such as was not since the beginning of the world to this time, no, nor ever shall be." However, if it denoted a future event ushering in the end of the world, it would hardly be necessary for Christ to add, "nor ever shall be." That tribulation would automatically end all tribulations. But Jesus knew of the ages to follow, and so prophesied, "nor ever shall be."

Considering the physical, moral, and religious aspects of

this horrible happening in history, one may safely say that the Jews have never experienced such a tribulation even up to this day. We must remember that Jesus is speaking about a tribulation to be experienced only by the Jewish nation. The Jews have suffered a great many tribulations since the destruction of Jerusalem, and particularly do we remember their sufferings during the second world war; yet these times of distress cannot compare with that which Jesus described in his Olivet Discourse.

It must be emphasized that the terribleness of the siege of Jerusalem was augmented by the suffering and horror which the Jews inflicted upon each other. Three vicious factions fought each other for control of the city. Each group robbed, tortured, and slaughtered the others who refused to join its own faction. Many of the crimes committed within the city are unmentionable. Aged men and women suffered so much from this internal war that they longed for the Romans to come in to deliver them from their domestic miseries. Although there was plenty of food to support the people in a siege for years, these factions by their evil passions set on fire those houses that were full of corn and other provisions.

Not even the Temple was spared but was used as a battleground by these warring parties. Worshipers were killed before the altar and hundreds of the dead were strewn within the Temple. Concerning this horrible situation Josephus laments: "O most wretched city, what misery so great as this didst thou suffer from the Romans, when they came to purify thee from thy intestine hatred! For thou couldst be no longer a place fit for God, nor couldst thou long continue in being, after thou hadst been a sepulcher for the bodies of thy own people, and hadst made the holy house a burying-place in this civil war of thine."

Josephus gives another picture of the plundering of those who possessed food. "But the seditious everywhere came upon them immediately, and snatched away from them what they had gotten from others; for when they saw any house shut up, this was to them a signal that the people within had gotten some food whereupon they broke open the doors, and ran in, and took pieces of what they were eating almost up out of their very throats, and this by force: the old men, who held their food fast, were beaten; and if the women hid what they had within their hands, their hair was torn for so doing; nor was there any commiseration shown either to the aged or to the infants, but they lifted up children from the ground as they hung upon the morsels they had gotten, and shook them down upon the floor. But still they were more barbarously cruel to those that had prevented their coming in, and had actually swallowed down what they were going to seize upon, as if they had been unjustly defrauded of their right. They also invented terrible methods of torments to discover where any food was. . . . And this was done when those tormentors were not themselves hungry; for the thing had been less barbarous had necessity forced them to it; but this was done to keep their madness in exercise, and as making preparation of provisions for themselves for the following day."

Josephus also uses expressions that are very similar to the words of our Lord in verse 21. He writes: "It is therefore impossible to go distinctly over every instance of these men's iniquity. I shall therefore speak my mind here at once briefly —That neither did any other city ever suffer such miseries, nor did any age ever breed a generation more fruitful in wickedness than this was, from the beginning of the world." This was the opinion of a Jew who was not a Christian and certainly reflects the words of our Saviour.

Another graphic word picture of the horribleness within the city of Jerusalem is given by the historian Josephus: "Now the seditious at first gave orders that the dead should be buried out of the public treasure, as not enduring the stench of their dead bodies. But afterwards, when they could not do that, they had them cast down from the walls into the valleys beneath. However, when Titus, in going his rounds along these valleys, saw them full of dead bodies, and the thick putrefaction called God to witness that this was not his doing; and such was the sad case of the city itself."

As to those who sought to escape to the Romans, this was their experience: "They were first whipped, and then tormented with all sorts of tortures, before they died, and were then crucified before the walls of the city. So the soldiers, out of the wrath and hatred they bore the Jews, nailed those they caught, one after one way, and another after another, to the crosses, by the way of jest, when their multitude was so great, that room was wanting for the crosses, and crosses wanting for the bodies."

Some of the deserters swallowed gold before leaving the city. "But when this contrivance was discovered in one instance, the fame of it filled their several camps, that the deserters came to them full of gold. So the multitude of the Arabians, with the Syrians, cut up those that came as suppliants and searched their bellies. Nor does it seem to me that any misery befell the Jews that was more terrible than this, since in one night's time about two thousand of these deserters were thus dissected."

The destruction which the Romans inflicted upon the Jews when finally they entered the city was also terrible. It is estimated that over a million lives were lost in the siege: the city had been filled with people because of the Passover Feast. As a last gesture the Romans even plowed up the ground upon which the city stood. Literally were these words of Christ fulfilled: "There shall not be left here one stone upon another, that shall not be torn down."

And with all the terrible physical suffering and the horrible, bestial morality of the people, there was bitter anguish of soul. Jerusalem had been the city of God. Constantly the cry arose, "Why these woes upon us, the chosen people?" Every moment they expected God would deliver them and when relief did not come, who can imagine the depth of anguish that racked the souls of these wretched people?

When all these factors are weighed, one can hardly deny that this was the greatest tribulation ever poured upon a people? If the physical suffering has been equalled to that of later dates in history, surely the bestiality of Jew to Jew and Roman to Jew has not. That, together with the anguish of a people forsaken by God, makes the words of Christ none too strong: "For then shall be great tribulation, such as was not since the beginning of the world to this time, no, nor ever shall be."

It was out of mercy that God decreed a limit to the terrible siege. This is the message in verse 22: "And except those days should be shortened, there should no flesh be saved: but for the elect's sake those days shall be shortened." If the siege had continued for long the war would have spread throughout Palestine and even the Christians would have suffered. But for the elect's sake the days were shortened. Even Titus acknowledged this as an act of God. "We have certainly had God for our assistant in this war," he remarked, "and it was no other than God who ejected the Jews out of these fortifications, for what could the hands of men, or any machines, do toward overthrowing these towers?"

120

Chapter VIII

No Personal Coming During the Siege

Then if any man shall say unto you, Lo, here is Christ, or there; believe it not. For there shall arise false Christs and false prophets, and shall shew great signs and wonders; insomuch that, if it were possible, they shall deceive the very elect. Behold, I have told you before. Wherefore if they shall say unto you, Behold, he is in the desert; go not forth: behold, he is in the secret chambers; believe it not. For as the lightning cometh out of the east, and shineth unto the west; so shall also the coming of the Son of man be. For wheresoever the carcass is, there will the eagles be gathered together (Matthew 24:23-28).

The disciples desired to know when the destruction of Jerusalem and its Temple would take place. In answer to that question Jesus first gave the preliminary signs in verses 4–14. Concerning these signs, he said: "For all these things must come to pass, but the end is not yet." The end would come only after the Gospel of the Kingdom had been preached for a witness to all nations. The actual sign of the destruction of Jerusalem was to be the gathering of the Roman armies round about her. Then the Christians were to flee without a moment of hesitation for the great tribulation was about to take place. And as there had been false christs and false prophets previous to the destruction of the city, so there would be the same during the siege. This is the prophecy of verses 23–26.

The adverb "then" which begins verse 23 marks precisely the point of time when false christs and false prophets would appear, namely, when the siege was taking place. Christ had warned about those who would seek to deceive the people before the siege; now he warns them against those who would be the deceivers during the time of the siege. The false christs of verse 24 are not those of verse 5.

In the midst of the terrible tribulation many longed and prayed for the coming of the Messiah. There were those in Jerusalem who took advantage of the people's desire for their own ends. Josephus has recorded an incident showing how literally the Lord's words were fulfilled in this regard. He writes: "The soldiers also came to the rest of the cloisters that were in the outer temple, whither the women and children, and a great mixed multitude of the people, fled, in number about six thousand. But before Caesar had determined anything about these people, or given the Commander any orders relating to them, the soldiers were in such a rage, that they set that cloister on fire; by which means it came to pass that some of these were destroyed by throwing themselves down headlong, and some were burnt in the cloisters themselves. Nor did any one of them escape with his life. A false prophet was the occasion of these people's destruction, who had made a public proclamation in the city that very day, that God commanded them to get upon the temple, and that there they should receive miraculous signs of their deliverance. Now there was then a great number of false prophets suborned by the tyrants to impose on the people, who denounced this to them, that they should wait for deliverance from God; and this was in order to keep them from deserting, and that they might be buoyed up above fear and care by such hopes. Now a man that is in adversity does easily comply with such promises; from when such a seducer makes him believe that he shall be delivered from those miseries which oppress him, then it is that the patient is full of hopes of such his deliverance."

Josephus records the extraordinary signs and wonders that appeared at the time. He writes of a star resembling a sword which stood over the city. A great light appeared for a half hour around the temple. Undoubtedly many of the signs were performed by false prophets under Satanic power. These things added to the tribulation of a people who daily expected deliverance through the appearance of the Messiah.

Christ stated definitely that during this tribulation he would not appear. In verses 23 and 26 he warns the disciples that if any man say "Lo, here is Christ, or there," they were not to believe it. Twice Jesus uses the expression "believe it not," and he pronounces it emphatically. Had the disciples been told that all the signs previously given were of a personal visible coming, then the declaration "Lo, here is Christ, or there" would not always signify a false Christ. Christ is speaking in this passage of an invisible, impersonal coming— a coming in judgment upon Jerusalem. The disciples were not to look for a deliverance by the personal coming of the Lord; any rumor to the contrary would be untrue.

Jesus said "Behold, I have told you before." In fine detail he had related to the disciples the preliminary signs, the actual sign, the terrible tribulation, and the appearance of false christs and prophets during the tribulation. He had done this in order that they might not be deceived. The signs, events, wonders, false prophets, and messiahs were such that even the elect, if it were possible, could be deceived. Now they were forwarned!

The Personal Coming of Christ

Not only were the disciples forwarned about false Christs but Jesus informs them that when he does come a second time it will be no local event. It will be a universal coming seen by all. He says in verse 27: "For as the lightning cometh out of the east, and shineth unto the west; so shall also the coming of the Son of man be."

This verse stands in contrast to the previous verses, for it speaks of Christ's second coming rather than his invisible coming in judgment upon Jerusalem. The disciples during the period of the siege were not to be deceived by anyone. When he comes the second time his coming will be as conspicuous as the lightning and will be witnessed by all men everywhere. From the east unto the west the coming of Christ will be seen. This means the entire world, not just Palestine.

So conspicuous then will this personal coming of the Lord be that it will require no announcement. The idea of this verse is not the suddenness of his coming but the self-manifestation of it. No one will need to believe the testimonies of other persons that Christ has appeared; nor will there be press and radio reports announcing his arrival on the Mount of Olives or at the gates of Jerusalem. The whole implication of this verse is that Christ's second coming will be manifested in the heavens and not upon the earth. Verse 27, then, stands in contrast to the message of its immediate context; that is, the second coming is contrasted to the coming in Divine judgment upon Jerusalem. It is profitable to note that Matthew uses the Greek *parousia* in this verse to express the thought of "coming." So far as we know, *parousia*, when used in connection

124

with Christ, refers to his second personal coming. Dr. Thayer states, "In N.T. esp. of the *advent,* i.e., the future, visible, *return* from heaven of Jesus, the Messiah, to raise the dead, hold the last judgment, and set up formally and gloriously the kingdom of God" (*Thayer's Greek-English Lexicon*).

It is also well to note that up to verse 27 in the discourse of Christ, there is no other reference to this coming. There are only warnings against false prophets about it. The signs which He gives plainly refer to the destruction of Jerusalem and not to the second coming of the Lord. Surely the disciples are not urged to flee to the mountains when Jesus comes in person!

Gathering of the Eagles

According to Jesus' prophetic words, there would be false christs and rumors of false christs during the time of tribulation, but the disciples were not to be deceived. The only deliverance for Jerusalem was to be a deliverance to destruction. This is the idea in verse 28. We quote from the American Revised Version because it correctly omits the conjunction "for." "Wheresoever the carcass is, there will the eagles be gathered together."

Carcass, meaning dead body, is figurative here for the Jewish nation which was morally, spiritually, and judicially dead. The denunciation of Christ in Matthew 23 reveals its moral and spiritual deadness, and at the conclusion of his denunciation he makes this pronouncement: "Behold your house is left unto you desolate." As a dead body attracts vultures so would Jerusalem, the center of the Jewish nation, attract those who would devour it.

Some may be puzzled to note the term "eagle" being used for vulture, but in Palestine this was a common usage. Gene Stratton-Porter in the *International Standard Bible Encyclopedia* explains how this came to be. He writes: "The Hebrew *nesher,* meaning 'to tear with the beak,' is almost invariably translated 'eagle,' throughout the Bible; yet many of the most important references compel the admission that the bird to which they applied was a vulture. There were many large birds and carrion eaters flocking over Palestine, attracted by the offal from animals slaughtered for tribal feasts and continuous sacrifices. The eagle family could not be separated from the vultures by their habit of feeding, for they ate the offal from slaughter as well as the vultures."

The Old Testament uses the term "eagle" to describe a foreign nation coming upon the Jewish nation as a punishment for sin. Moses is the first to use the term in Deuteronomy 28:49: "The Lord shall bring a nation against thee from far, from the end of the earth, as swift as the eagle flieth; a nation whose tongue thou shalt not understand." The term appears in Hosea 8:1 in the same sense: "He shall come as an eagle against the House of the Lord, because they have transgressed my covenant, and trespassed against my law." Again it appears in Habakkuk 1:8 where its sense is obvious: "Their horses also are swifter than the leopards, and are more fierce than the evening wolves: and their horsemen shall spread themselves, and their horsemen shall come from far; *they shall fly as the eagle that hasteth to eat."*

The picture that Christ presents us of the eagles gathering about the carcass is not difficult to perceive. It expresses the thought that a foreign army would come against Jerusalem because of its deadness in the sight of God. Christ makes this prophecy vivid because he wants it thoroughly understood on the part of the disciples that they were not to expect a personal coming nor a deliverance of Jerusalem from its just punishment.

126

Chapter IX

Signs in the Sun, Moon and Stars

Immediately after the tribulation of those days shall the sun be darkened, and the moon shall not give her light, and the stars shall fall from heaven, and the powers of the heavens shall be shaken: And then shall appear the sign of the Son of man in heaven: and then shall all the tribes of the earth mourn, and they shall see the Son of man coming in the clouds of heaven with power and great glory. And he shall send his angels with a great sound of a trumpet, and they shall gather together his elect from the four winds, from one end of heaven to the other (Matthew 24:29-31).

The above portion of Scripture employs such strong and vivid language that many think it can be descriptive of nothing else than the end of the world and the second coming of Christ. These descriptive terms would seem to indicate a catastrophic end of the earth. And yet when this passage is studied in the light of prophetic language and pronouncements, it can readily be that it is descriptive of the passing away of Judaism. We must remember that an apocalyptic language existed that was well known to the discerning reader of Old Testament Scripture. We would naturally expect that the traditional phraseology would be used to describe the eclipse of the Old Testament dispensation. The passing away of Jewish privileges and glories was certainly the greatest catastrophe that ever happened or would happen to the Jewish nation. Traditional apocalyptic language as used by the Old Testament prophets should not cause surprise here since Christ depicts the fall of the Jewish nation. One would naturally expect that Jesus would describe this catastrophe through the use of scriptural symbols well known to the Jews. In this passage, therefore, we have an opportunity to interpret Scripture with Scripture.

The first stumblingblock we encounter in the understanding of this portion of the Olivet Discourse is the word "immediately." Commentators who are inclined to believe that verses 4–28 relate to the siege and destruction of Jerusalem and that verses 29–31 relates to the end of the world have difficulty with this word and try to explain it away. However, it was to be immediately after the tribulation of those days to which verses 4–28 refer that the sun would be darkened, the moon would fail to give light, and the stars would fall from heaven. If the sun, moon, and stars referred to the Jewish nation and its prerogatives, then we have seen the fulfillment of this prophecy which, according to the words of Christ, was to be fulfilled within the period of the contemporary generation. It is a matter of history that the Jewish nation has been darkened and no longer shines for the living God. This has been true ever since the tribulation of those days. God in his righteous wrath has removed the Jewish nation from his heavens. The sun of Judaism has been darkened; as the moon it no longer reflects the light of God; bright stars, as the list of heroes in Hebrews 11, no longer shine in the Israel of the flesh. But are we justified in stating that the sun, moon, and stars are figurative of Judaism and its glories?

Apocalyptic Language

A study of Old Testament Scriptures discloses to us the fact that there is an apocalyptic language which describes great national disasters. Familiar symbols are used to articulate the destruction of nations. When disaster was overhanging Babylon, Idumea, and Egypt, the prophets used similar language to that which we find in Matthew 24:29-31:

> *For the stars of heaven and the constellations thereof shall not give their light: the sun shall be darkened in his going forth, and the moon shall not cause her light to shine* (Isa. 13:10).

The 13th chapter of Isaiah is introduced with the statement: "The burden of Babylon, which Isaiah the son of Amos did see." The entire chapter is related to the destruction of that mighty and glorious city. We may compare the fame and glory of Babylon to New York, London, and Moscow combined. In the days of Isaiah, the glory of Babylon shone as the sun, the moon, and the stars. This glory, Isaiah prophesies, was to be darkened. Babylon in all its shining beauty and marvelous glory was to be totally eclipsed; hence the prophet uses highly figurative language.

If the Holy Spirit speaking through the prophet Isaiah uses such figurative language to describe the downfall of a heathen nation like Babylon, how much *more* would not such language fit the downfall of the chosen nation of Israel?

> *And all the host of heaven shall be desolved, and the heavens shall be rolled together as a scroll: and all their host shall fall*

129

down, as the leaf falleth off from the vine, and as a falling fig from the fig tree. For my sword shall be bathed in heaven: behold, it shall come down upon Idumea, and upon the people of my curse, to judgment (Isa. 34:4, 5).

Idumea was by far a lesser nation than Babylon. But here again we find vivid symbols for the terrible and sudden judgment of God against it. Surely, no one will maintain that when the judgment of God came upon Idumea, the hosts of heaven were literally dissolved and the heavens actually rolled together as a scroll with all the stars falling down like leaves from a vine! Nor will one seriously maintain that a real sword came down from heaven upon the pagan nation Idumea. If these had been literal occurrences, then the end of the world must have have come at the time judgment fell upon Idumea, which is preposterous.

Can we not reason that as the Holy Spirit, speaking through Isaiah, used such figurative language to describe the downfall of Idumea, he would more than employ it in depicting the downfall of the Jewish nation?

And when I shall put thee out, I will cover the heaven, and make the stars thereof dark; I will cover the sun with a cloud, and the moon shall not give her light. All the bright lights of heaven will I make dark over thee, and set darkness upon thy land, saith the Lord God (Ezekiel 32:7, 8).

Within the context of Ezekiel 32 the judgment against Egypt was personalized in a lamentation for Pharaoh, king of Egypt, who was compared to the young lion and a dragon amidst the nation. Ezekiel prophesied that the king of Babylon would spoil the pomp of Egypt and destroy the inhabitants of that land. Again the vivid imagery of the sun, moon, and stars being darkened is used by the prophet to depict the end of the glory of Egypt.

130

If the Holy Spirit, speaking through the prophet Ezekiel, uses such figurative language to describe the downfall of Egypt and its Pharaoh, how much more would not such language be used to describe the downfall of the nation of Israel.

The same type of apocryphal language is employed in the second chapter of Joel, and the Apostle Peter quotes the prophecy of Joel on the day of Pentecost as recorded in Acts 2:16-21. This provides us with an infallible interpreter. On the day of Pentecost the Holy Spirit came upon the disciples and enabled them to speak with other tongues. Upon being accused of being drunk because of their manifestations, Peter declared that what was occurring was a direct fulfillment of that which was spoken by the prophet Joel. He quoted Joel 2:28-32 in these words:

"And it shall come to pass in the last days, saith God, I will pour out my Spirit upon all flesh: and your sons and your daughters shall prophesy, and your young men shall see visions, and your old men shall dream dreams: And on my servants and on my handmaidens I will pour out in those days of my Spirit; and they shall prophesy: *And I will shew wonders in heaven above, and signs in the earth beneath; blood, and fire, and vapour of smoke: the sun shall be turned into darkness, and the moon into blood, before that great and notable day of the Lord come:* And it shall come to pass, that whosoever shall call on the name of the Lord shall be saved."

In the second chapter of Joel we find two things predicted in the quotation of the Peter: fearful judgment upon Israel, and the outpouring of the Holy Spirit. In the first part of that chapter, and in the midst of the prediction of judgment, the same familiar figurative language is employed in verse 10: "The earth shall quake before them; the heavens shall tremble: the sun and the moon shall be dark, and the stars shall withdraw their shining." This determines for us the

131

meaning of these figurative expressions; as elsewhere, it is symbolic of the judgment of God.

In the latter part of this second chapter of Joel's prophecy, quoted by Peter, is the promise of the outpouring of the Spirit. Fearful judgments would accompany this outpouring, as the figurative language of judgments implies. What were these judgments? Surely those previous to and during the siege of Jerusalem. These judgments were related by Christ in the first part of Matthew 24. Peter could not have been mistaken that those in Jerusalem were witnessing the fulfillment of the prophecy of Joel. And if the outpouring of the Holy Spirit was being fulfilled, even so the portion which declares that "the sun shall be turned into darkness, and the moon into blood, before that great and notable day of the Lord comes." Thus the words of Joel, Christ, and Peter harmonize.

With the outflow of the Holy Spirit and the destruction of Jerusalem, the Kingdom was to be enlarged with the inclusion of the Gentiles as these words indicate: "And it shall come to pass, that *whosoever* shall call on the name of the Lord shall be saved" (Joel 2:32). The kingdom of God was no longer to be limited to the Jews. The mosaic economy with its levitical priesthood and ceremonial law was finished. The judgment against Jerusalem had brought all this to an end. And now as both Joel and Peter declared: "whosoever shall call on the name of the Lord shall be saved."

The Holy Spirit was and continues to be outpoured. That part of the prophecy has been fulfilled. Also, the Jewish nation has received the judgment of God. Its sun, moon, and stars have been darkened and are still obscured. It is the Gentiles that are calling on the name of the Lord and being saved. We witness that prophetic fulfillment to this day.

Because many do not consider the apocalyptic language of the prophets which Scripture itself translates, they look for a literal fulfillment of verse 29 in reference to the nation of the Jews. But there was no literal fulfillment ofthedescription in regard to Babylon, Idumea, and Egypt, and we do not need to look for any in respect to the Jewish nation. Peter declares the fulfillment of Joel's prophecy even though there was no literal evidence of it. The words are indicative of the severe judgment of God upon Israel for its rejection of the Messiah.

The last clause of Matthew 24:29 states: "and the powers of the heavens shall be shaken." This refers to Satan and his angels. With the coming of the Holy Spirit and the preaching of the Gospel, the powers of heaven were shaken. Christ revealed this after the successful mission of the disciples: "I beheld Satan as lightning fall from heaven" (Luke 10:18). And in John 12:31 He says: "Now is the judgment of this world: now shall the prince of this world be cast out." The fulfillment of the promise, "the powers of the heavens shall be shaken," clearly indicates the time of the Gospel dispensation. When one carefully follows the usage of apocalyptic language one can readily see that verse 29 is included in the statement of verse 34: "Verily I say unto you, This generation shall not pass, till all these things be fulfilled." This interpretation, following well-defined biblical usage, keeps the prophecy within the time prescribed by Christ. One need not project the prophecy of the sun, the moon being darkened, and the stars falling from heaven into the time of the second coming of our Lord if one understands that our Lord is using this figurative language even as the prophets of old employed it.

Analogy of New Testament

Some scholars have stated that one must be governed by the analogy of New Testament language rather than that of the Old. If it therefore can be demonstrated that the New Testament does use similar figurative language to describe an event other than the second coming then our contention should be

133

proven without a question of doubt. Fortunately, there is such a passage, namely, Revelation 6:12–17, "And I beheld when he had opened the sixth seal, and, lo, there was a great earthquake; and the sun became black as sackcloth of hair, and the moon became as blood; and the stars of heaven fell unto the earth, even as a fig tree casteth her untimely figs, when she is shaken of a mighty wind. And the heaven departed as a scroll when it is rolled together; and every mountain and island were moved out of their places. And the kings of the earth, and the great men, and the rich men, and the chief captains, and the mighty men, and every bondman, and every free man, hid themselves in the dens and in the rocks of the mountains; and said to the mountains and rocks, Fall on us, and hide us from the face of him that sitteth on the throne, and from the wrath of the Lamb: for the great day of his wrath is come; and who shall be able to stand?"

The above judgment came at the opening of the sixth seal. This judgment does not at all bear the character of the final judgment as the kings of the earth and others hid themselves and indeed pleaded for death whereas the final judgment is characterized by the resurrection of the dead, and their appearance before the judgment seat. Furthermore, time and history are still in process as the seventh seal was not yet opened.

In Revelation 8:1 the seventh seal was opened and there was silence in heaven about the space of half an hour. Then John saw the seven angels which had the seven trumpets. The trumpets are occupied with time and not with a cataclysmic act. They speak of a third part of trees burnt up; a third part of the sea becoming blood; one great star falling; a third part of the sun, moon, and stars smitten; men being tormented for 5 months; angels requiring an hour, and a day, and a month, and a year, for to slay the third part of men. Then after the blowing of the trumpets the seven vials are outpoured and occupied with a period of time. Now if the sixth seal finished the sun, moon, and the stars in one final cataclysmic act history would have been terminated and there would be no time for the trumpets and vials. If it be argued that the seals, trumpets, and vials are concurrent there is even greater proof that all are occupied with time and history as all indicate partial judgments and periods of time. As in Matthew 24:29, the language of Revelation is figurative; but a language that has been established and defined by the prophets.

Dr. Milton S. Terry makes a statement in his *Biblical Hermeneutics* which is well to the point. He writes, "We might fill volumes with extracts showing how exegetes and writers on New Testament doctrine assume as a principle not to be questioned that such highly wrought language as Matt. 24:29–31; I Thess. 4:16; and II Peter 3:10,12, taken almost *verbatim* from Old Testament prophecies of judgment on nations and kingdoms which long ago perished, must be literally understood. Too little study of Old Testament ideas of judgment, and apocalyptic language and style, would seem to be the main reason for this one sided exegesis. It will require more than assertion to convince thoughtful men that the figurative language of Isaiah and Daniel, admitted on all hands to be such in those ancient prophets, is to be literally interpreted when used by Jesus and Paul" (p. 466).

Chapter X

Appearance of the Sign

And then shall appear the sign of the Son of man in heaven: and then shall all the tribes of the earth mourn, and they shall see the Son of man coming in the clouds of heaven with power and great glory (Matthew 24:30).

Unless a student of the Olivet discourse is acquainted with the apocryphal language of the Old Testament prophets, he is apt to make a literal interpretation of such descriptive language as the sun being darkened, the moon hiding her light, and the stars falling from heaven. To him these terms can only be understood eschatologically and must refer to the end of the world which is to occur at the Lord's second coming. Anything less than that does not seem to do justice to the expressions employed by our Lord. But when one discovers that the same type of language is used to describe the passing away of Babylon, Idumea, and Egypt, he need be not surprised upon finding these terms and phrases in connection with the passing of the old dispensation. Jerusalem and its Temple were central in the worship of the Jews, and their destruction meant the end of the world so far as the Jews were concerned. If the use of such figurative judgment language against pagan nations was justified, how much more fitting would it not be to the passing away of Judaism?

While some commentators concede that the language of verse 29 possibly describes the passing away of the old dispensation, signalized by the destruction of Jerusalem and its Temple, nonetheless the words of verse 30, they believe, can only refer to the end of time. What is described in this verse cannot possibly refer to the generation living in the time of Christ's sojourn. Rather, the sign of the Son of man, the mourning of all the tribes of the earth, and the Son of man coming in the clouds must be eschatological terms about the second coming of the Lord.

The Sign of the Son of Man

The judgment upon Jerusalem was the sign of the fact that the Son of man was reigning in heaven. There has been mis-understanding due to the reading of this verse, as some have thought it to be "a sign in heaven." But this is not what the verse says; it says the sign of the *Son of man in heaven*. The phrase "in heaven" defines the locality of the Son of man and not of the sign. A sign was not to appear in the heavens, but the destruction of Jerusalem was to indicate the rule of the Son of man in heaven.

One must note that the verse speaks of a "sign" and not of the personal appearance of Christ himself. If Christ had re-ferred to his visible coming in the heavens, he would have said, "And then shall appear the Son of man in heaven." But he prophesied the appearance of a *sign* of the Son of man who dwells in heaven.

To what sign did Christ have reference? This had been the question of the disciples: "Tell us, when shall these things be? and what shall be the *sign* of thy coming, and of the end of the age?" Christ had informed them of the destruction of Jerusalem and its Temple, and when they asked, "when shall these things be?" he indicated to them the sign of his coming and the end of the pre-Messianic age. The sign of the passing away of the pre-Messianic age and the beginning of the Messianic reign was the destruction of Jerusalem and its Temple. As the old dispensation passed away, the sign would introduce the new dispensation. The Temple, made with hands, would vanish for the Temple made without hands.

If Judaism had been allowed to hold sway with its shadows and carnal ordinances, it would have been a hindrance to the spreading of the Gospel. The apostle Paul states in the eleventh chapter of Romans that the fall of the Jews was a blessing to the rest of the world. He speaks of it as the enriching of the Gentiles and the reconciling of the world. The catastrophe of Jerusalem really signalized the beginning of a new and world-wide kingdom, marking the full separation of the Christian Church from legalistic Judaism. The whole system of worship, so closely associated with Jerusalem and the Temple, received, as it were, a death blow from God himself. God was now through with the Old Covenant made at Sinai: holding full sway was the sign of the New Covenant.

Thus when it is kept in mind that it was no sign in heaven but rather the sign of the Son of man in heaven; that it is a *sign* spoken of rather than the personal appearance of Christ; and lastly, that it is a sign asked for by the disciples concerning the passing away of the age, then one has no difficulty in believing that the prophecy was fulfilled at the time of the destruction of Jerusalem and within the contemporary generation indicated by Christ in verse 34.

138

The Mourning of the Tribes

The second clause of verse 30 reads, "And then shall all the tribes of the earth mourn." This has reference to the division of the land of Palestine among the 12 tribes of Israel. All the Jews of the land were to mourn at that time. Some would mourn because of God's fearful visitation upon Jerusalem. Others would mourn because of true repentance.

It is interesting to note how this expression is enlarged in Revelation 1:7: "Behold, he cometh with clouds; and every eye shall see him, and they also which pierced him: and all kindreds of the earth shall wail because of him." The book of Revelation speaks of a number of judgments coming upon the world that are similar to the one experienced at Jerusalem. Here the expression "all kindreds (tribes) of the earth shall wail because of him" takes in all the nations of the earth, and not only Gentiles but Jews ("they also which pierced him"). By this is meant that the Jews could expect future afflictions throughout history, a fact that has been clearly verified.

The word "mourning" comes from the word meaning "beat themselves," or a smiting upon the breast when in deep fear or sorrow. A partial fulfillment of this prophecy occurred on the day of crucifixion: "And all the people that came together to that sight, beholding the things which were done, smote their breasts, and returned" (Luke 23:48). Another fulfillment is related in Acts 2:37: "Now when they heard this, they were pricked in their heart, and said unto Peter and to the rest of the apostles, Men and brethren, what shall we do?" Here the mourning turned to genuine repentance.

The Old Testament reveals two types of mournings. There was a mourning unto death and a mourning unto life. Jeremiah 4:28 reveals a mourning unto death, "For this shall the earth mourn, and the heavens above be black: because I have spoken it, I have purposed it, and will not repent, neither

139

will I turn back from it." But in connection with the destruction of Jerusalem there was also to be a mourning unto life as indicated in Zechariah 12:10: "And I will pour upon the house of David, and upon the inhabitants of Jerusalem, the spirit of grace and of supplications: and they shall look upon me whom they have pierced, and they shall mourn for him, as one mourneth for his only son, and shall be bitterness for him, as one that is in bitterness for his firstborn." There are some who would refer this prophecy of Zechariah to the second coming of the Lord. But the apostle John refers this prophecy to the first coming of Christ. He writes: "And again another scripture saith, They shall look on him whom they have pierced" (John 19:37). This prophecy of Zechariah's, therefore, is not limited to the second coming. With the preaching of Jesus Christ and him crucified, there were some Jews who mourned with the spirit of grace and supplication.

Thus we find ample justification for indicating the fulfillment of the second clause of verse 30 to the time of the destruction of Jerusalem. We know that there was deep mourning among not only citizens of Jerusalem and Judea but Jews scattered over the entire habitable world as they learned of the ruin of the beloved City and Temple. We know also that this judgment caused some to realize their sin and turn to the Lord for forgiveness. Deep grief of one type or another possessed the hearts of the tribes of the earth.

Coming in the Clouds

The third and final clause of verse 30 says: "And they shall see the Son of man coming in the clouds of heaven with power and great glory." This clause has been thought to relate definitely to the second, visible, and personal coming of the Lord. But in the light of well-defined biblical language, the reference is rather to a coming in terms of the events

140

of his providence in judgment against his enemies and in deliverance of his people.

It should be noted carefully that neither this verse nor this particular clause indicates a coming upon *earth*. Some have read into this clause that Jesus was actually descending to the earth for the purpose of taking up a reign in the city of Jerusalem. Nothing like that is indicated. As a matter of fact, there is not a single verse in the New Testament to indicate that Christ will reign upon a material throne in the material city of Jerusalem. This thought has been imported by a carnal interpretation of Old Testament passages. Christ is actually seated now upon his Messianic throne.

Many commentators have taken it for granted that the expression "coming in the clouds" refers to a visible coming of Christ. A careful study of the Scriptures, however, reveals that that is not a necessary interpretation. A similar expression occurs in Isaiah 19:1: "Behold, the Lord rideth upon a swift cloud, and shall come into Egypt: and the idols of Egypt shall be moved at his presence, and the heart of Egypt shall melt in the midst of it." Although this passage speaks of the Lord riding upon a cloud and of his presence, nevertheless we know that the Egyptians did not see the Lord in a personal, visible way. The Lord riding upon a swift cloud indicated a coming in judgment against the Egyptians.

A similar type of expression concerning judgment is found in Psalm 97:2,3: "Clouds and darkness are round about him: righteousness and judgment are the habitation of his throne. A fire goeth before him, and burneth up his enemies round about." In speaking of the mighty power of God the Psalmist uses this expression: "Who layeth the beams of his chambers in the waters; who maketh the clouds his chariot: who walketh upon the wings of the wind" (Psalm 104:3). The expression "who maketh the clouds his chariot," is no different from "coming in the clouds of heaven." In the Psalms there is no

141

thought of a personal visible coming of the Lord, but rather references to his judgment and power.

Following the well-defined biblical sense of such expressions the last clause of verse 30 may well be interpreted then to indicate a coming in judgment and power: judgment against his enemies and power in the establishment of his kingdom.

This interpretation is borne out by the words of Christ in other passages when he indicated that he was coming before the contemporary generation would pass away. He said: "Verily I say unto you, there be some standing here, which shall not taste of death, till they see the Son of man coming in his kingdom" (Matt. 16:28). Christ was saying that some of the people actually standing before him and listening to him would not die until they saw the Son of man coming in his kingdom. This could hardly refer to a personal and visible coming in that generation.

The same thought is conveyed in Christ's words to the High Priest: "Thou hast said: nevertheless I say unto you, Hereafter shall ye see the Son of man sitting on the right hand of power, and coming in the clouds of heaven" (Matt. 26:64). This high priest was to see Christ sitting on the right hand of power and coming in the clouds of heaven. Can this possibly refer to Christ's second coming when the description "sitting on the right hand of power" precludes such interpretation. It means rather that after the crucifixion and resurrection, Jesus would ascend into heaven and take his place on the right hand of God, the Father, as described in Daniel 7:13, 14: "I saw in the night visions, and, behold, one like the Son of man came with the clouds of heaven, and came to the Ancient of days, and they brought him near before him. And there was given him dominion, and glory, and a kingdom, that all people, nations, and languages, should serve him: his dominion is an everlasting dominion, which shall not pass away, and his kingdom that which shall not be destroyed."

When Christ ascended into heaven he was seated upon his Messianic throne. This is in full accord with the declaration of Christ as he was about to ascend into heaven: "All power is given unto me in heaven and in earth." One of the first manifestations of the power and the glory of the Messiah was the destruction of the city that refused to accept him as King and Saviour. This act of judgment gave evidence that all power had indeed been given unto him. He did come in the clouds of heaven and rained destruction upon those who had rejected and crucified him. This caused the tribes of the earth to mourn. The sign of the reigning Christ was seen in the destruction of Jerusalem. And the contemporary generation, indicated in verse 34, witnessed fulfillment of these things as Christ had prophesied.

Chapter XI

The Year of Jubilee

And he shall send his angels with a great sound of a trumpet,
and they shall gather together his elect from the four winds,
from one end of heaven to the other (Matthew 24:31).

The greatest event in the history of the world was the coming of Christ upon earth. The event of the Messiah called for a momentous decision on the part of the Jewish nation. By an acceptance of Jesus as Messiah, the Jewish nation would have led in the establishment of the kingdom of God upon earth. By rejecting him as Messiah, the Jews filled the cup of iniquity, and God took the kingdom away from them to give to other nations. That the prophets should use apocalyptic language to describe the judgment of God against the nation previously chosen to be the recipient of his oracles and blessings should be no surprise. It has been pointed out that this type of language was employed in judgments against pagan nations, and one would naturally expect to see it in reference to judgment against the chosen nation—particularly as we are limited by the infallible Prophet to the contemporary generation: "Verily I say unto you, This generation shall not pass, till all these things be fulfilled."

To many commentators the words of verse 31 are conclusive and can find fulfillment only in the event of the second coming. This denotes the end of time so far as the present earth is concerned and the beginning of the consummate kingdom. With the sound of a trumpet the angels gather the elect from all the earth. This, some maintain, is a description of the final resurrection at the second coming of the Lord.

That there is some ground for such an interpretation one cannot deny. The trumpet is associated with the resurrection of the dead in several passages: "In a moment, in the twinkling of an eye, at the last trump: for the trumpet shall sound, and the dead shall be raised incorruptible, and we shall be changed" (I Cor. 15:52). "For the Lord himself shall descend from heaven with a shout, with a voice of the archangel, and with the trump of God: and the dead in Christ shall rise first" (I Thess. 4:16). In both these passages the sound of the trump of God signalizes the resurrection of the dead. This is assigned for the beginning of the consummate kingdom. However, the Scriptures employ the figure of a trumpet in another sense, namely, its association with the year of Jubilee and with announcements of great deliverance.

The year of Jubilee was the fiftieth year occuring after seven times seven years from its inauguration. The name was derived from the custom of proclaiming it by a blast on the trumpet. "Jubilee" means "a joyful shout, sound of the trumpet." By the sound of the Jubilee trumpet, liberty was proclaimed to all Israelites who were in bondage to any of their countrymen, and those who had been compelled through poverty to sell their ancestral possessions received them back.

Also the ground during the year of Jubilee was to remain fallow.

The spiritual significance of the year of Jubilee is given in a beautiful passage in Isaiah: "The spirit of the Lord God is upon me; because the Lord hath anointed me to preach good tidings unto the meek; he hath sent me to bind up the brokenhearted, to proclaim liberty to the captives, and the opening of the prison to *them that are* bound; To proclaim the acceptable year of the Lord, and the day of vengeance of our God; to comfort all that mourn; To appoint unto them that mourn in Zion, to give unto them beauty for ashes, the oil of joy for mourning, the garment of praise for the spirit of heaviness; that they might be called trees of righteousness, the planting of the Lord, that he might be glorified" (61:1-3). Thus even in the Old Testament Scriptures the year of Jubilee was spiritualized to indicate liberty from sin and sorrow.

That the year of Jubilee was symbolic of the Gospel age is clearly seen from Jesus' identification of Isaiah's "acceptable year of the Lord" with his Gospel ministry. When Jesus attended the synagogue there was delivered unto him the book of the prophet Isaiah. He opened it to this particular passage and said to those who were present: "This day is this scripture fulfilled in your ears" (cf. Luke 4:17–21). The real significance of the year of Jubilee finds its fulfillment in the Gospel age. It was a time of preaching the Good News and healing those who were afflicted by sin. The Gospel was to be preached to the poor, the brokenhearted were to be healed, captives to sin were to be delivered, the spiritually blind were to recover sight, and those bruised by iniquity were to be set free.

Christ definitely associates his ministry to the beginning of the prophesied Jubilee. "This day," says he, "is this scripture fulfilled in your ears." This greater Jubilee was not to be limited to Jews nor to the land of Palestine. With the sound of the trumpet, redemption and freedom to all nations were to be inaugurated. That is the reason Jesus spoke of the angels gathering together his elect from the four winds, from one end of the heaven to the other. While the year of Jubilee for the whole earth actually saw its inception with the ministry of Christ, it formally started with the destruction of Jerusalem when the Old Dispensation gave way to the New. It was at this point that the Jubilee trumpet truly sounded.

Few people, who interpret this passage as the inauguration of the consummate kingdom rather than the Gospel dispensation, would look for a literal trumpet. They realize that this is a figurative expression. Yet, within the same context, many commentators fail to see the sun darkening, the moon not giving its light, and the stars falling as figurative expression indicating the end of the Old Dispensation.

The Angels

Another factor that has led some to refer verse 31 to the events at the second coming and the inauguration of the consummate kingdom is the use of the term "angels." Many passages in Scripture indicate that the angels will have a prominent part at the second advent. According to Matthew 13:41–42 Christ will send his angels to gather the wicked out of his kingdom and cast them into a furnace of fire. Another passage on the same thought is II Thess. 1:7–10: "And to you who are troubled rest with us, when the Lord Jesus shall be revealed from heaven with his mighty angels, In flaming fire taking vengeance on them that know not God, and that obey not the gospel of our Lord Jesus Christ. . . . When he shall come to be glorified in his saints, and to be admired in all them that believe (because our testimony among you was believed) in that day." Undoubtedly the angels, mentioned in these passages, are the heavenly spirits we associate with that term.

However, the Greek term *aggelos* does not always refer to

147

such heavenly spirits. The meaning of the term must be determined by the context. In the following passages the Greek word *aggelos* is translated by the word *messenger*: Matthew 11:10; Luke 7:24, 27; 9:52; Mark 1:2; James 2:25. John the Baptist is called an *aggelos*. The disciples of John the Baptist were also described as angels. And this was true in regard to the disciples of Christ. In James 2:25 the messengers sent to Raham were called "angels." In these passages the Greek word *aggelos* is translated *messenger* simply because we associate the word "angel" with a heavenly spirit.

Actually the context determines the meaning of the Greek word *aggelos* and one does not have to translate it "angel." The word does not always mean a heavenly spirit. As the word *aggelos* is used to describe a minister of Christ in other portions of the New Testament, so it may be translated in this particular passage. We know that Christ gave the function of preaching the Gospel and gathering in the elect to his disciples and through them to the Church. They were to go to the uttermost ends of the earth and proclaim the glad tidings of salvation, and by baptism receive the elect into the Church. From the day of the Great Commission unto this day his ministers have been fulfilling the function of *messengers* or *angels* in gathering the elect from all nations.

From the Four Winds

The Scriptures employ several expressions to indicate the universality of the Gospel—two of which are used in our verse: "from the four winds" and "from one end of the heaven to the other." The latter may have been borrowed from Deuteronomy 30:4: "If any of thine be driven out unto the outmost parts of heaven, from thence will the Lord thy God gather thee, and from thence will he fetch thee." This was a promise that if the Jews were scattered among the nations, the Lord would gather them back to the Promised

148

Land should they repent of their sins. Figurative terms are used to describe the fact that the elect—spiritual Israel—will be gathered from all nations of the world. A clear and distinct message of the Old Testament prophets was that the coming of the Messiah would see the extension of the kingdom of God to all the ends of the earth. "Look unto me, and be ye saved, and all the ends of the earth: for I am God, and there is none else" (Isa. 45:22). "All the ends of the world shall remember and turn unto the Lord: and all the kindreds of the nations shall worship before thee" (Psa. 22:27). The destruction of Jerusalem and its Temple signalized the end of a dispensation limited to one nation and the beginning of a new Israel composed of the elect from all nations of the world. The elect would henceforth be gathered from the four winds, from one end of the heaven to the other.

Our Lord used a very similar expression in reference to the universality of the Gospel when he said: "And they shall come from the east, and from the west, and from the north, and from the south, and shall sit down in the kingdom of God" (Luke 13:29). This statement is prophetic of the Gospel dispensation and is no different in meaning from "and they shall gather together his elect from the four winds, from one end of heaven to the other." The Lord's words recorded in Luke 13:29 had no reference to his second coming, and there is no need to interpret Matthew 24:31 as teaching his second coming. Both indicate the universality of the Gospel dispensation.

The Great Deliverance

Not only was the trumpet used as a symbol of the year of Jubilee but also of a great deliverance.

We find mention of the symbol in Isaiah 27:13: "And it shall come to pass in that day, that the great trumpet shall be blown, and they shall come which were ready to perish in

149

the land of Assyria, and the outcasts in the land of Egypt, and shall worship the Lord in the holy mount of Jerusalem."

No literal trumpet was sounded that was heard in Egypt and Assyria; it was a figure of speech denoting the time of a great deliverance. When all seemed lost, and the captive Jews were ready to perish, the Lord promised that he would deliver them from their terrible bondage. The trumpet of Matthew 24:31 indicated deliverance of universal scope, not from physical bondage but from bondage to sin and to Satan. As Isaiah's reference to trumpet sounding had nothing to do with the second coming of the Lord, so one must not feel that the trumpet mentioned in the Olivet Discourse refers to the inauguration of the consummate kingdom, especially in view of our Lord's clear indication that the sounding of it was to occur within the span of the contemporary generation. The trumpet sound was figurative for announcing the time of world-wide deliverance from sin through the Gospel now at hand.

The world-wide mission to conquer the world for Christ began actually on the day of Pentecost when the Apostle Peter preached to Jews, devout men, out of every nation under heaven. By a study of the book of Acts and the Epistles, we know that some of these devout Jews tried to shackle the world-wide mission with forms and rituals of the Old Dispensation. But the destruction of Jerusalem forever removed the shackles of Judaism, and the message of salvation was no longer impeded by those attempting to retain the carnal ordinances. All the nations of the earth were to benefit from the coming of the Messiah and his atoning death. And His words beautifully express this: "And he shall send his angels with a great sound of a trumpet, and they shall gather together his elect from the four winds, from one end of heaven to the other."

Chapter XII

Parable of the Fig Tree

Many prophesies of the Old Testament point to a glorious future under the rule of the Messiah. The Jews, living in the days of Christ's sojourn upon earth, misunderstood the nature of the Kingdom to be established and failed to recognize its King. Even the disciples of Christ, although confessing Jesus to be the Messiah, were dull in comprehending the death of Christ as a necessary step in the establishment of the Messianic Kingdom. Indeed Jesus rebuked several of the disciples with the statement, "O fools, and slow of heart to believe all that the prophets have spoken: ought not Christ to have suffered these things, and to enter into his glory?" Intermingled with prophecies of the coming kingdom were indications of terrible judgment that would fall upon the nation rejecting Christ. The Lord referred to this judgment in the statements: "But the children of the kingdom shall be cast out into outer darkness: there shall be weeping and gnashing of teeth" (Matt. 8:12); "Behold, your house is left unto you desolate"

(Matt. 23:38). Such was the mercy of God, however, that forty years were to elapse before the destruction of Jerusalem which signalized God's rejection and judgment. The events leading up to this judgment in the transition period might well cause bewilderment and discouragement in the hearts of the followers of Christ. But in the parable of the fig tree, Jesus informed them that all these untoward events to be experienced by the Jewish nation were harbingers of hope. He said:

Now learn a parable of the fig tree; when his branch is yet tender, and putteth forth leaves, ye know that summer is nigh: so likewise ye, when ye shall see all these things, know that it is near, even at the doors (Matt. 24:32, 33).

The summer is a time of fertility, growth, and fruit, and was figurative of the kingdom of God. With the removal of the old forms of Judaism, the Messiah's kingdom was to find fertile soil not only in Palestine but throughout the world; it was to grow unto the uttermost parts of the earth; it was to bring forth abundant fruit to the glory of God. The destruction of Jerusalem and the events preceding it were not terrible signs but harbingers of a summer that would spread its blessings throughout the earth. All the distressing events predicted by Christ, instead of discouraging the disciples, should encourage them, for by them they would know it was the beginning, not of winter time for this world, but of summer. They indicated the beginning of a world-wide harvest of souls.

Suppose for a moment that the parable of the Fig Tree applied to the second, personal, visible coming of Christ and that all the events prophesied were to occur in a period just before the second coming. The sense, then, of the parable would be somewhat as follows: "When you see the sun darkened, the moon not giving light, the stars falling, the powers of heaven shakened, the sign of the Son of man in heaven, all the tribes mourning, the Son of man coming in the clouds,

152

the sound of the trumpet, the final gathering of the elect: when ye shall see all these things, know that it is near, even at the doors." How superfluous such an admonition would be!

Imagine Christ informing his disciples that when they saw the sun and moon darkened and the stars crashing down about them, then they would know that his second coming was at the doors! Imagine Christ warning his disciples that when they saw him coming in the clouds then they would know that his second coming was at the doors! Imagine Christ communicating the news to his disciples that when they saw him sending his angels with a great sound of the trumpet to gather the elect from the four winds then they would know his second coming was at the doors!

If all the events predicted in Chapter 24:4–28 occurred and verses 29–31 were fulfilled literally, then the second coming would already be past. There would be no necessity of informing any one that the Lord's second coming was at the doors. The parable of the Fig Tree would not be needed. Only as one applies "all these things" to the events previous to and at the time of the destruction of Jerusalem does the parable of the Fig Tree have any point, significance and comfort. To the Christian, living in that generation when all these things would occur, every fulfilled event was a bud upon the fig tree. Summer was at hand.

All these Things

As already indicated in the course of the study of Matthew Twenty-four, many keys are provided for a proper interpretation. Another helpful key is the phrase, "all these things," which is repeated in the parable of the Fig Tree. Within the context of Christ's prophetic discourse it has a well-defined meaning. The phrase is employed in Matthew 23:36. Jesus had just made a scathing review of the hypocrisy and sins of the scribes and Pharisees of his generation and pronounced some terrible woes upon them for their iniquity. Then Christ indicated that "all these things" signified by the seven-fold woe would be fulfilled in the present generation: "Verily I say unto you, all these things shall come upon this generation." The woes would find fulfillment in the dissolution of Judaism and destruction of Jerusalem. That was the punishment for filling to the brim their fathers' cup of iniquity.

The destruction of the Temple was also part of the judgment pronounced upon the Jewish nation and was indicated previously by Jesus in the statement, "Behold, your house is left unto you desolate." Christ again uses the phrase, "all these things," after the disciples showed him the magnificent buildings of the Temple for they could hardly believe that it could be made desolate. But Jesus said, "See ye not all these things? verily I say unto you, There shall not be left here one stone upon another, that shall not be thrown down" (Matt. 24:2). It is, of course, obvious that the phrase here has definite reference to the destruction of the buildings of the Temple.

The phrase is next employed by the disciples as recorded in Matthew 24:3. They approached Christ and asked: "Tell us, when shall these things be?" "These things" referred definitely to the destruction of the Temple which Jesus had just announced but the disciples had also heard the expression in the denouncement of the scribes and Pharisees. Their minds were bewildered by the predicted events that were to include terrible judgments against the contemporary generation of Jews and the destruction of the magnificent buildings of the Temple. They wanted to know the time when "these things" would find their fulfillment.

Christ next employs the phrase in the parable of the Fig Tree, "So likewise ye, when ye shall see all these things, know that it is near, even at the doors." When the disciples had witnessed the fulfillment of the entire gamut of events then they would know that the summer time of the kingdom was at hand. These things would include the beginning of sorrows such as false christs, wars and rumors of wars, famines, pestilences and earthquakes; persecution of Christians and the falling away of some; preaching of the gospel as a witness to the world; the abomination of desolation spoken by Daniel; and the great tribulation of the Roman siege. Terrible as all these things were, they were heralds of the joys of summer.

The same phrase appears in the verse that follows the parable of the Fig Tree and which we have termed the "time text" of the chapter. Christ stated, "Verily I say unto you, This generation shall not pass till all these things be fulfilled." Here the Lord definitely limits "all these things" to the contemporary generation. Previously he had employed the phrase in reference to the woes upon the scribes and Pharisees of his generation and in reference to the destruction of the Temple. Here there can be no question as to its reference to the predicted events and especially to the destruction of the Temple for Jesus used the phrase ("See ye not all these things?") when the disciples showed him the buildings of the Temple. Furthermore, when Jesus prophesied that not one stone would be left upon another, the disciples asked, "When shall these things be?" Within the context "all these things" employed in the parable of the Fig Tree and the time text include all the events enumerated by Christ in answering the question of the disciples. If he meant something entirely different Jesus would have indicated it or else there would be utter confusion in the minds of the disciples.

How stunned and depressed the disciples of Christ would be if they beheld the fulfillment of the predicted judgments upon unbelieving Jews, without the knowledge expressed by Paul that the fall of the Jews would be "the riches of the world, and the diminishing of them the riches of the Gentiles" (Rom. 11:12). Even as the destruction of the old Jerusalem and the old Temple drew nigh, the new Israel, small and despised, would find hope and strength in the knowledge that soon her Beloved would speak, "Rise up, my love, my fair one, and come away. For, lo, the winter is past, the rain is over and gone; the flowers appear on the earth; the time of the singing of birds is come, and the voice of the turtle is heard in our land; the fig tree putteth forth her green figs, and the vines with tender grape give a good smell. Arise, my love, my fair one, and come away" (Song of Solomon 2:10–13). The entire earth had been in the throes of a spiritual winter to disappear with the advent of the Messiah. The summer of the everlasting gospel was to be delayed until the old Jerusalem was removed. The disciples were to exercise patience and to learn the parable of the Fig Tree: "When his branch is yet tender, and putteth forth leaves, ye know that summer is nigh: so likewise ye, when ye shall see all these things, know that it is near, even at the doors."

The Time Text

After the encouragement of the parable of the Fig Tree, Jesus concludes his prophetic discourse on the fate of Jerusalem with the time-text of Matthew 24:34, "Verily I say unto you, This generation shall not pass till all these things be fulfilled." This verse precludes the extension of times beyond the contemporary generation. While the figurative language of verses 29–31 proves a stumbling block of interpretation to some, careful attention to prophetic language in the Old Testament will remove difficulties. There is not a single figure employed whose use has not been already sanctioned and its meaning determined in the Old Testament. Prophecy has indicated and history has verified that all events mentioned by Christ have found their fulfillment.

To give emphasis to his startling predictions concerning the future of Jerusalem, Jesus gives a most solemn oath:

"Heaven and earth shall pass away, but my words shall not pass away" (Matt. 24:35). This is a declaration of infallible fulfillment and who but the Son of God could give such an explicit affirmation? What seems more stable and permanent than heaven and earth? Yet of greater stability were the words of Christ! All his utterances concerning the fate of Jerusalem would come to pass. And they did come to pass. His predictions were literally fulfilled.

Christ was no fallible prophet with mistaken notions of an imminent cataclysmal event falling upon the world. Matthew 24:4–35 refers to the destruction of Jerusalem. But there is to be a cataclysmal end of the world to occur at his second coming. Concerning this he speaks in the Second Section, Matthew 24:36–25:46. The fulfillment of the first section of our Lord's prophetic discourse should convince all of the fulfillment of the Second Section of the prophecy. With this second section we will be concerned in the following two chapters but not with such detail as there is greater agreement in the interpretation.

157

Chapter XIII

That Day and Hour

The first 35 verses of Matthew 24 relate to the destruction of Jerusalem and the events preceding that destruction. With verse 36 a new subject is introduced, namely, the second coming of Christ and the attendant final judgment. This forms the content of Matthew 24:36–25:46. The fact that the first 35 verses have been so completely fulfilled in the destruction of Jersusalem should impress all that the prophecies in regard to the second coming and final judgment will also be fulfilled. The one fulfillment is a guarantee of the other.

Many have recognized that with verse 36 a change of subject matter occurs. Spurgeon indicates this in his commentary on verse 36, "There is a manifest change in our Lord's words here, which clearly indicates that they refer to His last great coming to judgment." The verse reads as follows:

But of that day and hour knoweth no man, not the angels of heaven, but my Father only.

158

That Day and Hour

The expression, "that day and hour," gives immediate evidence of a change of subject matter. In the First Section (24:4–35) the plural "days" is employed; in the Second Section (24:36–25:46) the singular "day" comes to the fore. In verses 19, 22 and 29 of the First Section the plural "these days" describes the period under consideration and the singular "that day and hour" is not employed. But in the Second Section the period under discussion is described by the singular (24:36, 42, 44, 50 and 25:13). It is true that in verses 37 and 38 the plural "days" is found but that is in reference to the days of Noah previous to the "the day" when Noah entered into the ark. The distinctive use of the plural in the First Section and the singular in the Second Section points rather conclusively that the periods under consideration are different. The First Section concerns itself with the destruction of Jerusalem; the Second Section with the personal second advent of Christ and the final judgment.

The day, the great day, that day and *that hour* are known expressions in Scriptures for the final day of judgment. Christ had often spoken of the great judgment in connection with a certain *day*. Consequently the disciples had no difficulty understanding that Christ had changed the subject in verse 36 from the judgments upon Jerusalem to the judgment that was to occur at his second coming. Usage of the term, "the day," by Matthew in his Gospel, indicates that it would be understood by the Apostles to refer to the final judgment. Speaking of the final judgment, Jesus stated in Matthew 7:22, "Many will say to me in that day, etc." Matthew 11:22, 24 records, "But I say unto you, It shall be more tolerable for Tyre and Sidon at the day of judgment, than for you . . . But I say unto you, that it shall be more tolerable for the land of Sodom in the day of judgment, than for thee." And Matthew

12:36 states, "But I say unto you, that every idle word that men shall speak, they shall give account thereof in the day of judgment." All these statements refer to the final judgment. So when Christ speaks of *that day* in Matthew 24:36 the disciples knew that Christ had reference to the final judgment which they had confused with the destruction of Jerusalem.

Another startling fact that seems to have escaped notice of those who refer the prophecy of Matthew 24:1–35 to the second coming of the Lord is the fact that nowhere in the New Testament is the plural—*the days, days of vengeance, those days*—used in reference to the second coming of Christ or to the final judgment. One exception seems to be James 5:3, "Ye have heaped treasure together for the last days." But in the American Revised Version the expression, "for the last days" is corrected to "in the last days." It was the period of the last days that ungodly rich men heaped treasure.

A general impression prevails that the term, "last days," has reference to a short period just before the second coming of Christ, but that term is not so defined in Scriptures. The "last days" began with the first advent of Christ and will continue until his second advent. This is indicated in a number of scriptural passages. Hebrews 1:1,2 reads, "God, who at sundry times and in divers manners spake in time past unto the fathers by the prophets, hath *in these last days* spoken unto us by his Son, whom he that appointed heir of all things, by whom also he made the worlds." *In these last days* obviously refers to the time in which the author of Hebrews was writing and is contrasted to the time past of the prophets. The apostle Peter referred to the events of the day of Pentecost as events of the last days. He said, "But this is that which was spoken by the prophet Joel; and it shall come to pass *in the last days,* saith God, I will pour out my Spirit on all flesh" (Acts 2:16,17). John in his first Epistle writes, "Little children, *it is the last time:* and as ye have heard that antichrist shall come, even now are there many antichrists; whereby we know that *it is the last time.*" Peter in his first Epistle (1:20) uses the term in reference to the first advent of Christ. Following scriptural usage the term must be understood as the period from the first coming of Christ to his second coming. The Scriptures give no ground for believing that "the last days" indicates a short period just before the coming of the Lord. The plural does not refer either to the second coming or the final judgment.

Knoweth no Man

The day of Christ's second coming—the day of final judgment —"knoweth no man, no, not the angels of heaven, but my Father only." In the ARV Version the words, "neither the son," are included. As many authorities, some ancient, omit these words, they are not included in the King James Version. However, they are included in Mark 13:32, "But of that day or that hour knoweth no man, no, not even the angels which are in heaven, neither the Son, but the Father." The exact day and hour of the second coming is unknown not only to mortal man and immortal angels but was unknown to Christ while he was upon earth. As the Son of man, Christ did not seek that knowledge as it had no immediate connection with his work on earth.

How can this lack of knowledge be reconciled with Matthew 24:15 if this verse designates the second coming? The time mentioned in this verse is very specific; it was at the moment when they saw the abomination of desolation, spoken by Daniel, standing in the holy place. This would be followed by the great tribulation. Daniel is very specific as to the time of this desolation, "And from the time that the daily sacrifice shall be taken away, and the abomination that maketh desolate set up, there shall be a thousand two hundred and ninety days" (12:11). Was something revealed to Daniel that was not revealed to Christ? If the abomination of desolation indicates the second coming then Daniel knew the time and his knowledge would contradict Christ's statement that no man knoweth the day and the hour. Matthew 24:15, with such an interpretation, would contradict verse 36. But actually verse 15 revers to the destruction of Jerusalem while verse 36 relates to the second coming and thus there is no contradiction.

Contrast in Content

A definite and clear contrast exists between the subject matter of the First Section and that of the Second Section of Matthew 24 and 25. In the First everything is very specific; in the Second everything is general. In the First specific signs are given; in the Second there is an absence of explicit signs. In the First Section time is given for Christians to flee; in the Second there is no time for flight. Judgment upon earth is the subject of the First Section; judgment in the life to come forms the subject of the Second Section.

In Matthew 24:37–39 the time of the coming of the Son of man is compared to the suddenness of the flood in the days of Noah. The flood was the great judgment of the Old Dispensation. There were no "signs" given to the people; only the sign of Noah's preaching. The people lived in what appeared normal times: "eating and drinking, marrying and giving in marriage." Apparently there were no famines such as previous to Jerusalem's destruction and described in Section One. The picture of the days previous to the Noachin flood is a vivid contrast to the description of the days previous to the destruction of Jerusalem. No sign but the sign of Noah's preaching was given in the one case; many signs were given in the other case.

Another picture of normal times is given in Matthew 24:40,

41. Two people are working in the field: one is taken; the other left. Two women are grinding at the mill: one is taken; the other left. In the First Section the saints are urged to flee to the mountains; here they are "taken" while at their work. Why flee to the mountains when the Lord comes? What actually will happen is described in I Thess. 4:17, "Then we which are alive and remain shall be caught up together with them in the clouds, to meet the Lord in the air; and so shall we ever be with the Lord." The "fleeing" of the First Section contrasts vividly with the being "taken" of the Second Section.

The conclusion of Matthew 24:37-41 is given in verse 42: "Watch therefore: for ye know not what hour your Lord doth come." This watching for the unknown hour of the Lord's return forms the theme of the Second Section. No signs are to precede the coming: therefore watch.

The unexpectedness and suddenness of the Lord's return are illustrated by a thief coming in the night in Matthew 24:43. The thief gives no sign of his intention to rob. No indication of his coming is given. This exemplifies the coming of the Lord. Unmistakable signs are indicated as to the time of the destruction of Jerusalem but in regard to the coming of the Lord and the final judgment no definite signs were given. This thought is re-echoed in verse 44: "Therefore be ye also ready; for in such an hour as ye think not the Son of man cometh."

The three parables that follow reiterate the same thought. The parable of the Servants (24:45-51) stresses the fact that the Lord may delay his coming for a great length of time. No warnings or signs will herald his coming. This is emphasized in verse 50, "The lord of that servant shall come in a day when he looketh not for him, and in an hour that he is not aware of."

The same truth is revealed in the parable of the Ten Virgins

163

(25:1–13). The Lord came at midnight and there were no preliminary warnings by which the Virgins could make immediate preparations. There was no time to buy oil for the lamps. The Foolish Virgins may have been waiting for a special sign but no other is given than this general warning, "Watch, therefore, for ye know neither the day nor the hour wherein the Son of man cometh."

The possibility of a long delay for the second coming is taught in the parable of the Talents (25:14–30). The Master travels into a *far* country and *"after a long time* the Lord of those servants cometh, and reckoneth with them."

The three parables unite in teaching delay, lack of warning and absence of signs. The central theme is to be ever on the alert for no one knows the day nor the hour so as to receive warning that the second coming of the Lord is actually at hand. Alertness and preparedness are vital because the second coming will be attended by the final judgment. For this reason the discourse of Christ ends with a picture of the last judgment. This is an added motivation for watchfulness.

The careful reader cannot help but be impressed with the difference of content and emphasis between Matthew 24:1–35 and 24:36-25:46. The First Section gives impression of abnormal times: wars, famine, pestilences, earthquakes, persecution and great tribulation; the Second Section of normal times: eating and drinking, marrying and giving in marriage, peaceful employment. The First Section relates specific signs in relation to judgment upon Jerusalem; in the Second such specific signs are absent in regard to the final judgment. The First Section is concerned with "those days"; the Second, with "that day." The First Section limits the judgment to Palestine; the Second, embraces all nations. Warnings in the First; no warnings, except a general admonition to be prepared, in the Second. In the First the saints were warned to

164

flee to the mountains; in the Second, the saints are taken up. The First pictures a judgment upon earth; the Second, judgment in heaven. All this points to a vivid and clear contrast of content. The two sections have different subject matter.

Chapter XIV

The Last Judgment

The concluding portion of the Olivet Discourse of our Lord concerns itself with the second coming and the final judgment. The picture of the last judgment (Matt. 25:31–46) forms one of the most impressive and breath-taking passages of the Bible. The glorious and triumphant coming of the Lord will terminate history and inaugurate the final judgment at which all people who have dwelt upon the earth will be present. This is portrayed in verses 31–34:

> *When the Son of man shall come in his glory, and all the holy angels with him, then shall he sit upon the throne of his glory: and before him shall be gathered all nations: and he shall separate them one from another, as a shepherd divideth his sheep from the goats: and he shall set the sheep on his right hand, but the goats on the left.*

Other passages in Scripture corroborate the teaching that the second coming will be attended by the final judgment. I Corinthians 4:5 states, "Therefore judge nothing before the time, until the Lord come, who both will bring to light the hidden things of darkness, and will make manifest the counsels of the hearts: and then shall every man have praise of God." This passage teaches that Christ will judge both the evil and good at his coming. II Timothy 4:1 reveals the same truth, "I charge thee therefore before God, and the Lord Jesus Christ, who shall judge the quick and the dead at his appearing and his kingdom." All the dead and the living will be judged at the appearing of the Lord. Another clear revelation of that fact is Matthew 16:27, "For the Son of man shall come in the glory of his Father with his angels; and then he shall reward every man according to his work" (cf. II Thess. 1:7-10). All these passages confirm the teaching of Matthew 25:31–46 that the final judgment takes place at the second coming of Christ.

Universal in Scope

A vivid contrast presents itself between the particular judgments against Palestine described in Matthew 24:4–35 and the universal judgment described in Matthew 25:31–46. In the first passage judgment is limited to a specific locality and to the Temple of that locality. Those who would behold the desolation of abomination standing in the Temple are urged to flee from Judea to the mountains. The second passage is universal in its scope and reveals all nations standing before the throne of Christ. Surrounding the throne of glory are legions and legions of angels. All nations are present, according to this account; and we can be assured that not one nation will be missing. Thus one passage describes a judgment upon the small nation of Palestine; the other, judgment upon all nations. In one, the judgments are executed upon the earth; in the other, the scene is in heaven. The contrast is obvious.

It is rather difficult to picture all nations of the earth gathered together in the small land of Palestine. Crowding all nations that have ever existed in history into Palestine would be a physical impossibility. And yet some premillennialist writers would have us believe that the judgment scene described by Christ takes place in Palestine and even limit it to Jerusalem. To avoid the seeming physical impossibility, it is claimed that the nations will be present representatively. Dr. Henry W. Frost in his book, "The Second Coming of Christ," writes, "It is here that the judgment described in the twenty-fifth chapter of Matthew applies, where Christ, having come to earth and taken His seat upon His throne, brings before Him the nations—presumably representatively—and then and there settles the controversy which has existed through the ages as between Himself and those people who have rebelled against God and His holy commandments and ways (Joel 3:9-16)." According to this interpretation, men within the nations are judged representatively, placed on the right and left of the throne representatively, and enter into everlasting punishment and eternal life representatively. How fantastic and unscriptural!

That all people are to be judged on the day of final judgment as described in Matthew 25 is confirmed by other passages of Scripture. In the parable of the Tares in Matthew 13, both the tares and the good wheat grow together until the final harvest and Christ informs us definitely that the harvest is not until the end of the world. According to Romans 2 both Jews and Gentiles are to be judged "in the day when God shall judge the secrets of men by Jesus Christ according to my gospel." Paul does not speak of a judgment before the millennium and one afterwards. He does not intimate that there will be two or seven judgments which the premillennialist maintains. Our passage, too, conforms to another great picture of the last judgment, Revelation 20:11-13, "And I saw a great white throne, and him that sat on it, from whose face the earth and the heaven fled away; and there was found no place for them. And I saw the dead, small and great, stand before God;

and the books were opened: and another book was opened, which is the book of life: and the dead were judged out of those things which were written in the books, according to their works. And the sea gave up the dead which were in it; and death and hell delivered up the dead which were in them: and they were judged every man according to their works." In this passage, as in Matthew 25:31–46, a universal judgment is depicted and all people who have lived upon the earth are judged according to their works.

The average Christian reader of the Matthew passage believes that the final judgment is set forth. And he is right. The premillennialist has to explain this passage away because it does not fit in with his eschatological views. Actually he has to forsake his "literal" interpretation which he so stoutly maintains is the only proper way of interpretation. He has to explain that "all nations" are not "all" nations, and that the nations are at this judgment only "representatively." There is absolutely no basis for this type of interpretation. The "all nations" includes all those who have ever lived upon the earth.

Judged According to Works

Many passages concerned with the last judgment reveal that all are to be judged according to their works. In the passage under study Christ states as a principle of judgment: "Inasmuch as ye have done it unto one of the least of these, my brethren, ye have done it unto me." The premillennialist interprets this to mean that nations and individuals will be judged in relation to their attitude towards the Jews. But Christ gives no ground for this. He said that one would be judged by what had been done for "my brethren." Unbelieving Jews, whom Christ called the children of the devil, are not the brethren of Christ. The brethren of Christ are clearly defined in Matthew 12:49,50, "And he stretched forth his

169

hand toward his disciples, and said, Behold my mother and my brethren! For whosoever shall do the will of my Father which is in heaven, the same is my brother, and sister, and mother." Not an unbelieving Jew, but anyone who performs the will of God is a "brother" of Christ.

The good works mentioned by Christ are not to be construed as the meriting ground for receiving the blessing of eternal life but rather as evidence of a genuine faith in Christ. This is to guard against thinking that a mere outward profession of faith saves and thus gives hope to the hypocrite. Genuine faith changes the individual and produces good works. The apostle John indicates in his Epistle that one is not saved by mere profession of faith for "He that saith he is in the light, and hateth his brother, is in darkness even until now." The same principle is enunciated by Christ in the Sermon on the Mount, "Not every one that saith unto me, Lord, Lord, shall enter into the kingdom of heaven; but he that doeth the will of my Father which is in heaven." It is because good works and not mere profession of faith that gives evidence of genuine faith that they are used as the test in the last judgment. Such is the consistent teaching revealed in Scripture. Genuine works are bound to follow true faith in Christ. For that reason Jesus will state at the final judgment, "Inasmuch as ye have done it unto one of the least of these my brethren, ye have done it unto me" or "Inasmuch as ye did it not to one of the least of these, ye did it not to me."

The Throne of His Glory

That the scene of Matthew 25:31–46 is located in heaven is also manifested by the fact that Christ is seated upon "the throne of his glory." This is none other than the "white throne" of Revelation 20 whereupon Jesus also is depicted as judging "every man according to their works." This throne of glory was also seen by Isaiah in a vision, "In the year that

King Uzziah died I saw also the Lord sitting upon a throne, high and lifted up, and his train filled the temple" (Isaiah 6:1). The apostle John revealed in his Gospel that this was a vision of Christ, "These things said Esaias, when he saw his glory, and spake of him" (John 12:41). None of these descriptions locate the throne upon earth.

The premillennialist, however, maintains as a cardinal and fundamental tenet of his system of eschatology that the throne of glory is an earthly throne set up in the material city of Jerusalem. The temporal throne of David is to be reconstructed in Jerusalem. But David's throne was only a type of Christ's heavenly throne even as David was but a type of Christ. Surely the throne of David was of no more importance than David. The premillennialist by his peculiar interpretation mistakes the type for the antitype; he mistakes the shadow for the reality. David himself, though living in the Old Dispensation, beheld this superior and exalted throne and wrote of it in Psalm 110. The apostle Peter refers to this Psalm 110 in his sermon on the day of Pentecost, "Therefore being by the right hand of God exalted, and having received of the Father the promise of the Holy Ghost, he hath shed forth this, which ye now see and hear. For David is not ascended into the heavens: but he saith himself, The Lord said unto my Lord, Sit thou on my right hand, until I make thy foes thy footstool" (Acts 2:33–35). Thus David revealed a better understanding of the significance of Christ's throne and its location than do the premillennialists. As a matter of fact there is not one passage in the New Testament which gives definite information of a personal reign of Christ upon a temporal throne in the material city of Jerusalem! What seems to be hidden to the apostles has been revealed by uninspired men.

No preliminary signs will reveal the day and hour that

171

Christ will sit upon his throne of glory for the universal judgment. He states simply, "When the Son of man shall come in his glory, and all the holy angels with him, then shall he sit upon the throne of his glory: and before him shall be gathered all nations." There are no signs in heaven or commotions upon the earth to give the exact time of his coming and judgment. Again and again the warning rings forth, "Watch therefore: for ye know not what hour your Lord doth come." His coming will be like the coming of the flood in the days of Noah when the only warning was the preaching of the judgment. It will be like a thief coming in the night. The evil servant had no warning of his Lord's return. The virgins were all sleeping and evidently were not awakened by any fearful signs in the heavens. The return of the Lord who had journeyed to a far country was long delayed but on his unexpected return he demanded an account of the talents he had entrusted to his servants. One cannot help but be impressed as he reads the Second Section of the fact that no preliminary warnings will precede the second coming of the Lord.

Conclusion

The Olivet Discourse must be interpreted in accordance with the "apocalyptic dialect" employed by Old Testament Prophets. Our Lord used a well known prophetic language to answer the inquiry of the Apostles concerning the future of the Temple at Jerusalem. When Scripture is interpreted by Scripture erroneous conjectures of "prophetic students" will cease, recourse to "double meanings" will not be necessary, and the charge of error on the part of Jesus will be seen to be groundless. The prophecy of our Lord possesses a wonderful harmony and history has clearly manifested its truth.

Jesus was not in error when he declared, "This generation shall not pass, till all these things be fulfilled." How necessary is it, then, that all obey the infallible Prophet's admonition, "Watch therefore, for ye know neither the day nor the hour wherein the Son of man cometh." *Even so, come, Lord Jesus.*

SECTION THREE

REVELATION TWENTY

AN EXPOSITION

CONTENTS

Section Three

REVELATION TWENTY

FOREWORD

What about the Millennium? Will it be in history and upon the earth? Or will it occur after the second coming of Christ? Or is it descriptive of heaven? The answer to these questions surely should be sought for in Revelation Twenty in which the thousand-year period is mentioned six times. This Chapter is very important for the true conception of the Millennium.

The question of whether or not the earth will be the scene of the Millennium is coming more and more to the fore among Christians. Will all nations be converted to Christianity before the second coming of the Lord? Is history rapidly drawing to a close as predicted by some? Is there any possibility that nations will beat their swords into plowshares and spears into pruninghooks before the end of time?

While all the answers are not given in Revelation Twenty yet evangelical scholars have acknowledged that they have been influenced in their attitude towards prophecy by their interpretation of the Chapter. Many have entered into certain schools of thought because of what they felt this prophetic Chapter teaches. It is therefore very important to ascertain the true teaching of Revelation Twenty.

It is the habit of a few to read a few chapters of a book on prophecy to see to which school of thought the author belongs. Then if it does not agree with his particular school it is cast aside and condemned. It is my hope that the reader will not use the norm of any particular school of prophecy but will use the Scriptures. Does the Word of God teach this or does it not? The author does not feel any responsibility to any particular school of prophecy but he does feel his responsibility to interpret the Word of God correctly. I will feel grateful for any correction of error in interpretation.

While I have quoted from but few writers on the interpretation of Revelation, it is not because they have not been consulted. I owe a debt of gratitude to many who have enriched the Church with their writings. Among such are: Warfield, the Hodges, J. A.

Alexander, Vos, Lange, P. W. Grant, Alford, Hengstenberg, Garratt, Chr. Wordsworth, Moses Stuart, H. B. Swete, James Durham, Gauntlett, Bryce Johnstone, Alexander McLeod, Waldegrave, Fuller, Milligan, John Owen, John Lightfoot, Goodwin, Henry Gipps, Plummer, Thomas Newton. I have also consulted a number of recent writers on prophecy.

For the amillennialist position on the first resurrection I have taken as authorities Dr. Geerhardus Vos in his article on Eschatology in "The International Standard Bible Encyclopaedia" and Dr. L. Berkhof in the Second Revised Edition of his "Systematic Theology." A few, who classify themselves as amillennialists, do not accept the position of these authorities.

With the exception of several chapters, I have used the method of verse by verse exposition. The first two chapters, however, concern themselves with the two resurrections.

J.M.K.

Little Falls, N. J.

CHAPTER I

THE FIRST RESURRECTION

The Book of Revelation is a sealed book to many. It puzzles and baffles the reader. Because of this many avoid the reading of it as it makes no sense to them. And yet a blessing is promised to all those who hear and read this mysterious book. The Lord knew that Revelation would be difficult to understand and therefore graciously encourages the reader with a special blessing. In the very first chapter Jesus states that a blessing will attend the reading and hearing of the words of Revelation. This promise alone should cause every Christian to read and study it diligently. Where there is a promise of blessing the Lord will give light.

Of all the chapters of Revelation there is none considered more difficult than Chapter Twenty. It concerns itself with a thousand-year period which is called the millennium. This is associated in our minds with a period of peace and prosperity. It is called the golden age. Concerning the millennium there are three schools of thought. Within each school there are wide differences of opinion and interpretation. These schools of thought are called premillennial, amillennial, and postmillennial.

The premillennialist believes that the millennium will be ushered in after the second coming of Christ. The amillennialist believes that there will not be a millennium upon earth and that the thousand-year period refers to the intermediate state of the Christian soul in heaven. The postmillennialist believes that the thousand-year period is before the second coming of the Lord.

Without going fully into the merits and demerits of these various schools of thought, all held by able evangelical scholars, we will endeavour to give a verse by verse interpretation of this important Chapter. But before doing so it may be well to clear up a few matters which will help in the understanding of the entire Chapter. We feel that the apostle John through the Holy Spirit has given a key which will unlock the meaning of the Chapter. The key is given to us in verse 5. It is the expression: *This is the first resurrection.*

179

It is verse 4 that is most difficult to understand. It seems like a picture of a different type of life than that which is experienced at this present time upon earth. It pictures saints seated upon thrones, living and reigning with Christ a thousand years. The premillennialist says: "This must be upon earth and after the second coming of Christ. They must be resurrected saints reigning with the Lord upon earth." "No," says the amillennialist, "it must be the intermediate state in heaven because it speaks of souls." But the apostle John, the author of Revelation, states definitely: "This is the first resurrection."

The apostle John wanted no misunderstanding. He did not want anyone to think that verse 4 had reference to the General Resurrection and the period following. He halts us from such a thought by abruptly stating: "This is the first resurrection." If we can determine by Scripture what the first resurrection is, we will go a long way in the understanding of the entire Chapter. It is the key which will unlock the door.

All are acquainted with the simple meaning of the word *resurrection*. It is: "a rising again from the dead." That which was dead is brought to life again. This is very important to keep in mind. Whatever the term "first" may signify, the word "resurrection" means a rising again from the dead.

The fact that it is a resurrection knocks out the thought that it is descriptive of the life of the soul in the intermediate state. It has been maintained that when the soul leaves the body at death it enters into the millennial state and lives and reigns with Christ for a thousand years. But when the Christian soul leaves the body to dwell in heaven, it is not a *resurrection*. The soul in the Christian is alive; it is not in a dead state. Its removal from the body into heaven could be better termed an ascension or a translation. To state that the translation of the soul into heaven is a resurrection is to contradict directly the teaching of Christ that "whosoever liveth and believeth in me shall never die." The very fact that this Twentieth Chapter deals with a resurrection knocks out the whole amillennial interpretation that the Chapter is speaking of the intermediate state of the soul. Whatever Chapter Twenty describes, it is a raising from the dead and not a translation from earth to heaven.

But what is the *first resurrection* if it is not the translation of the soul to heaven? The best way to determine what is defined by the term "first resurrection" is to discover what is the "first death." What needs to be resurrected first?

THE FIRST DEATH

The first death is described to us in the first chapters of Genesis. God stated to Adam in Genesis 2:17, "But of the tree of the knowledge of good and evil, thou shalt not eat of it: for in the day that thou eatest thereof thou shalt surely die." The primary meaning of the expression, "Thou shalt surely die," is the death of the soul. Upon the act of disobedience the soul was separated from God. Adam and Eve upon disobedience did not immediately experience physical death but they did experience the death of the soul. They were separated from God. Included in the death of the soul was the death of the body which came later. However, the fundamental fulfilment of Genesis 2:17 was the death of the soul.

This is brought out strongly in the New Testament. The apostle Paul describes the state of the Ephesian Christians before conversion as those "who were dead in trespasses and sins." In I Timothy 5:6 it is declared: "But she that liveth in pleasure is dead while she liveth." Christ brings this sharply before us in His statement of Matthew 8:22, "Let the dead bury their dead." Even though the unregenerated man is physically alive he is dead in the sight of God. His soul is dead. This is the primary death. Involved in it and following from it is the death of the body.

Since the first death is primarily the death of the human soul, it is the soul that must be resurrected *first*. Consequently we must expect to find in the New Testament references to the resurrection of the soul. This we find in abundance.

THE FIRST RESURRECTION

An important passage is Ephesians 2:5, 6 which reads as follows: "Even when we were dead in sins, hath quickened us together with Christ (by grace ye are saved;), and hath raised us up together in heavenly places in Christ Jesus." The word "quickened" is translated in the American Revised Version as "made alive." The soul which was dead has been made alive. It has been resurrected. This is brought out even more clearly with the expression: "And hath raised us up together, and made us sit together in heavenly places in Christ Jesus." "To raise up" is to resurrect. Even while upon earth the resurrected saints sit with Christ in heavenly places. This points to the interpretation of verse 4. However, just now we are interested in pointing out that the first resurrection, as far as Christians are concerned, is the quickening of their souls from death.

Colossians 2:12, 13 teaches the same truth. It reads: "Having been buried with him in baptism, wherein ye were also raised with him through faith in the working of God, who raised him from the dead. And you, being dead through your trespasses and uncircumcision of your flesh, you, I say, did he make alive together with him, having forgiven us all our trespasses." Here the regeneration of the human soul is compared to the resurrection of Christ. They who were dead were made alive. They were raised with Christ. This is the first resurrection and surely the important one as far as the Christian is concerned. Ephesians 1:19, 20 brings out the fact that the same mighty power of God that was used to resurrect Christ was used in respect to the soul of the believer.

Another passage which brings out this same truth is I John 3:14, "We know that we have passed from death unto life, because we love the brethren." Each Christian can be assured that he has experienced the resurrection by one of the fruits thereof, namely, love for the brethren. It is a passing from death to life. That is the meaning of the word "resurrection."

The above verses clearly indicate that the rebirth of the soul is the first resurrection. The verses speak of "being made alive," "being raised," and "passing from death to life." This resurrection is the experience of believers upon earth. Surely it cannot be denied that it is a resurrection and actually the first resurrection in the experience of the Christian.

If the apostle John in Chapter Twenty of Revelation was not referring to the resurrection of the soul why would he use the term "first"? In his Gospel and Epistle he himself points to the resurrection experience of the soul. Certainly there would be confusion in the minds of his readers if in Chapter Twenty he referred to

182

something entirely different. They would say in effect: "The apostle speaks of the rebirth of the soul upon earth as the first resurrection experience of the Christian; but in Revelation he speaks of the translation of the soul to heaven as the first resurrection or he speaks of what is to happen at 'one phase' of the second coming as the first resurrection. Why did he not use some other term than *first?*" Undoubtedly if the apostle John was referring to another resurrection he would have used another term. However, by using the term "first resurrection" he was pointing to the well-known fact of the resurrection of the soul.

THE SECOND RESURRECTION

It may be well at this point to ask, What is the second resurrection? It is the resurrection of the body which is to take place at the second coming of Christ. This is the General Resurrection with which readers of the Bible are well acquainted. There are many references to it in the Scriptures. As a rule when one speaks of the resurrection people have that in mind. To indicate that the General Resurrection was not the one he had in mind the apostle John expressly used the term "first" so that there would be no confusion.

That there is to be a resurrection of the body as well as that of the soul is clearly taught in the Scriptures. In the Old Testament we have the classic passage of Job 19:26, "And though after my skin worms destroy this body, yet in my flesh shall I see God." And in Isaiah 26:19 we read: "Thy dead men shall live, together with my dead body shall they arise. Awake and sing, ye that dwell in dust: for thy dew is as the dew of herbs, and the earth shall cast out the dead." Notice how in Daniel 12:2 it speaks of the resurrection of both the wicked and the righteous: "And many of them that sleep in the dust of the earth shall awake, some to everlasting life, and some to shame and everlasting contempt."

The New Testament also teaches clearly the resurrection of the body. Romans 8:11 states: "But if the Spirit of him that raised up Jesus from the dead dwell in you, he that raised up Christ from the dead shall also quicken your mortal bodies by his Spirit that dwelleth in you." Our mortal bodies are to be made alive. The resurrection of the body is particularly dealt with in the fifteenth chapter of First Corinthians. There it is taught that as Christ was raised so will every believer be raised. Paul answers the objections that have been raised against the resurrection of the body.

The resurrection of the body will take place at the second coming of our Lord. In I Corinthians 15:23 it is stated: "But every man in his own order: Christ the first fruits; afterward they that are Christ's at his coming." That the wicked are also included in this resurrection is taught in Acts 24:15, "And have hope toward God, which they themselves also allow, that there shall be a resurrection of the dead, both of the just and the unjust." An important passage is John 5:21-29 with which we will deal in the next chapter. It speaks of two resurrections. Verses 28, 29 bring to the foreground the General Resurrection: "Marvel not at this: for the hour is coming, in the which all that are in the graves shall hear his voice, and shall come forth; they that have done good, unto the resurrection of life; and they that have done evil, unto the resurrection of damnation."

It is thus apparent that the Scriptures speak of two resurrections: that of the soul and that of the body. The resurrection of the soul is first. Unbelievers have no part in the first resurrection. The General Resurrection will witness the rising of all from the grave. We believe that it was to avoid any misunderstanding as to which resurrection he was writing about that the apostle John used the term *first*. He was writing about the resurrection of the soul. The expression, *first resurrection*, gives the key to the understanding of Revelation Twenty.

CHAPTER II

THE TWO RESURRECTIONS

There can be no understanding of Revelation Twenty without understanding what resurrections the apostle John had in mind when he referred to them in that Chapter. It is well, therefore, to study the other writings of the apostle which refer to the resurrections. John writes not only of two resurrections in Revelation but also in the Gospel which bears his name. They are referred to in John 5:19-29. This passage will give us light on Revelation Twenty. In quoting it below we have italicized what is known as the bodily or general resurrection.

> John 5:24, 25, 28, 29, "Verily, verily, I say unto you, He that heareth my word, and believeth on him that sent me, hath everlasting life, and shall not come into condemnation; but is passed from death unto life. Verily, verily, I say unto you, The hour is coming, and now is, when the dead shall hear the voice of the Son of God: and they that hear shall live.—*Marvel not at this: for the hour is coming, in the which all that are in the graves shall hear his voice, and shall come forth; they that have done good, unto the resurrection of life; and they that have done evil, unto the resurrection of damnation.*"

In our first chapter we expressed the thought that the key expression which would unlock the meaning of Revelation Twenty is that found in verse 5: *This is the first resurrection.* If we know what the apostle meant by that expression we are well on the way to the understanding of the entire Chapter. We have shown that the first death is that of the soul. It cannot be denied that the first resurrection experience of the Christian is that of his soul. The regeneration of the soul is referred to as a resurrection in a number of New Testament passages. The Scriptures also refer to a second resurrection which is that of the body.

It so happens that John records the teaching of Jesus on two resurrections in the passage which is quoted above. Jesus teaches that there is a resurrection of the soul and a resurrection of the body. If John in Revelation Twenty speaks of two entirely different resurrections than those spoken of by Christ it would, to say the least, be very confusing. However, we will discover that the Gospel of John gives light on the Revelation passage. It behooves us, therefore, to study John 5:24-29.

How Jesus came to teach about two resurrections must first be seen. Jesus had healed an impotent man on the Sabbath Day. This so enraged the Jews that they were ready to slay Him. But Jesus said to them: "My Father worketh hitherto, and I work." The Father did not stop His providential workings on the Sabbath and so neither did the Son. This further annoyed the Jews because therein Jesus made Himself equal with God.

Then Jesus goes on to say in John 5:19, 20 that the Son does only what the Father does. Furthermore the Father "will show Him greater works than these, that ye may marvel." Greater works were to be accomplished by the Son than the healing of an impotent man. These greater works consisted of the resurrection of the soul and of the body. Thus the incident of the miracle of healing led to the teaching of the greater miracles, namely, the two resurrections.

Up to the coming of Christ upon earth the work of raising the dead was the work of the Father. As Jesus states in John 5:21, "for as the Father raiseth the dead and giveth them life, even so the Son also giveth life to whom he will." This raising of the dead included both that of the soul and that of the body. These our Lord separates in verses 24, 25 (soul) and verses 28, 29 (body). The power which God the Father has in raising all manner of the dead is also the power of the Son.

THE RESURRECTION OF THE SOUL

The first resurrection is the resurrection of the soul. The first passing from death to life is that of the soul. This our Lord brings out clearly in John 5:24 which cannot be mistaken for a bodily resurrection of which our Lord speaks later. The verse reads:

"Verily, verily, I say unto you, He that heareth my word, and believeth on him that sent me, hath everlasting life, and

186

shall not come into condemnation; but is passed from death unto life."

The above cannot refer to the resurrection of the body because it is a conditional resurrection. It depends upon *hearing* and *believing*. We know that the resurrection of the last day does not depend upon hearing and believing. Everyone will be raised on the last day regardless whether believing or unbelieving. The Bible is very definite on the truth that all will rise upon the last day. But the resurrection mentioned in verse 24 is conditional.

That it is a resurrection is seen clearly from the expression: "is passed from death unto life." That is exactly what resurrection means. It is a rising again from the dead. That which was dead is brought to life again. The soul that is dead through sin is made alive by the word of Christ. Through hearing and believing the dead soul receives everlasting life. The greater miracle is not the resurrection of the body but it is the resurrection of the soul. With the resurrection of the soul, physical dying is no death at all as our Lord stated to Martha: "Whosoever liveth and believeth in me shall never die."

Notice, too, the expression: "is passed." It is no future resurrection but a present or past one. The American Revised version gives the correct rendering of the Greek perfect: "hath passed." To a believer his first resurrection is already past. He awaits only the resurrection of the body.

It must be remembered that the same tremendous power that God exerts in the resurrection of the body He exerts in the resurrection of the soul. This we read in Ephesians 1:19, 20: "And what is the exceeding greatness of his power to us-ward who believe, according to the working of his mighty power, which he wrought in Christ, when he raised him from the dead." That is, the same mighty power that God exerted in the raising of the body of Christ from the tomb He exerts in the resurrection of each Christian soul.

John 5:25 continues the same thought of verse 24. It also is introduced by the twofold "verily" which indicates the tremendous importance of the resurrection of the soul. The verse reads:

"Verily, verily, I say unto you, The hour is coming, and

187

now is, when the dead shall hear the voice of the Son of God; and they that hear shall live."

In the above verse there is again a limitation to the resurrection concerned. It is limited to those who hear: "And they that hear shall live." Not all hear the voice of the Son of God. There are some who do hear with their outward ears but not with the ears of their souls. Only those who truly hear the voice of Christ will live.

That this does not refer to the future resurrection of the body is indicated by the expression: "and now is." First our Lord states: "The hour is coming." This refers to the outpouring of the Holy Spirit upon the Church beginning at Pentecost. But even now by the Word of the Saviour there were those who were made alive. Among them were His disciples upon whom He breathed the Holy Spirit.

A few commentators refer this to the individual raising of the dead such as Lazarus, the little damsel, and the widow's son. But these were not raised to the "everlasting life" mentioned in verse 24. They were re-awakened to an earthly life which was again liable to death. The few individuals raised from the dead would not justify the language of those two verses nor of the word "life" as used by the apostle John.

There is no doubt but that the passage, John 5:24, 25, speaks of the resurrection of the soul which Christ and only Christ could bring about. This was part, and an important part, of the "greater work." *And this is the first resurrection.*

The Resurrection of the Body

Generally when people speak of the resurrection they think of the event that will occur at the Second Coming of Christ when the body will be resurrected and united with the soul. Concerning this resurrection, which is the second or general resurrection, verses 28 and 29 speak:

> "Marvel not at this: for the hour is coming, in which all that are in the graves shall hear his voice, and shall come forth; they that have done good, unto the resurrection of life; and they that have done evil, unto the resurrection of damnation."

Here there is no limitation or condition. *All* shall hear His voice. *All* shall come forth. It is not limited to those who believe. It is not limited to those who may hear. All that are in the grave shall come forth. This, of course, refers to the body as it is only the body that is in the grave.

In comparing the above passage with verses 24 and 25 one will notice important omissions. Christ does not use the expression, "and now is," regarding the resurrection of the body. This indicates that it is future. He omits the limiting expression, "they that hear." All hear when Christ makes the final resurrection call. He does not speak of only those "believing" being raised from the dead. The bodies of both believers and unbelievers will rise the last day. Christ does not speak of only one result: that of "life"; but He speaks of two results: "life" and "damnation." All this indicates so clearly that our Lord is speaking of two different resurrections. The first resurrection is that of the soul; the second, that of the body.

This distinguishing between the two resurrections guards against the heresy of Hymenaeus and Philetus, whom Paul mentions in Second Timothy. They denied the resurrection of the body, believing only in the resurrection of the soul. There are two resurrections according to the teachings of our Lord.

Some of our readers may be influenced by the teachings of the Scofield Bible which speaks of two different bodily resurrections separated by a thousand years. Our Lord contradicts this teaching in this passage when He states: "The *hour* is coming, in the which *all* that are in the graves shall hear his voice, and shall come forth; they that have done good, unto the resurrection of life; and they that have done evil, unto the resurrection of damnation." Both the good and evil shall hear the voice of Christ in that *hour*. According to this teaching of Christ the bodily resurrection of both the good and the wicked will take place in the same hour. There is no interval of a thousand years in this passage nor in any other passage of the Scriptures.

CONCLUSION

The importance of this passage in the fifth chapter of the Gospel of John for our study of Revelation Twenty is that it records our Lord's teaching of two resurrections: that of the soul and that of the body. The *first resurrection* is that of the souls of those who hear and believe. The *second resurrection* is that of the bodies of the righteous and the wicked.

In light of our Lord's teaching, which the apostle recorded, it is difficult to see how John would use the expression "first resurrection" in any other sense but that of the soul. It cannot mean, surely, the resurrection of the bodies of the righteous for that is not the first resurrection experience. It cannot mean the translation of the soul to heaven for that is not a resurrection from the dead. It can only mean the resurrection of the soul by the almighty power of God in Christ Jesus. The John of Revelation would not contradict the John of the Gospel.

CHAPTER III

THE ANGEL WITH THE CHAIN

Revelation 20:1, *"And I saw an angel come down from heaven, having the key of the bottomless pit and a great chain in his hand."*

There is no doubt that the book of Revelation is written for the purpose of giving encouragement to the believer. Encouragement is what one receives from reading the first part of Revelation Twenty. It gives a general picture of the defeat of Satan. This should give courage and hope to every follower of Christ. Satan has had so much power in the history of the world. From the fall of Adam to this very day Satan has brought havoc and ruin upon the earth. He is the great destroyer of souls. But here we read of his being bound and cast into the bottomless pit.

The binding of Satan was for the purpose of restraining his deception of the nations. For many centuries he had deceived nation after nation and empire after empire. Egypt, Assyria, Babylon, Medo-Persia, Greece, Rome, all were victims of his deceit. They were completely under his dominance. But now he was to be bound so that he could deceive the nations no more. An angel with a great chain in his hand would bind him and cast him into a bottomless pit.

Naturally, this picture of the Angel binding Satan gives rise to a number of questions. One main question is: "Do we have here a literal picture or figurative?" And the second main question is: "When is the time of fulfilment? Is it in the past? Is it in the process of being fulfilled? Is it in the future?" Another question concerns the identity of the Angel. And still another concerns the meaning of the chain. Let us seek the answers to these questions.

LITERAL OR FIGURATIVE?

Throughout the book of Revelation we have figures of speech. For instance, Jesus is described as the Lamb. Naturally we do not

191

expect to see a literal lamb when we behold Christ. Satan is pictured both as a serpent and a dragon. These are figures of speech as Satan is actually a spirit. From these examples we can readily see that the expressions, "key" and "chain," do not have to be taken in a literal way.

The first hint that the key and chain are not material objects is that the angel descended from heaven. One would not expect material objects in the realm of the spiritual heaven. Then Satan is himself a spirit and we cannot conceive of him bound with a material chain. It is thus evident that both the key and the chain are symbols or figures of speech.

The key, in the Scriptures, is a symbol of sovereignty and power. Christ states in Revelation 1:18, "I have the keys of hell and of death." Certainly we cannot think of material keys for hell and death. The same thought is brought out in Matthew 16:19 where Christ declared to Peter: "I will give unto thee the keys of the kingdom of heaven." There are no literal doors into the kingdom of heaven and no one would think that Christ meant literal keys. Christ was giving to Peter and to the true Church the power and authority as to whom should enter into the kingdom of heaven. *Key* is a symbol standing for sovereignty, authority, and power.

Likewise the chain is a symbol. It stands for restraining power. This will become apparent as we study several passages where the thought of binding is given yet where no literal chains can be meant. One such passage is Jude 6 and another is Matthew 12:29 where there is a reference to the binding of Satan. We will refer to these passages when we study the time of Satan's binding.

There is just a little misunderstanding in the minds of some people when you state that certain expressions in the Bible are figurative. They feel that it robs them of reality and makes them meaningless. That is not true. Figurative expressions stand for realities. The "Lamb" stands for the reality of the sacrificial atonement of Christ. The "Dragon" stands for the reality of Satan's power over ungodly nations. Even so the "key" and "chain" stand for realities. They stand for the real sovereign and restraining power of our Lord Jesus Christ. The figurative expressions help us to understand the spiritual realities and they help to portray them to the mind.

When does the Angel bind Satan? There are some Christians who believe that the binding is to take place in the future. It is at the time of the second coming of Christ. But when one examines the Scriptures it is easily seen that this binding is definitely connected with the first coming of Christ and is in the process of being fulfilled.

The first passage which we should consider is Matthew 12:28, 29 which reads: "But if I cast out devils by the Spirit of God, then the kingdom of God is come unto you. Or else how can one enter into a strong man's house, and spoil his goods, except he first bind the strong man? and then he will spoil his house." The Pharisees had attributed the casting out of demons by Christ to the power of Satan. But Jesus informed them that Satan would not cast out Satan. A kingdom divided against itself would not stand. Jesus cast out demons by the power of the Spirit of God. This meant that Satan had been bound. One cannot enter into what had been the domain of Satan without first binding him. Christ had bound Satan and therefore could cast out demons. Thus it is very apparent that this binding commenced with the earthly ministry of Christ. It did not have to wait until the second coming of the Lord.

That something drastic happened to Satan with the first advent of Christ is seen also by the words of John 12:31, "Now is the judgment of this world: now shall the prince of this world be cast out." The casting out of Satan was not to wait the second coming but was *now*. When the seventy disciples returned from a preaching mission they stated to Jesus: "Lord, even the devils are subject unto us through thy name." And Jesus replied: "I beheld Satan as lightning fall from heaven." This falling of Satan was not to await the second coming but took place during the ministry of Christ upon earth through the preaching of the Gospel.

In spite of the above passages there are people who will not believe that Satan is bound or that he has been cast out of his sphere of influence. They simply will not believe the words of Christ. "If Satan were bound and cast out," they argue, "why is there so much evil in the world? If we believe that Satan is bound we must deny our senses." It is better to believe Christ than it is to believe our senses. The difficulty, of course, is that such people do not understand what is meant by the binding of Satan.

In Revelation Twenty it is stated definitely what is meant by the binding of Satan. We are not left in doubt. Verse 3 reveals that the binding is in reference to the deceiving of the nations. Previous to the first coming of Christ, the Gentile nations were under the complete control and dominance of Satan. All nations were pagan and without true religion. But with the coming of Christ this was all to change. Nations were not to be deceived entirely. This does not mean that individuals within nations or even a great portion of them would not be deceived. But during the period of the binding of Satan the nations would not be entirely deceived as were Egypt, Assyria, Babylon, Persia, Greece and Rome. Never until that short period just before the second coming of Christ would the nations be deceived as they were before the first coming of Christ. To that end Satan was bound.

However, some people feel that if Satan were bound he would have no influence in the world and upon individuals. That this is not the significance of the binding of Satan is seen from a study of Jude 6. There we read that the fallen angels were bound with chains. Yet that did not prevent their activity in the world. That passage declares: "And the angels which kept not their first estate, but left their own habitation, he hath reserved in everlasting chains under darkness unto the judgment of the great day." The Gospels reveal the activities of these fallen angels. Therefore to be chained does not mean cessation of evil activity. Even so Satan, though bound, continues his evil work. But he is definitely restrained as to the sphere of his activity. He is bound by the decree of God. He cannot deceive the nations as he did previous to the coming of Christ.

THE ANGEL

Who is the Angel that binds Satan? Commentators are divided as to whether it is Christ or an agent of Christ. Personally we believe this Angel to be Christ. There is an Angel spoken about in the Old Testament who surely is the Son of God. He appears as a manifestation of God Himself, one with God and yet different from Him. This is the Angel who appeared to Abraham,

194

Jacob, and Moses. So it is entirely possible that the Angel of Revelation Twenty is Jesus Christ.

This is borne out by several other Scriptures. It is Christ who in Revelation 1:18 is said to "have the keys of hell and of death." It is Christ who in Genesis 3:15 is to crush the head of the serpent. It is Christ concerning whom John states in his first Epistle: "For this purpose the Son of God was manifested, that he might destroy the works of the devil." From these passages it is apparent that Christ is the supreme agent who binds Satan.

This does not mean that Christ does not use other agents in the binding of Satan. He uses the Church. In Romans 16:20 we read: "And the God of peace shall bruise Satan under your feet shortly." This is a reference to Genesis 3:15. Although Christ is meant in Genesis yet Paul infers that it is the Church who is to bruise the head of Satan. The Church is the Body of Christ. It is the Church through whom Christ destroys the work of the Evil One.

THE CHAIN

Knowing that it is the Church through whom Christ bruises the head of the Serpent, it is not difficult to ascertain by what means Satan is bound. The chain is the Gospel. Wherever a soul is released through the preaching of the Gospel there Satan is restrained and limited. As John declares in his Epistle: "that one toucheth him not." Satan is so bound in regard to everyone born from above that he cannot destroy such a one.

It is significant that immediately after announcing that the prince of this world was cast out, Jesus announced the means. He said in John 12:32: "And I, if I be lifted up from the earth, will draw all men unto me." It was through His death that He would destroy him that had the power of death, that is, the devil. The Gospel is: Christ died for the sins of His people. It is the cross. By the preaching of the cross Satan is to be destroyed. That is the chain which will limit his activity in the nations.

When the seventy disciples returned from a successful preaching mission, they reported that even the devils were subject to them through the name of Christ. To this replied Jesus: "I beheld Satan as lightning fall from heaven. Behold, I give unto you power to tread on serpents and scorpions, and over all the power of the

195

enemy: and nothing shall by any means hurt you." The Church, through the preaching of the crucified Saviour, has power to crush the Evil One and all his cohorts. It is the Gospel that is the chain which will bind Satan so that his activities will be restrained among the nations.

Unfortunately the Church of today does not realize the power that Christ has given her. Christ has placed in her hands the chain by which she can bind Satan. She can restrain his influence over the nations. But today the Church bemoans the fact that evil is becoming stronger and stronger. She bemoans the fact that the world is coming more and more under the control of the Devil. Whose fault is that? It is the Church. She has the chain and does not have the faith to bind Satan even more firmly. Satan is bound and the Church knows it not! Satan can be bound more firmly and the Church does it not!

CHAPTER IV

SATAN

Revelation 20:2a, *"And he laid hold on the dragon, that old serpent, which is the Devil, and Satan."*

In the beginning of history Satan in the form of a serpent tempted Adam and Eve. Many people wonder why God allowed Satan to bring about the fall of mankind. Concerning this there are many things which we do not know. But we do know this: that man was not coerced to fall. He had free will. He was not compelled to heed the temptation of the Devil. In the light of the manifested goodness of God to Adam, it is indeed amazing that he would listen to the Evil One. Nevertheless he did and that began the terrible reign of Satan over the ungodly world.

Satan was at one time the greatest angel in heaven. In Timothy we read that his downfall came about through his pride. He rebelled against God and influenced other angels to rebel against God. Since that time he and his demons have hated God and all that is good and pure. He has worked without ceasing for the destruction of mankind and the enlargement of hell.

The great ambition of Satan is to destroy the souls of men and to prevent them from being saved. He is constantly seeking to persuade man to sin. He did everything he possibly could to cause Job to renounce his God. He even sought to tempt Christ to renounce God the Father. We know from the Word of God that he is sometimes influential in bringing about sickness, financial loss, and death.

Satan is the ruler of the kingdom of darkness. He has under him principalities, powers, and demons. He is called the god of this age—the prince of this world. This does not mean that he has complete power over this world. It is over the evil world that he has power. It is over such who are termed the children of disobedience that he has his control. He is definitely limited when it comes to the children of God. He cannot touch them to their destruction. He can tempt and annoy them but he cannot conquer them.

It is the common conception that Satan rules over hell. It is thought that the great function of the Devil and his angels is to torment the dwellers in hell. That is not so. Satan and his angels are themselves to be tormented in hell. Hell was made for them and all those who ally themselves with the forces of evil. Satan and his demons fear hell even more than does mankind for they know the torments of it. They do not rule hell but are subject to the fires of hell.

We are happy to read in verse 2 that the Angel laid hold on the dragon, that old serpent, which is the Devil, and Satan. His four names are mentioned because he is going to be limited in his fourfold activity upon the earth. His universal sway over the earth, signified by his four names, is to be over. Let us consider his four names.

DRAGON

The Evil One is termed by the name *Dragon* to show that he is the animating principle which dominates the ungodly world-powers. It is he who influences ungodly nations and empires to wage war against the people of God. That the term *dragon* has a connection with pagan world powers is seen in the fact that Pharaoh of Egypt and Nebuchadrezzar of Babylon are compared to dragons. In Ezekiel 29:3 we read: "Behold, I am against thee, Pharaoh king of Egypt, the great dragon that lieth in the midst of his rivers." And in Jeremiah 51:34 we read, "Nebuchadrezzar the king of Babylon hath devoured me, he hath crushed me, he hath made me an empty vessel, he hath swallowed me up like a dragon."

Wherever we see paganism trying to crush and destroy the people of God there we see the Evil One manifested as a dragon. Egypt tried it by attempting to kill all the male children of the Israelites. The Assyrians conquered Palestine and took the Israelites captive. So did the Babylonian empire under the leadership of Nebuchadrezzar. Then for several hundred years Palestine was under the control of the Medo-Persian empire which was later succeeded by the Grecian Empire. The Roman Empire came in con-

198

tact with both the Old Testament Church and the New Testament Church. It sought to stamp out both. The opposition of these six pagan empires were all inspired by Satan. Whenever the opposition of ungodly nations comes to the fore the name of *Dragon* is used for the Evil One.

SERPENT

A very familiar name for the enemy of God and His people is *Serpent*. Satan first appeared on the scene of history in the form of a serpent. He succeeded in influencing Adam and Eve to mistrust the Word of God and to accept his word. He poisoned them in a subtle way. Whereas the name *Dragon* manifests his power, the name *Serpent* manifests his cunning.

Wherever deception is used, wherever error is spread, wherever doubt is implanted there is the work of the Evil One as the Serpent. It is the Serpent who sends out floods of heresy. It is the Serpent who sends out false prophets as angels of light. It is the Serpent who causes learned scholars to disparage the Bible by false criticism. Often the Serpent does more damage to the Christian Church than does the Dragon. The Church prospers under the fiery persecution of the great red Dragon but weakens under the subtle influence of the false teaching of the Serpent.

It is amazing how frequently in the Gospels and the Epistles that the Christian Church is warned to be on guard against deception and false doctrine. Our Lord warned His disciples against false doctrine and false prophets. In the Sermon on the Mount, He said: "Beware of false prophets, which come to you in sheep's clothing, but inwardly they are ravening wolves." And in the twenty-fourth chapter of Matthew He warns the Church against false Christs who would try to deceive even the elect.

Paul has this interesting passage in Second Corinthians which reflects on the work of the Serpent. He writes: "I fear, lest by any means, as the serpent beguiled Eve through his subtilty, so your minds should be corrupted from the simplicity that is in Christ. For if he that cometh preacheth another Jesus, whom we have not preached, or if ye receive another spirit, which ye have not received, or another gospel, which ye have not accepted, ye might well bear with him. Such are false apostles, deceitful work-

199

ers, transforming themselves into the apostles of Christ. And no marvel; for Satan himself is transformed into an angel of light. Therefore it is no great thing if his ministers also be transformed as the ministers of righteousness."

The study of church history will reveal that the Church has suffered more from false prophets and false doctrine than from persecutions. In times of persecution the Church grows stronger; in times of heresy the Church grows weaker. The Serpent is more to be feared than the Dragon. That is why in the New Testament there are more warnings of the activities of the Evil One as a Serpent than as a Dragon.

DEVIL

There is but one Devil and he is Satan. The King James version terms the fallen angels as "devils" but actually they are termed "demons" in the Greek. There is but one Devil.

The primary meaning of the Greek term is that of *false accuser, calumniator, slanderer*. That is what the term *devil* means. It is descriptive of the Evil One. He is so called because of his malignant spirit against the people of God. He is always suspecting evil of them and charging them with evil motives. A classic instance of this is Job. Satan said regarding Job: "Doth Job fear God for nought? Hast not thou made an hedge about him, and about his house, and about all that he hath on everyside? Thou hast blessed the work of his hands, and his substance is increased in the land. But put forth thine hand now, and touch all that he hath, and he will curse thee to thy face." The Devil could not believe that Job served God from a sincere heart and falsely accused him of serving God for gain.

So the Devil slanders all the children of God. He simply cannot believe the sincerity of those who truly worship God. He accuses them of hypocrisy day and night. It is a signal for great joy and praise when Satan was cast down as we read in Revelation 12:10, "And I heard a loud voice saying in heaven, Now is come salvation, and strength, and the kingdom of our God, and the power of his Christ: for the accuser of our brethren is cast down, which accused them before our God day and night."

The Devil does not lack followers upon earth who use the

same tactics in falsely accusing Christians as to their motives for serving God. Christians are accused of being hypocrites, of being evil doers, of doing more harm than good. It is inconceivable to the mind of a worldly man that a Christian loves Christ and serves Him because of this love. So the worldly man slanders the Christian even as his master, the Devil, slandered Job.

SATAN

The fourth name by which the Evil One is designated is that of *Satan*. This word properly signifies an adversary, an opponent. Truly the Evil One is the adversary of every human soul. He would destroy all into everlasting hell. We read in Revelation Twelve that it is he who deceiveth the whole world. He works evil on the bodies of men according to Luke 13:16; I Cor. 5:5; I Tim. 1:20. It was Satan who entered into the hearts of Judas and Ananias to turn them aside from Christ. It is Satan who hinders the work of the Church and transforms himself into an angel of light in order to deceive the Church. It is through his evil influence that what was once a church of God is transformed into a synagogue of Satan.

Woe unto the Christian Church if she underestimates the influence and power of the great adversary of the Church! We need but read the book of Acts and the Epistles to see what damage he did to the early Church. He is the enemy of all but especially of those who follow the Christ.

Thus the four names reveal the character and the power of the Wicked One. The number *four* designates the earth. He is the god of earth and those who are *earthy*. In the book of Revelation there is a difference made between "the dwellers on earth" and "the dwellers in heaven." The one is the seed of the serpent and the other is the seed of the woman. The one is the ungodly seed and the other the godly seed. The prince of darkness rules only over the dwellers on earth, the ungodly seed.

Lest we think that his power is supreme and that he is unconquerable let us note his defeat by Christ and His Church. In Revelation Twenty he is bound and cast into the bottomless pit. In Romans 16:20 it is stated by Paul to the early Christians: "And the God of peace shall bruise Satan under your feet shortly."

James tells the Christians: "Resist the devil, and he will flee from you."

And the Wicked One is overcome by the blood of Jesus Christ. Revelation 12:11 is a very important passage in regard to the method by which Satan is overcome. It states: "And they overcame him by the blood of the Lamb, and by the word of their testimony." It is true that we must not underestimate the influence and power of the Evil One; but it is also true that he can be easily overcome by those who believe in the power of the blood of Christ and are not ashamed to testify of it. They are the overcomers.

Yes, at one time his fourfold name indicated his sway over the four corners of the earth. But now the Angel has "laid hold on the dragon, that old serpent, which is the Devil, and Satan."

CHAPTER V

BOUND A THOUSAND YEARS

Revelation 20:2b, 3: *"And bound him a thousand years, and cast him into the bottomless pit, and shut him up, and set a seal upon him, that he should deceive the nations no more, till the thousand years should be fulfilled; and after that he must be loosed a little season."*

In Matthew Twelve Jesus asks this searching question of His enemies: "How can one enter into a strong man's house, and spoil his goods, except he first bind the strong man?" By this question Jesus taught that one cannot enter into the domain of Satan without first binding him. Jesus could not cast out demons except that He first bound the Prince of demons. Jesus could not release souls from the control of Satan except that He first bind Satan.

It is not difficult to see according to the words of our Lord that there has been a binding of Satan. Souls could not be rescued out of the kingdom of darkness except that the prince of darkness be bound. There has been a binding of Satan. It is such a binding that he cannot touch the Christian. This the apostle John verifies in his epistle when he states: "We know that whosoever is born of God sinneth not; but he that is begotten of God keepeth himself, and that wicked one toucheth him not." Every soul that has been born of God is safe from the clutches of the Devil. The Devil is definitely bound as far as the true Christian is concerned.

We read in Revelation Twenty that Satan is also bound as far as deceiving the nations is concerned. Where previously he had completely deceived the Gentile nations now he could no longer do so. This does not mean that no one within a nation could not be deceived. There might be many within a Gentile nation that would be deceived by the cunning of Satan. Even though Satan is bound as far as the individual Christian is concerned, yet a Christian may, for a period of time or concerning a certain doctrine, be deceived. So also in regard to the nation. It simply means that Satan would no longer be in complete control of the nations as he was before the coming of Christ.

The period of time that Satan is to be bound in regard to deceiving the nations is one thousand years. From the term "thousand years" we have the term "millennium." Whenever the term *millennium* is used we are apt to fill it in with our own ideas. But let us remember as far as Revelation Twenty is concerned all that it tells us of this millennium is: that the nations will not be deceived; that the saints sit upon thrones and judgment is given to them; that they live and reign with Christ; and that this is the first resurrection. No doubt this is the glorious period of which the Old Testament prophesies. However, let us definitely remember that this passage does not speak of Jesus seated upon a literal throne in the literal city of Jerusalem reigning with Jews over the Gentile nations of this world. The passage does not speak of this.

An important question to decide is whether the *thousand years* is to be interpreted as a literal thousand-year period. So far we have already seen that there are a number of figurative expressions used in this Chapter. We do not expect to see, for instance, a literal dragon or a literal serpent. Neither do we expect to see a literal key or a literal chain in the hand of the Angel. Figurative expressions are used in this Chapter and throughout the book of Revelation.

Whenever numbers are used in the book of Revelation they are used as symbols. For instance we read of *seven* spirits before the throne. Now we know that there is but one Spirit. The number *seven* is used to designate the fulness of the Spirit. Again we read of the Lamb having *seven* horns. We do not expect to see seven literal horns but we know that the completeness of the Lamb's power is signified by the number *seven*. *Twelve* is the number of the Church. Thus we find wherever the Church is mentioned we have twelve or its multiple. Hence twelve apostles, twenty-four elders, and 144,000 saints are mentioned.

Ten in the Bible stands for a rounded total. Thus we have the ten commandments and the ten plagues. A *thousand* is the cube of ten. This symbolizes vastness of number or time. Thus we have the number 144 *thousand* to indicate the totality of God's people. The same thought is brought out in the foursquare city of 12 *thousand* furlongs. Taken literally it would indicate a cube city of 1400 miles. The meaning of the term *thousand* is brought out in Deuteronomy 1:10, 11. In verse 10 it is stated that the Lord God made the Israelites as the stars of heaven for multitude. Then in verse 11 it is added: "The Lord God of your fathers make you a thousand times so many more as ye are." The *thousand* is not used in a literal sense but in a figurative way to indicate vastness. In Psalm 50:10 is the expression "the cattle upon a thousand hills." This does not mean that only the cattle on a literal thousand hills are the Lord's but the total amount of all the cattle on all the hills of the world are His.

The term *thousand years* in Revelation Twenty is a figurative expression used to describe the period of the Messianic Kingdom upon earth. It is that period from the first Advent of Christ until His Second Coming. It is the total or complete period of Christ's Kingdom upon earth. Christ Himself stated that with the casting out of demons the Kingdom of God had come and Satan was bound. If the binding of Satan began with the first coming of Christ then it follows that the *thousand years* began with His first coming.

Now the natural objection against this view is that the period from the first coming of our Lord to the present time can hardly be described as a Millennium. For one thing wars have not ceased and wickedness is still very much prevalent. As someone has stated: "if Satan is bound he must have a long tether." All appearances seem to be against the view that we are in the millennium now.

The trouble is that we have altogether a too materialistic concept of the millennial blessings. We fail to see that the greatest blessings are spiritual and they are in our midst. We are looking for a material kingdom, a material throne, and material prosperity. In this we fall into the same error of the carnal expectations of the Jews and the error with which our Lord had to contend with His own disciples. We fail to see that the greatest millennial blessings are already in our midst.

According to the prophets the great blessings of the "latter days" would be the coming of the Messiah and the establishment

205

of His Kingdom. This has been accomplished. The outpouring of the Holy Spirit was another blessing. This has been accomplished. Salvation for all that call upon the name of the Lord was another blessing of the Messianic reign. This has been accomplished. The inclusion and conversion of the Gentile nations in the covenant blessings was another thing to occur. This has been accomplished and is in the process of fulfilment.

An individual Christian may ask himself this question: "What more could the popular conception of the millennium give me than I already possess? I have a Saviour who is my Prophet, Priest, and King. God the Father is my covenant God. I have the forgiveness of sin. I have the promise of eternal life in heaven. I belong to the Church which is the Lamb's Bride. I have the Holy Spirit as my Teacher, Sanctifier, and Comforter. I have security against my greatest enemies: Death, Hell, and the Devil. I am standing on Mt. Zion and am a citizen of the Holy City. I belong to the commonwealth of Israel and am not a stranger from the covenants of promise."

What more does a Christian desire? More material prosperity? Is not the Lord wealth enough? Perhaps we desire less "tribulation, or distress, or persecution, or famine, or nakedness, or peril, or sword?" But are we not in all these things more than conquerors through Him who loves us?

What we really want is greater victory over personal sin. But is that not promised in this dispensation? We need not wait for the so-called future millennium. What we do want is peace amongst the nations and less wickedness. But that is promised if we go forth conquering and to conquer in the name of Christ. Let us not be blind to what has already been accomplished and thus rob God of glory. The absence of greater victories is due to our lack of faith, and not because of the absence of millennium blessings.

Besides a too materialistic conception of millennium blessings another difficulty is that we have not paid enough attention to the parables of our Lord which indicate that the millennial blessings will pervade the earth gradually. The Kingdom of Heaven is likened to a grain of mustard seed which grows and becometh a tree. The Kingdom of Heaven is likened to leaven which will gradually leaven the earth. Our Lord stated that the Kingdom cometh not with observation. That is, it will not be established with great fanfare. Our Lord is not slack concerning His promises but with Him one day is as a thousand years, and a thousand years as one day. There is the same indication in the Old Testament. Daniel's stone which smote the image became a great mountain, filling the earth. Ezekiel's river was ankle deep to start with but increased to a river in which to swim. Both the *amil* and the *premil* are in error when they maintain that the millennial blessings foretold in the Old Testament must come about by a cataclysmic act at the second coming of Christ. That is not the teaching of the Bible. Both in the Old Testament and in the New it is taught that the Kingdom blessings would come about by an almost imperceptible, gradual growth.

"But," some will object, "is not the new creation perfect?" I believe that I am a new creature born by the Spirit of God. But that does not mean I am perfect. But because I am not perfect that does not mean I am not a new creature. Isaiah gives us many beautiful pictures of the millennium. But even in the midst of the prophecies of the latter days he also points out those who will not receive the blessings of the Messiah's reign. In the pictures which Zechariah, the prophet, gives of millennial blessings there are indications of enemies and nations still to be converted. Our Lord indicates that there will be tares until the end of this age.

We are told definitely that Satan is to be bound in regard to the deceiving of the nations. And he has been bound. At no time since the coming of the Christ has he been able to deceive the entire world. Is it not true that in all nations Christ has His followers? Yet before the coming of the Lord there were only a handful in the little country of Palestine. Satan had complete control over the nations of the world. That is not true now. There is direct evidence that Satan has been bound.

The Bible does not teach that by the binding of Satan wickedness will be entirely eliminated and the activity of Satan entirely limited. We are told in Jude 6: "And the angels which kept not their first estate, but left their own habitation, he hath reserved in everlasting chains under darkness unto the judgment of the great day." Though these demons were chained yet we read of their activity in the Gospels. This is also told in II Peter 2:4. "For if

God spared not the angels that sinned, but cast them down to hell, and delivered them into chains of darkness, to be reserved unto judgment." Here again the chains of darkness did not limit the angels that fell. And let us remember that Satan was one of the fallen angels and thus also chained. These verses give us the right to our view that the chaining of Revelation 20:1-3 does not mean a complete cessation of activity on the part of Satan.

Satan has been cast into the bottomless pit. The Greek word for "pit" is *abussos*. The demons who possessed the Gadarene maniac besought our Lord that He would not cast them forth into the abyss, Luke 8:31. Though the abyss was their habitation yet under the permissive will of God and for His purposes they were allowed to be active on the earth until that day when they will remain in the abyss forever. Even so, Satan being cast into the abyss does not mean a cessation of his activity upon earth. He will remain active in a limited degree until the second coming of our Lord when he will be cast into the lake of fire and brimstone and where he will remain forever.

However, it should be carefully noted that as far as the deceiving of the nations is concerned Satan is shut up in the abyss and sealed. He cannot for the period designated "thousand years" deceive the nations as he did previous to the coming of Christ. That is, he cannot until a short time before the coming of the Lord. Then he is to be loosed for "a little season." This season is "little" in comparison to the time of the millennium. At that time he will be successful in deceiving many nations and the Church will face a time of persecution from which she will be delivered by fire from heaven.

CHAPTER VI

I SAW THRONES

Revelation 20:4a, *"And I saw
thrones, and they sat upon them."*

The apostle John in his vision beheld thrones. *What* thrones
were these? *Where* was their location? *When* were they in existence? *Who* sat upon them? These are very important questions
and the answers will determine to a great degree the interpretation
of Revelation Twenty. There is no doubt but that verse 4 is the
most difficult verse to explain in the entire Chapter.

While verse 4 is difficult it is not necessarily the key verse of
the Chapter. Nevertheless it must be shown that the interpretation
of this verse fits in with the general interpretation of the rest of the
Chapter and with the teaching of other portions of God's Word.
The interpretation of verse 4 and its comparison with other verses
of the Bible will require several chapters. In this chapter we will
concern ourselves chiefly with the *thrones.*

WHAT THRONES?

What thrones did the apostle John see in his vision? Surely
they were not literal material thrones such as those upon which the
kings of the earth sit? We do not expect to see a thousand or a
million little earthly kingdoms with a saint seated upon a throne
of gold ruling a number of subjects. While that may be pleasing
to the carnal mind and according to the expectations of Judaism,
it is not the teaching of the Scriptures.

An earthly throne set up within an earthly kingdom for His
followers, is against the teachings of Christ. This conception Jesus
rebuked when He said to His disciples: "Ye know that they which
are accounted to rule over the Gentiles exercise lordship over them;
and their great ones exercise authority upon them. But so shall it
not be among you: but whosoever will be great among you, shall be
your minister: and whosoever of you will be the chiefest, shall be

servant of all." In the light of this teaching of our Lord it is rather strange how a material, earthly, and carnal conception of the thrones continues to hold the minds of some people. The thrones are not literal.

Throne is a figure of speech indicating the reign of the saint. For instance, it is mentioned in Revelation 3:21 that the believer who overcomes will sit with Christ on His throne. That, of course, is not a literal throne for it would have to be a very large one, indeed, to hold all the saints. The throne indicates the Messianic reign of Christ. The Christian who overcomes will take part in the Messianic reign.

That the saints do reign is indicated in a number of verses. II Timothy 2:12 states: "If we suffer, we shall also reign with him." In Revelation 5:10 we read: "And has made us unto our God kings and priests: and we shall reign on earth." And in Romans 5:17 it is stated: "much more they which receive abundance of grace and of the gift of righteousness shall reign in life by one, Jesus Christ." The type of "lordship" the believer possesses in this life is revealed in I Cor. 3:21, 22, "For all things are yours: whether Paul or Apollos, or Cephas, or the world, or life, or death, or things present, or things to come; all are yours."

The thrones stand for the saints' spiritual dominion within himself and over the world. Through the grace of Christ they reign in life over the flesh, the world, and the devil. In all things he is more than a conqueror through Christ. He reigns over sin because sin has no dominion over him. He reigns over Satan who cannot touch him. He reigns over the world because of Him who has overcome the world.

There is a reign of the saint over the world. This he does by spiritual means and not by the power of the carnal sword. The saints bring about a state of society in which Christian opinion and morality will be dominant. This Jesus indicated when He stated that His followers are the salt of the earth and the light of the world. That Christian ideas rule the life of some nations is already in evidence. One need but compare a nominally Christian nation with a heathen country to see how Christian ideals have pervaded the life of certain nations. Christian morality has elevated many nations.

210

There is another sense in which it may be stated that the Christian is seated upon a throne. This is in respect to the power of keys given to the Church. The saints sit upon thrones judging those who would enter into the Church. This is referred to in Matthew 19:28 which is a text that we will seek to interpret in the following chapter. There is also a rule over the Church which must be considered later.

Thus the thrones of Revelation 20:4 are not literal thrones. Rather they signify the spiritual rule of the saint within his own heart; the rule over the world by spiritual means; and his rule over the Church.

WHERE LOCATED?

Where are these thrones located? Are they located in heaven and occupied by the departed saints during what is called the intermediate period? This cannot be. In verses 8 and 9 of Revelation Twenty we are informed that at the end of the thousand years Satan will deceive the nations again. These nations are upon earth. These deceived nations will compass the camp of the saints and the beloved city and the scene of this siege can only be upon earth. Satan and his hosts do not set siege to the saints in heaven. The scene is definitely upon the earth. The thrones, the camp, and the beloved city all have reference to the Church upon earth.

It is apparent that the binding of Satan has some effect on the reigning of the saints. The reigning of the saints is synchronous with the binding of the Evil One. It is because Satan is bound that the saints are able to reign upon earth. Surely the binding and the loosing of Satan does not have any influence whatsoever on the life of the saints in heaven. But it does to those who live upon earth.

Furthermore, Revelation 5:10 tells us definitely that the reign of the saints is upon earth: "And hast made us unto our God kings and priests: and we shall reign upon the earth." There are those who say that the reign will be upon the renewed earth after the second coming of Christ and the final judgment. But that cannot be. Christ gives up the Mediatorial Kingdom after the final judgment. And we must not forget that the thrones exist during the thousand-year period. After this period Satan gathers Gog and

Magog to oppose the saints. Surely this would not happen on the "renewed earth"! Surely this would not happen in heaven! No, the scene is upon this present earth. That is the location of the thrones.

WHEN DID THEY EXIST?

When were these thrones in existence? In verses 4-6 we have a period synchronous with the binding of Satan. While Satan is bound for the thousand years the saints are reigning. You will notice how verse 7 takes up where verse 3 leaves off. Verse 3 concludes: "and after that he must be loosed a little season." Verse 7 picks up that thread: "And when the thousand years are expired, Satan shall be loosed out of his prison." John pauses, as it were, in verses 4-6 to tell us what is happening to the saints. Then he continues in verse 7 to finish the story of Satan. The time of the saints reigning upon earth is the same time as the binding of Satan which we believe to be from the day of Pentecost to the "little season" just before the second coming of Christ.

In verses 8 and 9 we read that the saints are subject to the onslaught of Gog and Magog. This again indicates that the time of the thrones is before the second coming of the Lord. The last judgment takes place after Satan's final defeat. The reigning of the saints must, therefore, take place before the final judgment.

Another indication as to time is the fact that it takes place during the Messianic reign. Many interpreters are apt to forget I Corinthians 15:24, 28: "Then cometh the end, when he shall have delivered up the kingdom to God, even the Father; when he shall have put down all rule and all authority and power. And when all things shall be subdued unto him, then shall the Son also himself be subject unto him that put all things under him, that God may be all in all." At the end of this world the Messianic reign is over along with that of the saints.

Then another important thing must be noted in regard to the time of the thrones. According to the King James Version the verbs *sat, was given, lived, reigned,* are in one tense; while the verbs *had worshipped, had received* are in another tense. It would seem from this that the period of not worshipping the beast and not receiving his mark was before the sitting, living, and reigning. Actually all the verbs are in the same tense in the Greek. The

212

tense of all verbs is the aorist. This is corrected in the American Revision Version which reads: "and such as worshipped not the beast, neither his image, and received not the mark upon their forehead and upon their hand; and they lived, and reigned with Christ a thousand years." The time of sitting on the thrones and reigning with Christ is the same as that of not worshipping the beast.

It was while the saints were actually seated upon the thrones that they were refusing to worship the Beast and to receive his mark. It really was an evidence that they were reigning with Christ —that they did not receive the mark of the Beast and refused to pay him homage. However, we will deal with this matter further when we consider the martyred saints and those who were living during the period of the Beast and his image.

WHO WERE ENTHRONED?

Who are they that are seated upon the thrones? Perhaps the reader has gathered that it is our opinion that every saint of the New Dispensation is seated upon a throne. The thrones were not limited to those who were martyred when the Beast prevailed nor were they limited to those who refused to worship him. Otherwise the thrones are limited to only a small portion of the saints of Christ. All are not martyred nor do all live during the period of the Beast.

Every saint is seated upon a throne. Every saint is a king. Every saint rules over sin. Every saint is a victor over the world, the flesh, and the devil. Every saint is more than a conqueror. *All things* in this world and in the world to come belong to every saint. The apostle John through the symbol of the "throne" gathers up the teaching of the New Testament that the saint reigns upon earth.

Thus these thrones are not literal and material for that would be against the teaching of our Lord and Saviour Jesus Christ. These are not thrones in heaven during the intermediate period for the scene is upon earth. These are not thrones after the second coming of Christ for Satan is not yet cast into the lake of fire and brimstone. Rather they are thrones occupied by the saints on earth during the period of thousand years.

213

CHAPTER VII

THE REGENERATION

In the previous chapter we showed that the thrones of Revelation 20:4 are not literal thrones. *Throne* is a figure of speech indicating the reign of the saint. The saints reign over the flesh, the world, and the devil. The place of this reigning is upon earth. The time is during the Messianic reign of Christ.

In this chapter we digress from the study of Revelation Twenty to see whether our interpretation of "thrones" is according to the general teaching of the Word of God. How does it fit with other verses which speak of the reign of the saints? There is an important passage in Matthew's Gospel which speaks of thrones. It is Matthew 19:28 which states:

> *And Jesus said unto them, Verily I say unto you, That ye which have followed me, in the regeneration when the Son of man shall sit in the throne of his glory, ye also shall sit upon twelve thrones, judging the twelve tribes of Israel.*

The setting of the above verse is as follows. A rich young ruler turned sadly away from Jesus. He wanted eternal life. The Lord had asked him to give up his earthly possessions and follow Him. This led Jesus to comment: "How hardly shall they that have riches enter into the kingdom of God!" This caused Peter to say: "Lo, we have left all, and followed thee; what then shall we have?" Jesus replied: "Verily I say unto you, That ye which have followed me, in the regeneration when the Son of man shall sit in the throne of his glory, ye also shall sit upon twelve thrones, judging twelve tribes of Israel." He added also: "And every one that hath left houses, or brethren, or sisters, or father, or mother, or children, or lands, for my name's sake, shall receive a hundredfold, and shall inherit eternal life."

The promise that the apostles would sit upon twelve thrones judging the twelve tribes of Israel in the regeneration has been variously interpreted. Some refer this to a period when the Lord will reign upon earth over the Jewish kingdom and that the apostles will also occupy thrones in this period. This interpretation has no foundation in the Scriptures. For instance, there is not even one verse in the New Testament which speaks of Christ sitting on a literal throne and reigning upon earth in the literal city of Jerusalem during the millennium.

Others have interpreted this to have reference to the Consummate Kingdom. At His second coming the earth will be renovated. Upon this renovated earth the apostles will have a prominent place in ruling over the saints. The fatal objection to this interpretation is that this takes place during the reigning of the *Son of man*. It is during the reign of Christ in His Messianic capacity. At His second coming He delivers the kingdom to the Father as it states in I Corinthians 15:24: "Then cometh the end, when he shall have delivered up the kingdom to God, even the Father; when he shall have put down all rule and all authority and power." The Messianic reign ceases at the second coming. This is stated in verse 28 of the same chapter: "And when all things shall be subdued unto him, then shall the Son also himself be subject unto him that put all things under him, that God may be all in all."

While we have not seen it in print, we have heard Matthew 19:28 referred to as describing the intermediate period. It is thought that Christ had reference to the abode of the departed saints. It is the life of the souls in heaven. However, heaven would hardly be called the regeneration. The word properly means "born again" or "born anew." It is a rebirth; it is a re-creation. It refers to such a radical change that it might be properly called a second birth. This, of course, cannot refer to heaven, the abode of God. The Scriptures speak of no radical change or the necessity of it in heaven which is the abode of God, the good angels, and the departed saints. It must have some reference to this earth which has need of renewal, renovation, and re-creation.

With Calvin I believe that the regeneration has reference to the Gospel dispensation. It has reference to the new order of things which was started with the advent of Christ. The regeneration is another expression for the Kingdom of God. This is confirmed by Luke 22:30 where Christ also refers to the apostles sitting on thrones judging the twelve tribes of Israel. There He states:

"And I appoint unto you a kingdom, as my Father hath appointed unto me: that ye may eat and drink at my table in my kingdom, and sit on thrones judging the twelve tribes of Israel." In this verse "the kingdom" takes the place of the expression "in the regeneration."

The regeneration is that period of time in which the Son of man reigns as the Messiah over the earth. As a reward for His suffering upon the cross God the Father has exalted God the Son and has given Him all power in heaven and in earth. God the Father does not reign over the world now; it is God the Son. God the Son is seated upon the throne of His glory and reigns over this world. This is the period of regeneration which will be terminated with the second coming of Christ when He delivers the kingdom to the Father.

That the period of the regeneration relates to the earth is also indicated in the two parallel passages: Mark 10:29, 30 and Luke 18:29, 30. In these two passages the fact that the apostles would be seated upon twelve thrones is omitted. They do mention, however, the fact that those who sacrifice in this life for Christ will be compensated a hundredfold in this life. The reward is also related to the earth and life upon the earth. It is in the period of the regeneration that this compensation will be made.

THREE MISCONCEPTIONS

There are three misconceptions which have caused people to fail to recognize that the regeneration is the period of the Gospel dispensation upon earth. The first misconception is that which speaks of Christ being glorified only at His second coming. Christ is seated upon the throne of glory now. Jesus stated to the two disciples on the way to Emmaus: "Ought not Christ to have suffered these things, and to enter into his glory?" Through the cross Christ entered into His glory. Peter on the day of Pentecost shows how God raised up Christ to sit on His throne: "being by the right hand of God exalted." The exaltation of Christ has already taken place. This Paul also states in Philippians: "Wherefore God also hath highly exalted him, and given him a name which is above every name." The exaltation does not await the second coming but has already taken place. The glory and reign of Christ are present. Christ is seated upon the throne of His glory now. After all the events which shall take place at the second coming Christ will give up this Messianic throne of glory so that God may be all in all.

The second misconception about this period of the regeneration is that it is thought of as a state of society in which perfection and sinlessness prevails. It is claimed that all the saints living in "the regeneration" will be perfect and without sin. However, this is not the picture which the Scriptures give us. The very word "regeneration" should teach us that. In Titus 3:5 the same word is in reference to the Christian upon earth: "Not by works of righteousness which we have done, but according to his mercy he saved us, by the washing of regeneration, and renewing of the Holy Ghost." The Christian upon earth, though *regenerated*, is not perfect. The old nature still clings to him. He is not perfect and sinless. As we need not look for a perfect and sinless man who is regenerated neither need we look for a perfect and sinless society which has been regenerated. Upon earth regenerated society, like the regenerated individual, is not perfect.

The third misconception about the period of the regeneration is that it will be brought about by a sudden cataclysmic act to occur at the second coming of the Lord. This present earth and heavens will be suddenly destroyed and a new material earth and heavens will take their place. Upon this new earth and heavens the resurrected saints will dwell. The *regeneration* is thought of as a *regenerated* earth. In other words, the "new heaven and new earth" of Revelation 21:1 is thought of as a material concept rather than spiritual. This is an error.

It is not the purpose of this book to enter into the question of the "new heaven and new earth." However, we ask our readers to compare two statements of Revelation 21:4, 5 with II Corinthians 5:17. The two statements are: "For the former things are passed away" and "Behold, I make all things new." Paul states that these things are true upon earth in this present dispensation in II Corinthians 5:17, "Therefore if any man be in Christ, he is a new creature: old things are passed away; behold, all things are become new." Paul refers to the regenerated individual; John in Revelation refers to regenerated society, namely, the Church.

217

Yes, to a new creature in Christ old things are passed away. For him the first heaven and the first earth are passed away. He is no longer bound by its lusts and ambitions. He is no longer ensnared by its fleeting pleasures. He lives in a new heaven and new earth. All things have become new. His conversation now is in heavenly places. His relationship to God has been changed. Everything has changed for the Christian. A new world has been opened up before him. And what is true of the individual who has been born from above is true of the entire Church of the firstborn.

JUDGING THE TWELVE TRIBES

Coming back to Matthew 19:28 we read that in the regeneration the apostles will sit upon twelve thrones, judging the twelve tribes of Israel. Without going too much in detail, the meaning of this is that the apostles through their teachings rule the Church of God. This is just another way of stating that the Church is "built upon the foundation of the apostles and prophets" as stated in Ephesians 2:20. It is stated in still another way in Revelation 21:14, "And the wall of the city had twelve foundations, and in them the names of the twelve apostles."

In this dispensation the apostles are still ruling the Church through their teachings. We read in Matthew 23:2, 3: "The scribes and the Pharisees sit in Moses' seat: all therefore whatsoever they bid you observe, that observe and do." Moses through the giving of the law ruled the old Israel until the coming of Christ. Now the apostles rule the new Israel. The "twelve thrones" of the apostles take the place of Moses' seat.

We are now in the period of the regeneration. True Christians who form the "Israel" of God are judged (ruled) by the apostles. The "thrones" of the apostles are no more literal than the "seat" of Moses. All this is in agreement with our interpretation of Revelation 20:4 where the thrones of the saints are not to be considered as literal and the period of their reigning has reference to this earth. It is the period of the Messianic reign. It is the period of the regeneration.

218

CHAPTER VIII

THE JUDGING OF THE SAINTS

Revelation 20:4b, *"And judgment was given unto them:* . . .
and they lived and reigned with Christ a thousand years."

During the millennium judgment is given to the saints. Because we associate the condemnation and punishment of evil doers with the word "judgment" we are apt to think that this judgment has reference to the condemnation and punishment of the wicked in the last day. Some think that this has reference to the final judgment which will vindicate the saint. A little reflection, however, will show that this cannot be the final judgment.

Whatever this judgment is, it is continuous throughout the millennium. It is during the entire period of the thousand years. As the saints are seated upon thrones throughout this period even so they are occupied in judging during the entire period. Then one must remember that only Christ is the Judge during the final judgment. All stand before His throne of judgment. Thus it is clearly seen that this judgment given to the saints is not the final judgment.

Those who are acquainted with the teachings of the Scriptures know that the word "judge" has several meanings. One meaning is seen in the book of Judges. There the word "judge" indicated one that ruled; one who delivered Israel from slavedom and oppression; one who restored the wayward Israelites to religious purity.

In the book of Judges these men are also called "saviours." In the American Revised Version of Judges 3:9 we read: "And when the children of Israel cried unto Jehovah, Jehovah raised up a saviour to the children of Israel, who saved them, even Othniel the son of Kenaz, Caleb's younger brother." In Judges 3:15, Ehud is also called a saviour.

Prophetically Obadiah speaks of these *saviours* in the 21st verse of his prophecy: "And saviours shall come up on mount Zion to judge the mount of Esau; and the kingdom shall be the Lord's."

The mount of Esau here stands for the ungodly world which shall be judged and ruled by the saints. The *saviours* will conquer the world and establish the kingdom of the Lord's. Paul states the same thing in I Corinthians 6:2, "Do ye not know that the saints shall judge the world?" While some refer this to the final judgment we know that the saints are nowhere in the Scriptures represented as taking an active part in the final judgment of the world. In the next verse Paul states: "Know ye not that we shall judge angels?" The significance of this is stated by the disciples: "Lord, even the devils are subject unto us through thy name." Whereas before the Devil and his angels ruled the world, in the new dispensation the saints would take over.

That this is the meaning of the word "judgment" is also revealed by our Lord in the Gospel of John. There we read in chapter 12:31, "Now is the judgment of this world: now shall the prince of this world be cast out." This is not the final judgment as is indicated by the word *now*. It refers to the ruling of Christ and His saints over the world. The prince of this world is cast out. He no longer rules completely as he did previous to the coming of Christ. As Luther has stated it: "And the gospel shall not only be judge over flesh and blood, nay, not only over some of Satan's angels or devils, but over the prince himself, who has the whole world mightily in his hands."

This ruling is a fulfilment of many Old Testament prophecies which speak of Christ judging the world in the sense of ruling the world. Psalm 96:13, "For he cometh to judge the earth: he shall judge the world with righteousness, and the people with his truth." Isaiah 2:4, "And he shall judge among the nations." Isaiah 42:4, "He shall not fail nor be discouraged, till he have set judgment in the earth." Daniel 7:22, "Until the Ancient of days came, and judgment was given to the saints of the most High; and the time came that the saints possessed the kingdom." Psalm 72:2, "He shall judge thy people with righteousness, and thy poor with judgment." All these passages prophesy the righteous rule of Christ over the earth to which Christ refers in John 12:31.

Included, of course, in this judging is the ruling of the Church. This is indicated in the statement of Matthew 19:28, "Ye also shall sit upon twelve thrones, judging the twelve tribes of Israel." This clearly has no reference to the final judgment or of judging in the sense of condemning and punishing wrong doers. This is the ruling of the Church. This is the power of the keys. This concerns matters of discipline. This concerns such matters as Paul discusses in I Corinthians 6.

LIVING WITH CHRIST

Another privilege of the saints is that they live with Christ. Only Christians live. They have experienced the resurrection of the soul. At one time they were dead in trespasses and sin but they have been quickened in Christ Jesus. They are alive in contrast with the rest of the world who are dead even though they think that they are alive.

Christians are alive because they have fellowship with the living God through Jesus Christ. They know God. They know His justice and they know His love. They know His power and they know His wisdom. They truly can address God as their Father who is in heaven. This is life. This is living in Christ.

The saints live with Christ in that they are recipients of spiritual blessings and comforts. The Holy Spirit dwells in their souls. He sanctifies them. He enables them to mortify the deeds of the body. He teaches them wisdom that is hid from the wise of this world. This is a spiritual life that is unknown to souls who have not been quickened in Christ Jesus.

The Christians also live with Christ in that their affections are on those things which are above where Christ sitteth on the right hand of God. Their conversation is in heaven. This is true even while they are dwelling upon earth. Their present life is hid in Christ even though they dwell upon earth. Upon earth they are living with Christ.

REIGNING WITH CHRIST

Not only do the saints upon earth live with Christ but they also reign with Christ. Notice carefully that it does not state that Christ is reigning with the saints upon earth but that the saints are reigning with Him. Nowhere in Revelation Twenty do we read that Christ reigns bodily upon earth. As a matter of fact there is not one text in the New Testament which speaks of Christ literally reigning upon earth in the literal city of Jerusalem. That is a teaching which is prevalent in some circles but is not taught by Christ or the apostles.

But how can the saint reign with Christ while the saint lives upon this sinful earth? In the very same manner as Enoch walked with God. The fact that Enoch walked with God did not mean that Enoch was in heaven. Nor did it mean that God was in bodily form upon earth. Enoch walked with God in a spiritual sense as everyone understands. The saint upon earth reigns with Christ in the same manner as Enoch upon earth walked with God.

As Christ dwells in His saints even so do the saints dwell in Christ. So near is Christ to His saints upon earth that whatsoever is done to them is done to Him. Christ reveals this in the picture of the Judgment given in Matthew 25: "Verily I say unto you, inasmuch as ye have done it unto one of the least of these my brethren, ye have done it unto me." Christ considers Himself as dwelling in all faithful Christians in such a way that whatever is done to them is done to Him. Needless to say, this does not mean His bodily presence on earth.

Christ stated to the persecutor of the Christian Church: "Saul, Saul, why persecutest thou me?" Paul thought that he was persecuting heretics but he was persecuting Christ in His saints. Even as Christ lives and suffers with His saints on earth, even so do they reign with Him in heaven. He is persecuted in them; and they reign with Him. As is stated in II Timothy 2:11, 12: "It is a faithful saying: for if we be dead with him, we shall also live with him: if we suffer, we shall also reign with him." Though dead, we live; though suffering, we reign. The one is no different from the other. As He partakes of our suffering, so we partake of His glory. As the one does not require His bodily presence upon earth, neither does the other require the presence of the saints in heaven. The saints reign with Christ even while they dwell upon earth.

One reason why it is so difficult to have a proper estimation of the reign of the saints is because of the carnal conception of such a reign. It is associated with an earthly kingdom and earthly power. But as Christ's kingdom is not of this world neither is the believer's. The kingship of the believer does not require a literal throne with a subject people under him. His reign is spiritual. He reigns over the devil, the flesh, and the world. Even death is subject to him. This is a much superior reign than is generally conceived. Yet people seem to be fascinated by the lesser and carnal type of reign.

The apostle Paul speaks of the present reign of the believer in I Corinthians 3:21, 22: "For all things are yours; whether Paul or Apollos, or Cephas, or the world, or life, or death, or things present or things to come; all are yours." Notice that among other things the world belongs to the Christian. But is not the world in opposition to the child of God? Yes, but even that opposition works for the glory of the believer. The very fires of temptation of the world are so controlled by God that they are used to burn away the dross of the believer. All things work together for good to those who love God. The world does not reign over the Christian but the Christian reigns over the world. One might just as well deny the present reign of Christ as to deny the present reign of the saint.

The Twentieth Chapter of Revelation indicates that the reign of the saints is upon earth in that the opposition of Gog and Magog is upon earth. This is stated in verses 8 and 9: "And shall go out to deceive the nations which are in the four quarters of the earth, Gog and Magog, to gather them together to battle: the number of whom is as the sand of the sea. And they went up on the breadth of the earth, and compassed the camp of the saints about, and the beloved city: and fire came down from God out of heaven, and devoured them." By no possible interpretation can this be a picture of heaven. We are told definitely that the scene is upon earth. It is upon earth that the saints who reign are beset by Gog and Magog. This should prove conclusively that the reign of the saints mentioned in Revelation Twenty is upon earth.

CHAPTER IX

THE REIGN OF MARTYRS

Revelation 20:4c, *"And I saw the souls of them
that were beheaded for the witness of Jesus, and for
the word of God, and which had not worshipped
the beast, neither his image, neither had received
his mark upon their foreheads, or in their hands."*

In the preceding chapters it has been shown that Revelation
20:4 gives a picture of the present Gospel dispensation. This
verse does not deal with the intermediate state of the souls of
believers. It does not deal with a kingdom to be established after
the second coming of our Lord. It deals with the present dispensation upon earth.

It has been shown that the terms *thrones, judgment, living,*
and *reigning,* relate to the life of the saint upon earth. Like terms,
or equivalent terms, are used throughout the New Testament. It
is no strange teaching that Christians are kings upon earth. Christ
has made them kings. They form a royal priesthood. Their reign
is not to be likened to the reign of an earthly king over an earthly
kingdom. Their reign is spiritual. They reign over the flesh, the
world, and the devil. All things belong to the Christian.

Now what may seem to contradict all this is the experience
of the Christian martyrs and others who lived in periods of persecution. There have been periods in the history of the Christian
Church when the saints suffered tribulation and the enemy seemed
to triumph. Verse 4 refers to two such periods of persecution: the
first under the Beast; and the second, under the Image of the Beast.
These two periods of persecution are pictured to us in Revelation
Thirteen.

Two Beasts and an Image of the first Beast are mentioned in
Revelation Thirteen. The first Beast is pagan Rome. He is described as "like unto a leopard, and his feet were as the feet of a
bear, and his mouth as the mouth of a lion." For several centuries

under the leadership of cruel Emperors, pagan Rome persecuted the Christian Church. An incidental verification of the fact that it was the persecution by pagan Rome is seen in the use of the verb "behead." It means literally "to cut off with an axe." This was the Roman method of execution.

The second Beast is described in Revelation Thirteen as one who "had two horns like a lamb, and he spake as a dragon." This is papal Rome. It is the Roman Catholic Church which is described by this figure. This second Beast, however, is not referred to in our verse. It refers to the first Beast and its Image. The Image of the first Beast is the Holy Roman Empire. This was an Empire that sought to bring back the old Roman Empire. It is a matter of history that the Papacy sought to use the Holy Roman Empire to persecute true Christians.

It may be well to point out that there were those who lived during the reign of the two Beasts who were not martyred. They were not put to death for their faith in Christ. Nevertheless they suffered. Some were deprived of their living and suffered terrible poverty. Their wealth was confiscated. The boycott was employed against them. Others were imprisoned or suffered other inconveniences for the sake of the Gospel. Nevertheless they did not worship the Beast, neither his Image, neither received his mark upon their foreheads or in their hands. The mark implies likeness in spirit and character. In spite of all pressure used against them they remained Christian in spirit and character.

Now it is said of both martyrs and sufferers that they were seated upon thrones and that they lived and reigned with Christ. How can that be? How can they be said to be enthroned when the Beasts had the upper hand? How can they be said to live in the midst of the terrible persecution of the Beasts? How can they be said to reign in the midst of apparent defeat? How can they be pictured as triumphant when it is apparent that the two Beasts were triumphant over the Christians?

The question is, did the Beasts triumph? Their aim was to crush Christianity and cause Christians to apostatize from the faith. In this the Beasts failed and the Christians were triumphant. The martyrs never showed their kingship more strongly than when confronted with the axe, the lion's den, and the torch. They had control over their souls, over sin, over temptation, over the Beasts, and over the Devil. They could not be dethroned! They were living! They were reigning! They were in all these things more than conquerors.

In his second epistle to Timothy and the second chapter Paul tells of his suffering for the sake of Christ. Then he states: "It is a faithful saying: For if we be dead with Him, we shall also reign with Him." In the midst of death one lives with Christ. In the midst of suffering, a Christian reigns with Christ.

PSUCHAI

However, it is claimed by the amillennialist that the apostle John did not see living persons; he saw *souls*. These *souls*, he explains, are disembodied spirits. A recent writer of this school states: "The word here translated *souls* (psuchai) is found a hundred times or more in the New Testament for the soul, as distinct from the body." This statement is open to serious challenge. The New Testament, as we shall see, very seldom uses the Greek term "psuche" to describe the disembodied spirit.

The premillennialist, on the other hand, thinks that he is perfectly justifiable in translating the Greek term "psuche" by the word "person." This would include both body and soul. This is a possible interpretation if the context warrants it. In the following passages the term "psuche" is used of the entire person: Acts 2:41, 43; 3:23; 7:14; 27:37; Romans 13:1; I Peter 3:20; Revelation 16:3. The passage would then read: "I saw the persons (bodies and souls) of them who had been beheaded." But John tells that he is describing the first resurrection which is that of souls only. The context, therefore, forbids this translation of "psuche."

There is another sense in which "psuche" is used frequently in the New Testament and that is in the sense of "life." There are over thirty-five clear cases where "psuche" is translated in this sense. Among them are Matthew 2:20, "For they are dead which sought the young child's *life*." Luke 12:22, "Take no thought for your *life*, what ye shall eat." Acts 20:10, "Trouble not yourselves; for his *life* is in him." The apostle John who wrote the book of Revelation uses "psuche" almost exclusively in that sense: John 10:11, 15, 17; 12:25; 13:37, 38; 15:13; I John 3:16; Rev. 8:9; Rev. 12:11.

226

It is therefore entirely permissible to translate the "psuchai" of Revelation 20:4 by the word "lives." The clause would then read: "And I beheld the lives of them that were beheaded for the witness of Jesus." It might seem, on the face of it, that the martyrs had not reigned in life. But the apostle sees them also as enthroned in life. In their lives upon earth they also were more than conquerors.

Verse 4 of Revelation Twenty may be paraphrased in this fashion: "I beheld the saints seated upon thrones, ruling over the flesh, the world, and the devil; yea, I beheld the victorious lives of those who had been beheaded and also those who suffered because they refused to worship the beast; as a matter of fact all saints lived and reigned with Christ a thousand years."

To come back to the question of translating the term "psuche" to mean "disembodied soul." There are very few cases in the New Testament where it can be translated in this sense. Thayer's Lexicon gives four examples: Acts 2:27, 31; Rev. 6:9; 20:4. The passages in Acts cannot possibly refer to the disembodied soul of Christ for his body was in the tomb. The disembodied soul is never committed to the grave which seems to be the sense of "hades" in the passage. Christ committed His spirit to the Father as it stated in Luke 23:46. If His soul in distinction from His body were in the grave, how could He say to the thief: "This day thou shalt be with me in paradise." The passages in Acts refer to the fact that Christ was not left in a state of death. And concerning Revelation 6:9 Hengstenberg has this to say: "The souls of the martyrs in verse 9 are not the souls in the intermediate state, as expositors commonly suppose; the souls are meant of which it is said in the Old Testament, that they are in the blood —the animal souls (see, for example, Genesis 9:5); they are murdered souls; but the blood itself might as well have stood, and in verse 10 indeed is actually put instead of the souls here. This is plain from comparing the original passage, Genesis 4:10, where the blood of Abel cries to God from the ground."

From the above it can be clearly seen that it is not so evident that the reference to "souls" indicates the intermediate state. And if it were the intermediate state that is indicated why are only the martyrs mentioned? All departed saints are in this intermediate state.

227

That verse 4 is speaking of the lives of the saints upon earth is again indicated by the tense used in speaking of those who did not worship the beast, neither his image, neither received his mark upon their foreheads. In the King James version the verbs *sat, was given, lived, reigned,* are in one tense; while the verbs *had worshipped, had received,* are in another. But in the Greek the same tense is used for all—the aorist. Since they are all in the same tense they must refer to the same time. That is, the time of not worshipping the beast and not receiving his mark is the same time as that of sitting on thrones and living and reigning with Christ. The American Revised Version thus correctly translates the passage: "And I saw thrones, and they sat upon them, and judgment was given unto them: and I saw the souls of them that had been beheaded for the testimony of Jesus, and for the word of God, and such as worshipped not the beast, neither his image, and received not the mark upon their forehead and upon their hand; and they lived, and reigned with Christ a thousand years."

Another question which remains is: how can it be said concerning the saints upon earth that they live and reign with Christ *a thousand years*? Three score years and ten is the average life of the saint upon earth. This, however, is no more different than stating that the Romans ruled over the world for many centuries. This does not mean that each individual Roman lived for that period. It refers to the Roman Empire. Even so the apostle John is speaking of the Church in relation to the binding of Satan. He is speaking, as it were, of the Body of Christ. As the Roman Empire is one so is the Body of Christ. The Body of Christ is always represented upon earth. The Church never ceases but reigns throughout the thousand-year period.

It is our contention that Revelation 20:4 speaks of the Gospel dispensation. It reveals the victorious reign of the saints upon earth regardless of martyrdom and suffering. In all these things they are more than conquerors. The use of the word "psuche" in the New Testament shows how difficult it is to apply it to the intermediate state of the believer's soul. And to relate this verse to a kingdom to be established after the second coming of Christ brings such a host of problems and contradictions as to bring hopeless confusion.

CHAPTER X

THE DEAD AND THE LIVING

Revelation 20:5, 6, *"But the rest of the dead lived not again until the thousand years were finished. This is the first resurrection. Blessed and holy is he that hath part in the first resurrection: on such the second death hath no power, but they shall be priests of God and of Christ, and shall reign with him a thousand years."*

In our study of verse 4 we have seen that Christians upon earth live and reign with Christ. By the power of the Gospel the Christian has been translated from death to life. His soul has a living communion with God through Jesus Christ. He is the recipient of spiritual blessings and comforts. In Christ he has conquered the world, the flesh, and the devil. He has conquered death and hell. Through the resurrection of his soul he truly lives.

But the rest of the dead lived not until the thousand years were finished. All men are dead through trespasses and sin. Some are resurrected by the grace and power of God. They experience life. Their souls live. But the rest of the dead lived not. The remainder of mankind continues in the state of death. They have no communion with God. They have no spiritual blessings and comforts. They are dead. They live not.

It is unfortunate that in the King James version the word *again* is used. It does not appear in the Greek. The dead thus described never lived. Their souls continued in death. They were dead even in the midst of life.

It might seem that these dead would remain so only during the thousand-year period. They lived not *until the thousand years were finished.* One might think that when the thousand-year period ended that these dead would live. But the conjunction *until* is used in the sense "to the time that." The rest of mankind remained in spiritual deadness to the time that the thousand years ended. They had no part in the first resurrection. Their souls remained dead. An illustration of this use of the conjunction *until* is seen in I Samuel 15:35, "And Samuel came no more to see Saul until the day of his death." This does not mean, of course, that after Samuel died he began to see Saul. It simply means that up to the time of his death he did not see Saul. Another illustration is Isaiah 22:14 where it is stated: "Surely this iniquity shall not be purged from you till ye die." Here the word *till* excluded them from ever having their iniquity purged. Even so the conjunction *until* has an excluding sense in that the dead never come to life.

THE FIRST RESURRECTION

In the first two chapters of this book we dealt with the question of the first resurrection. The amillennarian would fain refer this to the intermediate state of the disembodied soul. Geerhardus Vos in his article on the Eschatology of the New Testament in the *International Standard Bible Encyclopaedia* refers the first resurrection to "the state of glorified life enjoyed with Christ in heaven by the martyrs during the intermediate period preceding the parousia."

The above view forgets the meaning of the word *resurrection*. It is: "a rising again from the dead." When the Christian soul leaves the body to dwell in heaven, it is not a *resurrection*. The soul in the Christian is alive; it is not in a dead state. Its removal from the body into heaven could be better termed an ascension or translation. To state that the translation of the soul into heaven is a resurrection is to contradict directly the teaching of Christ that "whosoever liveth and believeth in me shall never die." The very fact that Revelation Twenty deals with a resurrection eliminates the interpretation that the Chapter is speaking of the intermediate state of the soul.

As has been shown in the first chapter the logical way to determine the meaning of the *first* resurrection is to discover what is the *first* death. When Adam and Eve sinned their first experience of death was the death of the soul. The apostle Paul describes the state of the Ephesian Christians before conversion as those "who were dead in trespasses and sins." And in I Timothy

5:6 it is stated: "But she that liveth in pleasure is dead while she liveth." That can only refer to the soul. The primary death is that of the soul.

In the New Testament there are a number of passages which speak of the dead becoming alive in reference to their conversion. For instance, it is stated in Colossians 2:12, 13: "Having been buried with him in baptism, wherein ye were also raised with him through faith in the working of God, who raised him from the dead. And you, being dead through your trespasses, and uncircumcision of your flesh, you, I say, did he make alive together with him, having forgiven us all our trespasses." Here the regeneration of the human soul is compared to the resurrection of Christ. They who were dead were made alive. This is the first resurrection. And John states in his epistle: "We know that we have passed from death unto life." Surely this is the first resurrection of which the Scriptures speak.

The second resurrection is that of the body which will occur at the second coming of our Lord. The apostle John speaks of both resurrections in John 5:24, 25, 28, 29. In part of this passage it is stated: "Verily, verily, I say unto you, He that heareth my word, and believeth on him that sent me, hath everlasting life, and shall not come into condemnation; but is passed from death unto life." This is a conditional resurrection. It depends upon *hearing* and *believing*. Through hearing and believing the dead soul receives everlasting life. Notice that our Lord states "is passed" from death unto life. This is not contingent on the death of the body. As a matter of fact the American Revised Version renders the Greek perfect: "hath passed." To a believer his first resurrection is already past.

In the second part of the passage in John 5 it is stated: "Marvel not at this: for the hour is coming, in which all that are in the graves shall hear his voice, and shall come forth; they that have done good, unto the resurrection of life; and they that have done evil, unto the resurrection of damnation." All shall hear His voice. All shall come forth. Both believers and unbelievers are mentioned. This is the second or general resurrection. The first is that of the soul; the second, that of the body.

231

BLESSED AND HOLY

Blessed and holy is he that hath part in the first resurrection. To be blessed means to be happy. And such is the experience of every true believer. He is blessed because he has been raised from death to life. He is blessed because he has Christ as his Saviour. He is blessed because he had fellowship with the living God. He is blessed because his sins are forgiven. He is blessed because heaven is his. His conversion is indeed a raising from the dead.

Moreover he is holy. He has been separated from sin and consecrated to the service of God. Holiness means separation and consecration. The believer has been set apart by God. He is set apart from the rest of the world. His portion is to serve God and enjoy Him forever.

On such the second death hath no power. The second death is the casting of both soul and body into everlasting hell. But on the Christian this terrible second death has no power. As his soul has been resurrected so will his body. As Christ stated: "He that believeth on me shall never die." As the Christian's soul has been changed from death to life in the first resurrection so his body will be raised in the second resurrection. This is stated in Romans 8:11, "But if the Spirit of him that raised up Jesus from the dead dwell in you, he that raised up Christ from the dead shall also quicken your mortal bodies by his Spirit that dwelleth in you." Neither body nor soul of the true believer will experience the second death.

But they shall be priests of God and of Christ. The apostle Peter wrote to believers. "Ye are a royal priesthood." And in the first chapter of Revelation John states that Christ hath made believers to be "priests unto God and his Father." The same truth is revealed in Revelation 5:10. The common priesthood of the believer is a cherished doctrine of the evangelical Church. It is a priesthood that is experienced in this life.

As priests the believers have direct access to God. In the old dispensation only the high priest once a year could enter into the Holy of holies. But now every believer by virtue of his priesthood can enter into the Holy of holies—into the presence of God. Through the blood of the atonement he can come before the mercy seat.

As priests, believers present unto God their spiritual sacrifices. They offer to God the sweet incense of their praise. They present their bodies as living sacrifices unto their God. Instead of a material temple they worship Him in the spiritual temple. It is not necessary for them to offer animals as sacrifices upon the altar for Christ offered Himself once and for all. That part of the priesthood is no longer necessary.

As priests, believers intercede for others. They are not mediators between man and God. There is only one Mediator and that is Christ. But as priests they pray for others. They pray for such who are not able to pray for themselves. They pray for those who are unsaved. They pray for those who are burdened and afflicted. In their intercession they perform the office of priests.

And they shall reign with him a thousand years. To every believer there is given a crown. He reigns upon earth. He reigns over the world, the flesh, and the devil. He conquers death and hell. He shares in the victories of Christ.

All this belongs to the blessedness of the first resurrection. The body does not have to die to experience this blessedness. Through the resurrection of the soul the Christian is raised into heavenly places even while on earth. This is not apparent to the world and often is not appreciated by the Christian. However, as the Christian grows in grace and knowledge, he learns of the riches of Christ which are his. But the evil world knows not the blessedness of the first resurrection. The world is dead in trespasses and sin and the dead live not until the thousand years are finished. And then they only experience the dreadful power of the second death.

CHAPTER XI

SATAN IS LOOSED!

Revelation 20:7, 8, *"And when the thousand years are expired, Satan shall be loosed out of his prison, and shall go out to deceive the nations which are in the four quarters of the earth, Gog and Magog, to gather them together to battle: the number of whom is as the sand of the sea."*

Satan is loosed! The chains which held him in the bottomless pit are removed. No longer is he confined to his prison. No longer is he limited as to the sphere of his wicked operations. No longer is he restrained from deceiving the nations. What a woeful day that will be for the inhabitants of the earth!

There are those who believe that the loosing of Satan will occur after the second coming of Christ. It will be, it is claimed, towards the end of His thousand year reign upon the earth. Jesus is to reign on a literal throne in the literal city of Jerusalem. Suddenly towards the end of the thousand years His reign is to be challenged by Satan. Christ and those who remain faithful to Him are to be contained in the city of Jerusalem. He and His army are seemingly helpless against the onslaught of Satan and his hosts. Only the miraculous intervention of God in sending fire from heaven will save the situation.

If the above were true, it would mean that Christ would suffer a second humiliation. Though all power has been given to Him both in heaven and upon earth yet He must wait for a miraculous deliverance from the Father. The Scriptures, of course, do not speak of a second humiliation of Jesus. His humiliation ended with the cross. Further, this is in contradiction to several passages of Scripture which speak of Christ coming at the day of judgment. Hebrews 9:27, 28 states: "And as it is appointed unto men once to die, but after this the judgment: so Christ was once offered to bear the sins of many; and unto them who look for him shall he appear the *second time*, without sin, unto salvation." The appearance here spoken of is the appearance of Christ at the day of judgment to complete the salvation of His Church. But how could He so come if He were bodily upon earth during the millennium which is to take place before the day of judgment? This view also contradicts such passages as I Thessalonians 4:16 and II Thessalonians 1:7, 8, 10. How could Christ be revealed from heaven if He were upon earth in His human nature? And still further there is not a single text in the New Testament which indicates clearly that Christ will actually reign in the earthly Jerusalem in His human nature.

Satan's loosing will be that period just before the second coming of the Lord. It will take place after a long period of peace and prosperity. The "thousand years" is a symbolical number indicating a long period of time. As we have already shown, it is that period from the ascension of Christ until His second coming.

The period of the millennium is a time of great blessings. The greatest of the millennium blessings are spiritual. It is the time when the Holy Spirit is given in abundance to the Church. It is a time when many experience salvation through faith in the crucified Saviour. It is a time when many possess eternal life and fellowship with the living God. It is a time when God dwells with the Church. It is a time when the middle wall of partition is broken down between Jew and Gentile believer. It is a time when the Church receives the protecting care of Christ the Lord. The many Messianic blessings predicted in the Old Testament are experienced by the saints upon earth.

Gradually, the by-products of spiritual blessings will prevail upon the earth. Carnal minded men look upon these as the primary blessings of the millennium but actually they are secondary. We will always be sojourners upon the earth even as David declared in the midst of temporal blessings: "For we are strangers before thee, and sojourners, as were all our fathers: our days on the earth are as a shadow, and there is none abiding" (I Chronicles 29:15). Nevertheless, it is the teaching of Scripture that at times that nations are righteous there will be material blessings. In Psalm 67 where it speaks of the time when all nations will be governed by God, it states: "Then shall the earth yield her increase;

and God, even our own God, shall bless us." It is evident that earthquakes, hurricanes, floods, and other calamities of nature will cease when God is pleased with the nations. Another picture of material prosperity is given in Isaiah 30:23, "Then shall he give the rain of thy seed, that thou shalt sow the ground withal: and bread of the increase of the earth, and it shall be fat and plenteous: in that day shall thy cattle feed in large pastures." Isaiah 65:21-23 and Ezekiel 34:23-31 give other pictures of material prosperity that may be expected during the reign of the Messiah.

But the important thing to realize is that before the loosing of Satan all nations will become predominantly Christian. This is clearly implied in the Covenant promise: "And in thee shall all families of the earth be blessed." Paul interprets this to mean that the seed of Abraham will inherit the world in Romans 4:13, "For the promise, that he should be the heir of the world, was not to Abraham, or to his seed, through the law, but through the righteousness of faith." That is why Christ in the Great Commission commanded His followers to make disciples of all nations. He promised that the meek shall inherit the earth. The Bible is rich with promises that all nations will turn to the Lord. Typical of them is Psalm 22:27, 28: "All the ends of the world shall remember and turn unto the Lord: and all the kindreds of the nations shall worship before thee. For the kingdom is the Lord's: and he is the governor among the nations."

It is after the fulfilment of such prophecies that Satan will be loosed again. But this, according to verse 3, will be for "a little season." Verses 4-6 form a parenthesis between verses 3 and 7. In verse 3 it is mentioned that Satan would be loosed for a little season and now from verse 7 it is disclosed as to what will take place with this event.

THE NATIONS DECEIVED

Before the advent of Christ Satan held sway over the nations of the world. With the coming of Christ his control was broken. He was bound as far as the nations were concerned. At present there is no nation that is totally pagan. There are believers everywhere. The Gospel has gone forth to the four quarters of the earth. Of course, there is much land still to be occupied. But the Church has gradually grown from the few disciples in Palestine to millions of Christians throughout the world. This growth will continue till the loosing of Satan. Then he will deceive the nations as he did before the advent of Christ.

Notice that Satan does not break out of prison by his own power. He does not break his own chains. He is loosed by the Lord. Why the Lord withdraws His restraints is within the secret counsel of the Godhead. We know that just before the flood God withdrew His Spirit from among men to reveal the exceeding wickedness of man and God's righteous judgment. Even so before the final judgment day the Spirit will be withdrawn from the great majority of men. Satan will have his way. This will be the great apostasy.

The nations to be deceived are called Gog and Magog. The mention of Gog and Magog immediately recalls Ezekiel 38 and 39 where these names indicated the enemies of Israel. It was popular at one time (and still may be) for premillennialists to associate Gog with the dictator of Russia because in Ezekiel he is ruler over Meschech and Tubal. With the use of imagination they associate Meschech with Moscow and Tubal with Tobolsck. Because both start with the same letter it does not indicate they are the same cities. You might just as well state that heaven is hell because both start with the letter *h*. Besides this, in Revelation 20 Gog is a nation and in Ezekiel Gog is a prince. This shows the utter foolishness of such an interpretation. And further, the Gog of Ezekiel comes from the north and the Gog and Magog of Revelation come from the four quarters of the earth.

The names of Gog and Magog are used much as we might use the names of Hitler and Nazi after our experience in World War II. *Hitler* and *Nazi* bring before our minds cruel enemies who wrought much damage. We might well term some future tyrant *Hitler* and some future nation *Nazi Horde* without having Germans in mind. In Revelation the names of the old enemies are used to designate new ones. Gog and Magog represent the future enemies of the Church whose names are as yet unknown. This type of interpretation is taught in Revelation 11:8, "And their dead bodies shall lie in the street of the great city, which spiritually

is called Sodom and Egypt, where also our Lord was crucified."
Sodom and Egypt are "spiritualized." Even so we "spiritualize"
Gog and Magog.

The nations represented by Gog and Magog are in the four
quarters of the earth. This term is to be considered in its symbolical import rather than geographical. It means world-wide.
It is an ecumenical movement. Every nation is deceived. The
number of the enemy is as the sand of the sea.

It is difficult for some to conceive of the nature of the opposition. The language is so vivid that it is hard for us to realize
that this is not a battle of arms—of sword and gun. Our Lord
clearly indicates that the battle for Christianity is not fought with
carnal sword. It is a battle between the true Gospel and the false
Gospel. It is a battle of truth against error. It is a battle of light
against darkness. It is not a war against flesh and blood "but
against principalities, against powers, against the rulers of the
darkness of this world, against spiritual wickedness in high places."
The Old Testament wars were but types of the spiritual battles to
be fought in the New Dispensation.

Nor must we think that this happens in a moment, a day, a
week, a month, or a year. The deception of the nations is a subtle
thing. Even as we have seen an evangelical generation being
changed into a modernistic generation so it will be at the end of
the millennial period. Peace and prosperity incline the human
heart to become careless. Satan plants doubt; unbelief becomes
the fruit. Rebellion against God may not be open at first. It
will be secret as it was in the heart of Judas. Eventually the
rebellion will come out in the open. It will grow like wildfire.
Nation after nation will be poisoned by Satan. In this particular
period it will not be restrained for Satan is without chains and
out of his prison.

It may seem strange that it will be possible to turn a host of
happy people, prospering under the blessing of God, into such a
world-wide rebellion. It would almost seem impossible that Satan
could influence people to their own hurt. But alas it is a repetition of history. Who could be more happy than the angels in the
presence of God? But Satan and a host of angels rebelled. Who
could be more happy than Adam and Eve in the beautiful Para-

dise? But a simple temptation of Satan caused them to rebel against the commandment of God. Look at the prosperity of Israel during the rule of Solomon but Israel, too, turned against the God who blessed them so abundantly. In the light of history it is not so difficult to see how the subtlety of Satan will turn a people blessed of God to rebel against Him and His Christ.

Chapter XII

THE SIEGE OF THE BELOVED CITY

Revelation 20:9, *"And they went up on the breadth of the earth, and compassed the camp of the saints about, and the beloved city: and fire came down from God out of heaven and devoured them."*

We are aghast at the power and influence of Satan in this present generation. The evil that is present in the world has led some Christians to feel that we are in the midst of the Great Apostasy. Yet a little knowledge of history will reveal that the fate of the Church in this present generation compares favorably to the fate of the Church during the days of Roman persecution, or during the dark ages, or during the days previous to the Reformation. We who have the freedom of worship and can propagate the Gospel without fear of persecution cannot say that we are living in the midst of the greatest apostasy the Church has ever witnessed. Such a view betrays ignorance of history. An honest appraisal of conditions will indicate that Satan is still restrained. He is still weighed down with chains. And surely more so in this present generation than in some of the generations of the past.

But the day is coming just previous to the second coming of the Lord when there will be a world-wide apostasy. What fearful days they will be for the Christian Church! Gog and Magog will cover the breadth of the earth. The number of hostile enemies will be as the sand of the sea. Only a remnant will remain faithful to the cause of Christ. The enmity will be fierce. The struggle will be the greatest since the first advent of the Lord. It is Satan's last attempt to crush the followers of Christ.

It will be a world-wide conflict. Again we state that it is not to be a military clash of carnal weapons. Christians will not use guns, missiles, planes, tanks, and atom bombs to defend themselves. There will undoubtedly be persecution. The enemy may use physical violence. But the main weapons will be in the realm of the spirit. The false doctrines of Satan will enter in the life of the Church. New heresies will prevail. Satan will use his poison intensively and extensively. Nation after nation will become predominately pagan. The apostasy will be world-wide. It will be in America as well as Russia. It will be in England as well as in Japan. It will be in Europe as well as in Asia. The apostasy will cover the earth. Only a remnant represented by The Beloved City will remain faithful.

It must be borne in mind that the Church will be in a measure responsible for this apostasy among the nations. She is supplied with sufficient armor to face and defeat Satan. But while the Lord tarries and delays His coming, the Church will become careless. Discipline will not be exercised as it should and heresy will be tolerated. The defensive weapons with which the Lord has endowed the Church will be neglected. The Church will also forget that she is militant. The offensive sword will remain in the scabbard. Even at the present day the Church little realizes her responsibility for the darkness that prevails. It is the Church that is the light of the world.

THE CAMP OF THE SAINTS

They compassed the camp of the saints about. The Church is likened to a military camp. This is a figure borrowed from the time of Moses and Joshua when the Church even externally presented the form of a military camp. The twelve tribes with their banners surrounded the Tabernacle on four sides. The camp was in the form of a square; of which the four sides were to be placed toward the four quarters of the compass. This was a type of the heavenly city as seen by Ezekiel 48:20 and the city foursquare of Revelation 21:16. The Camp and the City are but different figures of speech to describe the Church upon earth. The Church in heaven will never be surrounded by enemies such as are pictured to us in Revelation 20.

The ancient camp of the Israelites was both for defensive and offensive purposes. But it was chiefly for offense. They were on their way through the wilderness to the promised land. They were on their way to drive the heathen tribes out of the land. The

Church of today is too much on the defensive and not enough on the offensive. The Church has not only been given the shield of faith but also the sword of the Spirit. She is to go forward conquering and to conquer. This is what the apostles did and also the early Church. The Church must never forget that in the sight of God she is a military camp formed for the purpose of driving the heathen out of the promised land.

THE BELOVED CITY

The Church is also termed The Beloved City. To many this is a figure of speech to describe heaven. This, of course, cannot be true of that expression as used in Revelation 20. Satan and his host do not surround the saints in heaven. They do not set siege to heaven. The scene is upon the earth. The nations of the earth battle the Church upon earth. The Beloved City is a figure of speech to describe the Church upon earth.

To others this is the literal city of Jerusalem. Just a little thinking will show how impossible this is. Imagine all the armies of the nations of the world laying siege to one city in Palestine! And you must picture modern armies equipped with missiles, bombs, and planes. The land of Palestine could not contain all the armies of the world. This is figurative language. This is the language of the Old Testament to express the enmity of the world against the Church.

This is verified by the Scriptural use of the term *Jerusalem*. The Beloved City is not like the old material Jerusalem but it is the new spiritual Jerusalem. The Scriptures themselves do the "spiritualizing." This Paul does first in Galatians 4. He states that he uses the two *Jerusalems* in an allegorical sense. And in verse 26 he writes: "But Jerusalem which is above is free, which is the mother of us all." This can only be a spiritual Jerusalem because no future material Jerusalem can be "the mother of us all."

The writer of Hebrews also "spiritualizes" Jerusalem. He writes in chapter 12:22, "But ye are come unto mount Sion, and unto the city of the living God, the heavenly Jerusalem." Notice that it is stated "ye *are* come." This is no future material city but a present spiritual city. And notice that this is not the Consummate Kingdom for believers are citizens of that City even while they are upon earth.

There are many interpreters who feel that the Holy City of Revelation is a picture of the Consummate Kingdom—of heaven after the second coming of Christ. How then can it be stated in Revelation 11:2, "But the court which is without the temple leave out, and measure it not: for it is given unto the Gentiles: and the holy city shall they tread under foot forty and two months." Surely it does not mean that heaven will be trampled under foot by heathen nations for a short period of time!

The Holy City of Revelation 11 and of Revelation 20 and of Revelation 21, 22 are one and the same City. It represents the Church of God upon earth. Because it is attacked and besieged by enemies it cannot refer to the abode of the saints either in the intermediate period before the second coming of Christ or to the Consummate Kingdom. Of course, it may be argued that while the Holy City of Revelation 11 and 20 refers to the Church upon earth surely the Holy City of Revelation 21, 22 refers to the Consummate Kingdom—to heaven after the second coming of the Lord. But a careful exegesis of the last two chapters of Revelation will indicate that this is not so.

It is one of the mysteries of the history of interpretation that so many commentators take for granted that the last two chapters of Revelation form a picture of the Consummate Kingdom. It is taken for granted that after the picture of the final judgment in Revelation 20 the next would be a picture of heaven in the consummate state. This, however, is an error. In Revelation 21, 22 we have a recapitulation of all the glorious promises of the Word of God. The apostle John gathers together various prophetic pictures of the Old Testament and relates them to the Church. This he himself reveals clearly.

John tells us in Revelation 21:2 that he saw "the holy city, the new Jerusalem, coming down from God out of heaven, prepared as a bride adorned for her husband." This immediately indicates the Church; and the Church before the consummation for she is the bride of the Lamb. We are told definitely in I Corinthians 15:24, 28 that at the second coming Christ will deliver the kingdom to the Father so "that God may be all in all." But during the Gospel dispensation the kingdom is the Lamb's.

In verse 9 one of the angels said to John: "Come hither, I will shew thee the bride, the Lamb's wife." And what did the

243

angel show him? The angel showed him "that great city, the holy Jerusalem." The Bride, the Church, and the Holy Jerusalem are one and the same thing. Furthermore, it cannot be heaven for it descends out of heaven.

There are two errors we wish to combat. The first is the conception that the Holy City is a material city. The very measurements of the City should indicate that the author is giving figurative description. Revelation 21:16 reads: "And the city lieth foursquare, and the length is as large as the breadth: and he measured the city with the reed, twelve thousand furlongs. The length and the breadth and the height of it are equal." Twelve thousand furlongs amounts to practically fourteen hundred miles. Here then is a picture of a city fourteen hundred miles long, fourteen hundred miles wide, and fourteen hundred miles high! The land of Palestine could not contain such a city. Surely it must be interpreted figuratively. The next verse indicates that the protecting wall is 216 feet. The height of the city is 7,000,000 feet while the wall around it is only 216 feet! Surely this passage fairly shouts that we are not to take the description in a literal way.

The second error is that the Holy Jerusalem is the consummate state. We have pointed out that it is the Lamb's Bride which indicates the Messianic or Gospel state. There would hardly be a necessity for a wall to protect it from enemies if it were the consummate state when all the enemies of the Church are in hell. There is yet a division of nations which indicates an earthly scene: "And the nations of them which are saved shall walk in the light of it: and the kings of the earth do bring their glory and honour into it." There are still tears for it is said that God will wipe them away. There are still wounds of sin for we read that "the leaves of the tree were for the healing of the nations." Is that a picture of heaven where healing is needed and medicine provided? The gates are open to those who have as yet not entered. After the description of the Holy City there is still the invitation to come to the river of water of life which is in the center of the city: "And the Spirit and the bride say, Come. And let him that heareth say, Come. And let him that is athirst come. And whosoever will, let him take the water of life freely."

We are conscious that this is but a very brief indication of what the Holy City really signifies. There are questions of interpretation which we have not answered. This we trust to do in a book on the interpretation of Revelation 21, 22. But surely enough has been indicated that the Holy City is situated in time and history and that the consummate state is not indicated.

FIRE FROM HEAVEN

And fire came down from God out of heaven and devoured them. This is the fire which the Jews looked for in vain during the siege of the earthly Jerusalem in the year 70 A.D. They looked in vain for a miraculous deliverance. But those in the New Jerusalem at the time of the final onslaught of Satan look not in vain for deliverance. It will come.

The expression "fire from God out of heaven" alluded to Genesis 19:24, "Then the Lord rained upon Sodom and upon Gomorrah brimstone and fire from the Lord out of heaven." And again it is based upon Ezekiel 39:6, "And I will send a fire on Magog, and among them that dwell carelessly in the isles: and they shall know that I am the Lord." These are types of the final outpouring of the wrath of God upon the enemies of the Church.

Since nothing more is written in this prophecy concerning an intervening period between the destruction of Gog and Magog and the resurrection of the dead this must be the final destructive blow. It is the revealing of Christ as described in II Thessalonians 1:7-9, "And to you who are troubled rest with us, when the Lord Jesus shall be revealed from heaven with his mighty angels, in flaming fire taking vengeance on them that know not God, and that obey not the gospel of our Lord Jesus Christ: who shall be punished with everlasting destruction from the presence of the Lord, and from the glory of his power."

CHAPTER XIII

THE DOOM OF THE DEVIL

Revelation 20:10, *"And the devil that deceived them was cast into the lake of fire and brimstone, where the beast and the false prophet are, and shall be tormented day and night for ever and ever."*

How terrible and revolting would be the history of the Devil if it were written with all its horrible details! Even to review the broad outlines of his activities is depressing. It started with his rebellion in heaven. Then he led a host of angels astray and changed them into demons whose abode is hell. Then he poisoned Adam and Eve and robbed them of Paradise. He left his venomous trail of murder and deceit throughout all the pages of history. Up to the first advent of Christ he controlled the nations by his deceit.

How thankful we are that with the advent of Christ Satan was cast out of the heavens. He fell like lightning from the height of his power. For the thousand-year period he was bound. He could no longer deceive the nations as he did formerly although his poison still remains to bring misery and woe. At the end of the millennium period he is again to be released to deceive the nations. That will be a woeful day for the world. Fortunately it is to be only for a short season. Then will come the final doom. The Devil will be cast into the lake of fire and brimstone and shall be tormented day and night.

There will be no sympathy with the lot of the Devil. Even those who have been deceived will howl with glee at the terrible punishment of Satan. It is a terrifying picture that the lake of fire and brimstone presents. A lake of fire! drowned in flames and yet fully conscious. A lake of brimstone! surrounded by suffocating fumes and nauseating odors and yet alive. This is the deepest hell. How deserving a fate for one who has brought such terrible misery and woe upon earth for so many centuries.

There is no relief from this torment of fire and brimstone. There is no drop of water to alleviate pain from the tormenting flames. The Devil shall be tormented day and night. The suffering is unending. There is no pause; there is no rest; there is no comfort. The torment is eternal; it is everlasting; it is day and night without end.

It may be questioned whether or not the lake of fire and brimstone is to be considered in a literal way. Personally we believe that it is not literal fire and brimstone. One reason for so believing is that the Devil is a spirit. This does not in the least lessen the severity of the punishment but actually makes it more intense. Spiritual suffering is more intense and painful than physical suffering. If fire and brimstone are the figures, the reality is worse. One does not soften the anguish and torment by not believing in a literal fire and brimstone. The torment is so horrible that only these figures of speech can describe it. One must remember that the sufferings of the soul of Christ on the cross were more intense than the sufferings of His body. The Devil might well wish that his only suffering was that endured by a body.

Usually the Devil is pictured as ruling over hell and tormenting others. But on the contrary he will be tormented by those whom he deceived and led into hell. It is not difficult to imagine that they will gnash upon him and curse him for his deceptions. How they will hurl at him his first lie: "Ye shall not surely die." They will cast at him his false promise: "Ye shall be as gods." The torment of those whom he deceived will undoubtedly be part of the lake of fire and brimstone.

How deceived indeed has the world been by the Devil since the creation of Adam and Eve. His great aim has ever been to plant doubt in the minds of men concerning the veracity of God's Word. This he started with Eve with the question: "Yea, hath God said, Ye shall not eat of every tree of the garden?" This way of planting doubt has ever been the method of the great Deceiver. Is Genesis authentic? Was Moses the author of the Pentateuch? Was there a flood? Did David actually write some of the Psalms? Was there only one author of Isaiah? Was Jonah swallowed by a big fish? Did Jesus really perform miracles? What parts of the Gospels are reliable history? What was the real source of Paul's

247

theology? These are but a few of the thousand questions the Devil has asked in order to implant doubt in the minds of people. What new doubts he will plant in The Great Apostasy only the future will reveal.

And the Devil always seeks to give a false picture of God. He suggested that God was envious of the power mankind would obtain through eating of the forbidden fruit. The God of the Bible has been pictured as crude, as blood-thirsty, as cruel and harsh. What kind of God is the God of revelation who would allow people to suffer? What kind of God is the God of nature who allows earthquakes, floods, and hurricanes? The Devil has ever sought to give a false picture of God throughout all generations. His power is seen in that he convinced some of the angels who dwelt in the presence of God; Adam and Eve who dwelt in the midst of every evidence of God's goodness; and the Israelites who were living in a land flowing with milk and honey. So will he deceive those who are living at the time of the greatest manifestation of millennium blessings.

His special desire is to poison minds concerning Christ. He has set up false Christs. He has implanted doubts concerning the deity of Christ and he has implanted doubts concerning the humanity of Christ. He has acknowledged Him to be a prophet but has denied that He is truly the Son of God. He has taken away from Him a place in the Trinity. The deceptions that Satan has practiced concerning the Christ have been various and manifold.

Millions upon millions have been deceived by the Devil as to the way of salvation. They have been led to put their trust in idols. They have been led to put their trust in human works. They have been led to put their trust in penances, indulgences, and human priests. Mary has been substituted for the Son of God as mediator. Others have been led to put their trust and faith in human wisdom and false philosophy.

What a welcome will the Devil receive from those whom he has deceived! What curses, what vituperation, what abuses, what reviling, what berating will be heaped upon his head. He will be surrounded by a lake of curses. His nostrils cannot escape the stench of vituperation. It is part of his torment day and night. He will be hated, despised, and rejected throughout all eternity.

THE BEAST AND THE FALSE PROPHET

The Devil will find the lake of fire already occupied when he is cast into it. It will be occupied by the Beast and the False Prophet. Some time previous, while the Devil was chained, the Beast and False Prophet were defeated and cast into this terrible lake of fire and brimstone. To identify the Beast and False Prophet we must go back to the previous chapters of Revelation where they are described and their history given.

Revelation 13 to 19 gives a description and history of the Beast and the False Prophet. It is not our purpose to enter into a detailed study as to the identification of these two figures. Needless to say they do not represent any individuals. They embody and represent two anti-Christian forces which persecuted the Christian Church. As we search into history we may say that there were three great persecutions experienced by the Church up to this time. The first was from the Jews which sought to crush the Christian Church in its infancy. The second was pagan Rome which sought to stamp out the Christian faith in the first three centuries. The third was that of papal Rome.

The first persecution which appeared from the moment that Christ was born upon earth is described in Revelation 12 which is that of the Jewish nation. Then in Chapter 13 a beast appears upon the scene. This was the next persecuting power—the pagan Roman Empire. It is described in Revelation 13:2 as being like a leopard, bear, and lion. This points back to the vision of the prophet Daniel in the seventh chapter of his book. He describes four great beasts arising out of the sea. The first was like a lion, the second like a bear, and the third like a leopard. The fourth was the most terrible. This fourth beast of Daniel 7 was the fourth Empire from the time of Daniel. This was the Roman Empire which Daniel states was greater than the three previous empires: Babylon, Medo-Persia, and Greece. This John indicates by stating that this Beast was like a leopard, and his feet were as the feet of a bear, and his mouth that of a lion. That is, the Roman Empire combined the vastness, the power, and the ferociousness of the three previous Empires.

Actually the Roman Empire was the sixth head of the Dragon which had seven heads. The seven heads represent the seven pagan empires that have opposed themselves to the true God. Although they come at different times on the scene of history yet they are but one beast animated by the same opposition to true religion. This sixth head received a fatal wound. But this deadly wound was healed. The Roman Empire died in the year 476 but was revived again under Charlemagne in 800. It became the main support of the False Prophet or, as it is pictured to us with another figure of speech, the harlot woman seated upon a scarlet colored beast.

The first Beast was defeated by the year 313 when Christianity defeated pagan Rome. The False Prophet was defeated at the time of the Reformation when the papacy received a fatal stroke. We must remember, of course, that in Revelation images are used which do not give us the proper conception of time. For instance, the red dragon with seven heads represents seven empires and covers centuries of time. So when we read in Revelation 19:20 of the defeat of the Beast and the False Prophet we must not take that to mean that it occurred in the matter of a day, month, or year. It covers the course of centuries.

These two enemies were conquered by the word of God. In the description of the battle in Revelation 19 Christ is pictured as having a sword coming out of His mouth. That, of course, is the Gospel as preached by His followers. This is indicated in Revelation 12:11, "And they overcame him by the blood of the Lamb, and by the word of their testimony." That is how pagan Rome was overcome. That is how the papacy was defeated during the time of the Reformation. It is by the power of the Gospel that the Beast and the False Prophet were cast into the lake of fire and brimstone.

That there is still a remnant of paganism and papalism in this world is chiefly the fault of the Church. The Word of God is just as powerful in this generation as it was during the early history of the Church. The power of the Gospel is just as strong in this century as in the days of the Reformation. These enemies could be completely vanquished if the Christians of this day and age were as vigorous, as bold, as earnest, as prayerful, and as faithful as Christians were in the first several centuries and in the time of the Reformation.

Chapter XIV

THE GREAT WHITE THRONE

Revelation 20:11, *"And I saw a great white throne, and him that sat on it, from whose face the earth and the heaven fled away; and there was found no place for them."*

Fire has come down from God out of heaven and devoured the nations. The Devil has been cast into the lake of fire and brimstone. Now is the Day of Judgment. This is the Day concerning which the Scriptures speak so much and concerning which all are warned. This is the Day in which all must give an account of their lives upon earth. It is here called the judgment of The Great White Throne.

The Throne is the great symbol of the sovereignty of God. The sovereignty of God is a sweet doctrine to all who believe. It is wonderful to know that one is under the rule of God and that God is a ruler over all the nations. It is a doctrine that has been denied frequently. To deny the sovereignty of God is part of the sinful rebellion of Satan's followers. Man is the master of his fate, is the doctrine that the unbeliever fain would believe. But the foolishness of that doctrine will especially be seen at the sight of The Great White Throne. God is sovereign and every knee must bow to Him.

The Throne is called Great for it is greater than any earthly throne. It is greater than the throne of the Pharaohs. It is greater than the throne of Nebuchadrezzar, Cyrus, or Artaxerxes. It is greater than the throne of Alexander of Antiochus. It is greater than the throne of the Caesars. It is greater than the throne of France, Germany, or England. Yea, it is greater than all the thrones of earth combined. It is the throne of the King of kings.

The Throne is called Great because of the multitudes to be judged before it. All who ever lived upon earth stand before this great Throne. As we are told in Matthew 25:32, "And before him shall be gathered all nations." There are those who maintain that the throne of Matthew 25 and the throne of Revelation 20 are not the same. It is maintained that the first throne concerns the judgment of nations as such. But upon examining the scene described in Matthew 25 we find that it concerns individuals within the nations. Both thrones concern the Judgment after the second coming of the Lord. And all, whether great or small, will stand before it.

The Throne is also called Great because of the issues involved. It will issue into eternal life for some and it will issue into eternal death for others. Some will hear the King saying: "Come, ye blessed of my Father, inherit the kingdom prepared for you from the foundation of the world." Others will hear the King saying: "Depart from me, ye cursed, into everlasting fire, prepared for the devil and his angels." Some will go to the right and others will go to the left of The Great White Throne.

It is the White Throne because it reveals the purity and glory of Him who is seated upon it. Those who stand before this white throne need not fear any miscarriage of justice. He will not judge according to appearances but according to the heart. Even Pharaoh had to acknowledge that the Lord is righteous in His judgments. Pharaoh is revealed as saying in Exodus 9:27, "I have sinned this time: the Lord is righteous, and I and my people are wicked." And so in the Day of Judgment all will acknowledge the purity of the White Throne.

White is also a symbolical color which reveals glory. The White Throne will reveal the glory of Him who sits upon it. It will be like the glory of the transfiguration: Matt. 17:2, "And he was transfigured before them, and his face did shine as the sun, and his raiment was white as the light." It will be the throne of glory by the majesty of His royal attendants: "and all the holy angels with him." It will be a throne of glory for it will vindicate His righteousness. It will be a throne of glory because Christ will be revealed as God-man to whom all judgment has been given. In Him is revealed the Godhead. The throne is white for it is all glorious.

As has already been indicated it is the throne of Christ. He sits upon it, not as the second person of the Trinity, but as God-

252

man. It is the Son of man as Matthew 25:31 reveals: "When the Son of man shall come in his glory, and all the holy angels with him, then shall he sit upon the throne of his glory." As God the Son He had the right to judge those whom He had created. As God-man He was appointed to be the final judge of the world.

There are a number of passages which indicate the above fact. It is said in John 5:27, "The Father hath given him authority also to exercise judgment, because he is the Son of man." And Acts 10:42, "He is ordained of God to be the judge of the quick and the dead." And again Acts 17:31, "He hath appointed a day in which he will judge the world in righteousness by that man whom he hath ordained." This Jesus Himself claims in John 5:22, 23, 27, "For the Father judgeth no man, but hath committed all judgment unto the Son that all men should honour the Son, even as they honour the Father.—And hath given him authority to execute judgment also, because he is the Son of man." As God, Christ does not need authority, ordination, or appointment. But as God-man He does.

This appointment as Judge of the world is the reward of His obedience unto death while upon earth. It is part of His exaltation. This is revealed in Philippians 2:8-11, "And being found in fashion as a man, he humbled himself, and became obedient unto death, even the death of the cross. Wherefore God also hath highly exalted him, and given him a name which is above every name: that at the name of Jesus every knee should bow, of things in heaven, and things in earth, and things under the earth; and that every tongue should confess that Jesus Christ is Lord, to the glory of God the Father."

The Great White Throne brings out, of course, the divine nature of our Lord. It brings out His omnipotence. Think of the power that is required to raise the dead bodies and to unite each to its soul! Think of the power that is required to arrange all before His throne! Think of the power that is manifested in separating the sheep from the goats! Think of the power that is required to cast the wicked into hell! Only God has the power to accomplish these things. Christ is God.

His omniscience is also revealed. Open before Him is the life of all that have dwelled upon earth. He is acquainted with every thought, every word, and every deed of every individual. This wisdom defies the imagination. This omniscience was in evidence even while Christ was upon earth as John testifies in the second chapter of his Gospel: "But Jesus did not commit himself unto them, because he knew all men, and needed not that any should testify of man: for he knew what was in man." And this will be in evidence at the Day of Judgment when the thoughts of men will be revealed.

No Place for Earth and Heaven

From whose face the earth and the heaven fled away; and there was found no place for them. These words teach us the end and annihilation of the material earth and heaven. They fled away and there was no place for their existence in eternity.

They fled away from the face of Christ. They fled away from the holiness that was manifested. The earth since the fall of man has been contaminated with sin. Thorns and thistles have infested it. It has witnessed murder, adultery, theft, deceit, and covetousness. It has been the scene of strife and battle. And no doubt the sun, the moon, and the stars would blush to witness what they have seen of evil during the course of the centuries. They, too, have been contaminated by the sin of man. As someone has written: "Not only impenitent sinners cannot abide His holiness but the earth upon which they trod; the heavens upon which they gazed." Even as the Israelite could not enter into the sanctuary after he had touched a dead body or an unclean thing even so there is no place for the earth and the heaven through their contact with sin.

This is one of the clearest statements in Scripture of the non-eternity of the earth and the heavens. There are other passages such as Psalm 102:25, 26, "Of old hast thou laid the foundation of the earth: and the heavens are the work of thy hands. They shall perish, but thou shalt endure: yea, all of them shall wax old like a garment; as a vesture shalt thou change them, and they shall be changed." This is also taught in such passages as Isaiah 51:6; 54:10; Matt. 24:35; Luke 21:33; Mark 13:31.

But what about the new heaven and the new earth? Will there not be a renovated material heaven and earth? When the

Scriptures speak of a new heaven and new earth it is not a material concept but a spiritual concept. It is first spoken of in Isaiah 65:17, "For, behold, I create new heavens and a new earth: and the former shall not be remembered, nor come into mind." In its context it cannot refer to the Consummate Kingdom. J. A. Alexander, in his commentary on this verse, writes: "That the words are not inapplicable to a revolution of a moral and spiritual nature, we may learn from Paul's analogous description of the change wrought in conversion (II Corinthians 5:17; Galatians 6:15), and from Peter's application of this very passage, 'Nevertheless, we, according to his promise, look for new heavens and a new earth wherein dwelleth righteousness' (II Peter 3:13). That the words have such meaning even here, is rendered probable by the last clause, the oblivion of the former state of things being much more naturally connected with moral and spiritual changes than with one of a material nature."

Sometimes Revelation 21:1 is quoted to indicate that there will be a renovated material earth and heavens after the second coming of the Lord. It reads: "And I saw a new heaven and a new earth: for the first heaven and the first earth were passed away; and there was no more sea." If that is a material concept then Revelation 21:2 must also be a material concept. On this new earth will be a material holy city. This city is a cube of 1400 miles. It has a wall 216 feet high. It contains all the saints whose multitude no man can number yet within the confines of this measured city. The new heavens (sun, moon, and stars) will be somewhat useless to the city for "the city had no need of the sun, neither of the moon, to shine in it: for the glory of God did lighten it, and the Lamb is the light thereof." Even the nations outside of it do not need the sun and the moon for they walk in the light of the city. There will be a literal throne for the Lamb and the Infinite God. From that throne will come a literal stream from which the saints will refresh themselves. The literal tree of life will straddle this stream and bear fruit for the saints and healing leaves for the nations.

Just a little reflection will show that to take Revelation 21 and 22 in a literal way is to make utter foolishness of that which John revealed. In that figurative passage you cannot say that the "new heaven and new earth" is a material concept while the rest is to be taken in a figurative way. The "new heaven and new earth" is but the same as "the holy city" and "the Lamb's bride." They just bring out different aspects of the Gospel dispensation.

As far as the material earth and heaven are concerned there is no place for them in the Consummate Kingdom. Revelation is completely silent as to what type of environment will be the enjoyment of the "spiritual body." Paul says concerning his experience of that other life: "I knew a man in Christ above fourteen years ago (whether in the body, I cannot tell; or whether out of the body, I cannot tell: God knoweth;), such an one caught up to the third heaven.—How that he was caught up into paradise, and heard unspeakable words, which is not lawful for a man to utter." Life in the Consummate Kingdom will be unspeakably glorious but for the revelation of it we must wait until we enter into the other life.

CHAPTER XV

THE BOOKS ARE OPENED

Revelation 20:12, 13, *"And I saw the dead, small and great, stand before God; and the books were opened: and another book was opened, which is the book of life: and the dead were judged out of those things which were written in the books, according to their works. And the sea gave up the dead which were in it; and death and hell delivered up the dead which were in them: and they were judged every man according to their works."*

These verses describe the Final Judgment. It is a scene which defies the imagination. Christ is seated upon the great white throne. He is surrounded by myriads of holy angels. In front of the throne will be gathered all that have ever lived upon the earth. There is not one exception. It is a multitude which no man can number. Small and great will all stand before the the judgment seat of God.

In this description the multitude to be judged are pictured as standing before God. In Matthew 25 where a similar scene is described it is the Son of man seated upon the throne. It is the Lord Jesus Christ in both instances. It cannot be God in His absolute essence. In I Timothy 6:16 it is stated: "Who only hath immortality, dwelling in the light which no man can approach unto; whom no man hath seen, nor can see." Finite man cannot comprehend the infinite God. God in His absolute essence dwells in an inaccessible light. But Christ is the image of the invisible God. Therefore Christ stated in John 14:9, "He that hath seen me hath seen the Father." And in John 12:45, "He that seeth me seeth him that sent me." To stand before Christ is to stand before God.

Sometimes it is thought that only the wicked dead will stand before the Judgment Seat of God. But it is obvious both from Matthew 25 and the passage before us that those before the throne consist of the righteous dead and the wicked dead. They are described as "small and great." This is a term which may describe both the righteous and the wicked. Then it is stated: "and another book was opened, which is the book of life." The book of life contained the names of the elect and was needed for the judgment of the righteous. Also it is stated that "the sea gave up the dead which were in it." The sea would contain the bodies of the righteous as well as the bodies of the wicked. There is no reason to doubt that all will stand before the judgment seat of God as is taught in other passages of Scripture (Matthew 16:27; 25:32; Romans 14:10; II Corinthians 5:10; II Timothy 4:1; Hebrews 9:27).

This Final Judgment involves the body as well as the soul of both the righteous and the wicked. This is taught in the words: "And the sea gave up the dead which were in it; and death and hell delivered up the dead which were in them." This expression conveys the idea that every place where there are any dead, gives them back. The sea giving up the dead indicates the resurrection of the body. Death and Hell (Hades) giving up the dead indicates the soul. Death and Hades are viewed as localities here and in Revelation 1:18 where Jesus states: "I have the keys of hell and of death." That is, Christ is sovereign over all phases of human experience. He is in complete control as to whom death can touch and as to the time when death can reach out towards an individual. Christ has complete control over Hades the abode of departed souls. So at the end of time Christ as supreme ruler and judge summons and the sea will give up the dead. Death and Hades must yield those whom they have swallowed. There is a yielding up of both bodies and souls.

The fall of man damaged both soul and body. The greatest harm was to the soul. The soul died immediately. It was separated from God which is death. The body, however, did not die immediately. That was due to the grace of God. Nevertheless, the sentence of death was upon it. Sooner or later the body dies and gives evidence of the judicial sentence of death. Through Christ it is the soul which recovers first. It is resurrected and restored to fellowship with God. This is the first resurrection. Upon the death of the body the soul of the believer enters into the intermediate state of heaven. The soul of the unbeliever remains in a dead state and is never restored to fellowship with God. It enters into the abode of the wicked which Christ describes as the place of torment. The bodies of both believers and unbelievers enter into the grave to await the final resurrection.

THE BOOKS OPENED

And the books were opened. We must not understand these as literal books. John speaks in anthropomorphic language, not that God needs any record, but because men do keep such books. It indicates that all things are held in remembrance in the mind of God. This reveals the omniscience of the Lord who knows all things. In judging every individual all things are brought out. There is nothing hid. Because there is such a complete and accurate account of everything that an individual has done there is no room for argument or debate. In the courts of the land there is continual argument as to whether this or that actually happened. But in this Judgment there is an accurate and true record because of the omniscience of the Judge.

The individual will undoubtedly have his memory sharpened in the Day of Judgment. It has been the experience of individuals at time of danger that their lives stand out in bold relief in a few minutes of time. This will be intensified at the time of judgment. The conscience then will be fully awakened. It will not be dull or dead. Forgotten sins will come vividly to mind.

All deeds of the body will be revealed. In II Corinthians 5:10 it is stated: "For we must all appear before the judgment seat of Christ; that every one may receive the things done in his body, according to that he hath done, whether it be good or bad." One will have to give an account for every word spoken according to Matthew 12:36, 37, "But I say unto you, That every idle word that men shall speak, they shall give account thereof in the day of judgment. For by thy words thou shalt be justified, and by thy words thou shalt be condemned." Not only the deeds and words but the very thoughts of men are recorded and manifested as indicated in I Corinthians 4:5, "Therefore judge nothing before the time, until the Lord come, who both will bring to light the hidden things of darkness, and will make manifest the counsels of the

259

hearts: and then shall every man have praise of God." Whatever one has been able to hide from others will be manifested in that day as is written in Romans 2:16, "In the day when God shall judge the secrets of men by Jesus Christ according to my gospel." Deeds, words, thoughts, and innermost secrets will stand out in bold relief in that Day of days. What a terror that should be for sinful man!

It is not even a pleasant thought for the Christian to realize that his deeds, words, thoughts, and secrets may be revealed on the Judgment Day. They are, of course, already known to Him concerning whom the Psalmist says: "Yea, the darkness hideth not from thee; but the night shineth as the day: the darkness and the light are both alike to thee." But there is a different factor as far as the Christian is concerned which is brought out in the special mention of another book. "And another book was opened, which is the book of life." This book of life records things in a different fashion than the other books.

The wonderful fact is that God does not remember the sins of His elect in the same sense as those of the reprobate. There are many passages in Scripture which teach that God blots out the sin of His people. In Psalm 85:2 it is recorded: "Thou hast forgiven the iniquity of thy people, thou hast covered all their sin." In Psalm 103:12, "As far as the east is from the west, so far hath he removed our transgressions from us." In Isaiah 1:18, "Come now, and let us reason together, saith the Lord: though your sins be as scarlet, they shall be as white as snow." In Isaiah 43:25, "I, even I, am he that blotteth out thy transgressions for mine own sake, and will not remember thy sins." So also Jeremiah 31:34 and Ezekiel 33:16. All these verses give comfort to the Christian that the Lord does not remember his sinful deeds, words, thoughts, and secrets. It is because these sins have been imputed to another.

It is the Lamb's book of life. The sins of the elect have been imputed to Him and He has erased them by His sacrificial death on Calvary's cross. The garment of life of the Christian has been washed in the blood of Christ. The question is asked in Revelation 7: "What are these which are arrayed in white robes and whence came they?" The answer was: "These are they which came out of great tribulation, and have washed their robes, and made them white in the blood of the Lamb."

There is a remembrance, however, of the good works performed by the righteous. Malachi 3:16 records: "Then they that feared the Lord spake often one to another: and the Lord hearkened, and heard it, and a book of remembrance was written before him for them that feared the Lord, and that thought upon his name." And those who bear the name of Christian and have no good deeds, words, and thoughts have deceived themselves as to their standing before God. This the passage of our study calls to our attention twice with the expression: "according to their works."

ACCORDING TO THEIR WORKS

Not only in the passage before us but in many other parts of Scripture we are told that the final judgment will be according to works performed. In Matthew 25, for instance, Jesus invites certain ones to enter into the kingdom because they performed such works of charity as feeding the hungry and visiting those in prison. This has puzzled some Christians for they feel that they are justified not by works but by faith in Jesus Christ. Actually the works of the believer give a reason for the sentence but do not express the fundamental cause of the reward received.

We may use this illustration. A man with considerable property makes a free offer to any person for lots on this property. At the end of a certain time he gives formal deeds to those who have accepted his offer because, as he might say: "You have built houses on my property and you have developed the land." Now no one would say that he gave the deeds because of individual merit. He gave the deeds because they gave evidence that they had received his free offer. God of His marvellous grace has given the free offer of forgiveness of sin and eternal life to all who repent and turn to the Lord Jesus Christ. A new life and good works issue from the acceptance of this offer. This new life and good works are not the cause but the evidence that people have accepted the free offer of salvation.

This is a protection from the assumption that mere profession of faith in Christ will entitle one to heaven. It must be a *true* profession of faith. Jesus states in Matthew 7: "Not every one that saith unto me, Lord, Lord, shall enter into the kingdom of heaven; but he that doeth the will of my Father, which is in heaven. Many will say to me in that day, Lord, Lord, have we

261

not prophesied in thy name? and in thy name have cast out devils? and in thy name done many wonderful works? And then will I profess unto them, I never knew you: depart from me, ye that work iniquity." In other words, as He stated just previous to this: "By their fruits ye shall know them." Their fruits are not the meriting cause of salvation but the evidence that they have been truly saved.

On that great Day of Judgment all will appear on the same footing. They will all be judged according to their works. This is true of the believer as well as the unbeliever.

CHAPTER XVI

DEATH AND HADES VANQUISHED

Revelation 20:14, 15, *"And death and hell were cast into the lake of fire. This is the second death. And whosoever was not found written in the book of life was cast into the lake of fire."*

There are two things which confront all mankind: Death and Hades. Death is that experience wherein the soul is separated from the body. Death is viewed by most people as a grim and terrifying reaper. Death still represents the curse of God against sin. This Death is the physical experience which confronts all.

It is unfortunate that in the minds of most people the term "hell" is associated only with the abode of the wicked. The Greek word is *Hades*. In the Biblical sense it is used to designate the invisible realm into which all souls depart. It is the intermediate state of both the righteous and the wicked. The concept of hades includes heaven the abode of the righteous and hell the abode of the wicked.

The physical experience of death and the entrance into the abode of hades confronts all with the exception of those who are upon earth at the second coming of the Lord. While Death is a terrifying figure for the believer, as it may prove an unpleasant experience for a short time, nevertheless Christ has taken the sting out of death. Hades as indicating the intermediate state is a place of delight for the Christian. It is the place where Christ is and into which Paul longed to enter. For the wicked both Death and Hades are terrifying. Of course, through ignorance these two experiences may not seem so terrible. But the actual experience will because death means entrance into the place of torment for the wicked.

Death and Hades are here personified. This is also true in Revelation 6:8, "And I looked, and behold a pale horse: and his name that sat on him was Death, and Hell (Hades) followed with him. And power was given unto them over the fourth part of the earth, to kill with sword, and with hunger, and with death, and with the beasts of the earth." Here Death is personified as a terrible killer with Hades following as a hearse picking up the dead. And so in our passage Death and Hades are personified and are pictured as two persons being cast into the lake of fire.

Death and Hades are cast into the lake of fire after the general resurrection which takes place at the second coming of Christ. From that time Death and Hades cease to exist for the saint. The resurrected body of the saint will never be confronted with Death. Death has relinquished his hold on the body of the saint and will never have another opportunity to do so. Death, as far as the saint is concerned, is cast forever into the lake of fire. Even so Hades has ceased to exist for him. Hades is the abode of his soul. It is a wonderful place but it is not the place for the fulness of what has been promised. His soul leaves Hades and enters what is indicated in these words of the Lord: "Come, ye blessed of my Father, inherit the kingdom prepared for you from the foundation of the world." Hope for the redemption of his body (Romans 8:23) has now passed into reality. Hades as the abode for his soul ceases to exist. As useless, it is cast into the lake of fire.

Death and Hades also cease to exist for the wicked. The wicked will not experience Death again in the sense that his soul will be separated from his body. At the general resurrection his body, too, is united with his soul. They will never be separated. As far as he is concerned, Death has been cast into the lake of fire. Even so Hades ceases to exist for him as it was the abode of his soul alone. This present Hades is the place from which his soul will be called. He will enter, body and soul, into the place designated by these words of our Lord in Matthew 25: "Depart from me, ye cursed, into everlasting fire, prepared for the devil and his angels." They leave the former Hades and enter into the place which had been especially prepared for the Devil.

What the apostle John has vividly placed before us in the language of symbols the apostle Paul tells us in direct words in I Corinthians 15:26, 54, "The last enemy that shall be destroyed is death.—So when this corruptible shall have put on incorruption, and this mortal shall have put on immortality, then shall be brought to pass the saying that is written, Death is swallowed up in victory." This is also expressed in Isaiah 25:8, "He will swallow up death in victory; and the Lord God will wipe away tears from off all faces; and the rebuke of his people shall he take away from off all the earth." And again it is expressed in Hosea 13:14, "I will ransom them from the power of the grave; I will redeem them from death: O death, I will be thy plagues; O grave, I will be thy destruction." The truth of these verses John sums up: "And death and hell were cast into the lake of fire."

THE SECOND DEATH

No doubt it sounds strange that Death will be cast into the lake of fire and that this is the Second Death. It is because the Second Death swallows up the First Death as the ocean swallows up a river. There are a number of differences between the two. Both are the results of the fall of man in Paradise. Both are the results of sin. Both are because of the sentence: "for in the day thou eatest thereof thou shalt surely die." However, the first death was but the partial fulfillment of that sentence. The second death was the complete fulfillment.

The first Death had its greatest effect on the soul. The soul became dead in trespasses and sin. It was separated from the source of its life—God. There was, however, the possibility of a resurrection. By the grace and power of God some souls experience resurrection. The souls become alive and are restored to communion with God. All possibility of resurrection is ruled out by those who experience the Second Death. That state is final and eternal.

The effect of the First Death upon the body is to destroy it. This it does in a process of time. The body is not immediately destroyed. But the marks of death constantly show. The body becomes weaker through age and disease. Eventually it succumbs and becomes as Paul states corrupt, dishonored, and weak. There is, however, the possibility of resurrection. There is a possibility that the body may become incorruptible, glorious, and powerful. But all possibility of such a resurrection is ruled out by the Second Death. Whatever the state of the body is when united with the soul, so it remains throughout eternity. It is not a matter of revelation as to just what the state of the resurrected body of the wicked is except that it is a state of torment and misery.

It may also be stated that the effects of the First Death are restrained by God's common grace. No human soul is as evil as it might be. By environment, by civic law, and by direct influence of the Holy Spirit the souls of the wicked are curbed and checked. But in the Second Death there are no restraints or good influences. All is evil. Greed is unrestrained. Hatred is not checked. Envy is not curbed. Deceit holds sway. Strife is ever present. And all these vices and a thousand more bring on their attendant miseries and woes. The unrestrained evils of men and demons is what makes hell such a black pit of torment and agony. That plus the constant remorse which bites into the conscience is what makes the torment of hell. As words fail in the description of eternal bliss so words fail in the description of the Second Death.

THE BOOK OF LIFE

And whosoever was not found written in the book of life was cast into the lake of fire. This expression does sound as though he who will be cast into the lake of fire is the exception rather than the rule. We are of the opinion that those in the kingdom of light will be more numerous than those who will be in that terrible kingdom of darkness. History so far would not back us up in that opinion. But history is not finished. We do believe that time will come when the knowledge of God will cover the earth as the waters cover the sea. The period of the loosing of Satan is short but the period of the millennium is long. We are told that the number of the saints will be as the stars of the heavens and the sand upon the sea shore. It is a multitude without number. Many will be enrolled in the book of life.

This book of life is called the Lamb's book of life in Revelation 13:8 and 21:27. It is the register with the names of those whom God the Father has given to the Son. "All that the Father giveth me shall come to me," said Christ. They are the elect. The names in the book of life are those which have been written by God. No man can write his own name upon this register. Only those whose names appear in the book of life can enter into the Holy City according to Revelation 21:27, "And there shall in no wise enter into it any thing that defileth, neither whatsoever worketh abomination, or maketh a lie: but they which are written in the Lamb's book of life." This is the book that has been written in heaven.

There is a comforting thought expressed in Revelation 13:8, "And all that dwell upon the earth shall worship him, whose names are not written in the book of life of the Lamb slain from the foundation of the world." This speaks of those who worshipped the Beast. The only exceptions to the worship of the Beast at that period were those whose names were written in the Lamb's book of life. They were preserved from this blasphemous worship not by their own power and virtue but because they were the elect of God. God will take care of His elect. Not one will be lost.

By the title of *Lamb's* book of life all saints are reminded that their names are written there because of the sacrificial death of Christ upon the cross. They would have no entrance into heaven if Christ had not died for them on Calvary's cross. God gave Christ a people on the basis of Christ taking upon Himself their sins and guilt. There would not be a heavenly register of names if Christ had not died for His people.

It is a book of life. It is not a register of nominal Christians. It is not a register of dead Christians. The elect prove that they are elect by being living sacrifices unto God. They will manifest that their names are written there by true repentance, a living faith in Christ, and love towards God and man. Peter in his second Epistle speaks of faith, virtue, knowledge, temperance, patience, godliness, brotherly kindness, charity. Then he adds: "Wherefore the rather, brethren, give diligence to make your calling and election sure: for if ye do these things, ye shall never fall." It is by manifesting a Christian life that one is assured that his name is in the book of life.

Thus we come to the end of our study of Revelation Twenty. The Chapter tells us about Satan being bound so that he cannot deceive the nations. It speaks of the lot of the saints during the thousand-year period. It speaks of the first resurrection. Then the Chapter relates of what will occur when Satan is loosed again. It reveals the finish of Satan, Death, and Hades. It brings us

267

before the Great White Throne. And then it reveals the books which will be opened. It may be fitting to close our study with these words from Luke 10:17-20, "And the seventy returned again with joy, saying, Lord, even the devils are subject unto us through thy name. And he said unto them, I beheld Satan as lightning fall from heaven. Behold, I give unto you power to tread on serpents and scorpions, and over all the power of the enemy: and nothing shall by any means hurt you. Notwithstanding in this rejoice not, that the spirits are subject unto you; but rather rejoice, because your names are written in heaven."